TRAIN ON LINE

Tim Helme

Published by

Top Link Press

toplink@btinternet.com

CONTENTS

ABOUT THE AUTHOR

Tim Helme was born in Derby and raised in Derbyshire. More truant than student, he joined the Junior Leaders aged sixteen then later, the regular Forces. Turning his back on a promising military career, he joined British Rail in 1990 to follow his true calling of railwayman, but this aspiration was cut short owing to industry privatisation in 1994. He then followed the well-trodden paths of security, building and groundwork, interspersed with several years' truck driving. Returning to the railway in 2006, he served as signalman on the North Staffordshire Line for fourteen years, having the rare perspective of seeing the job from both sides, that of train driver and signalman.

OTHER BOOKS BY THE AUTHOR:

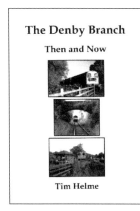

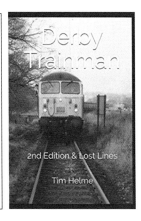

In memory of Skye

(Friend, companion and inspiration 2010-14)

ACKNOWLEDGEMENTS

Train On Line is only superior to *Derby Trainman* because I finally managed to obtain a keyboard where the full stop works all the time, instead of having to rely on exclamation marks to finish most of my sentences! (That one was intentional, by the way.) Also, it is because of the sterling efforts of numerous long-suffering friends who proof read the manuscript, instead of me just sending it to the printers after one bleary-eyed session in the pub. And last, but by no means least, it is largely because of Frank and Helen Chadfield, Bryn Davies, Richard King and my brother Phil, for their outstanding contributions to the project. I would also like to thank certain people for making some of those relentless shifts a little more bearable. You may not have realized it, but your brief appearances often made the difference between me merely surviving a shift and having a rewarding one.

Front Cover
The author in silhouette at Egginton Junction, February 2008. *Richard King.*

Back Cover
Skye on duty at Scropton, June 2011. *Philip Helme.*

Title Page
Scropton's Up block indicator. *Bryn Davies.*

Maps by the author. All other illustrations by Helen Chadfield.

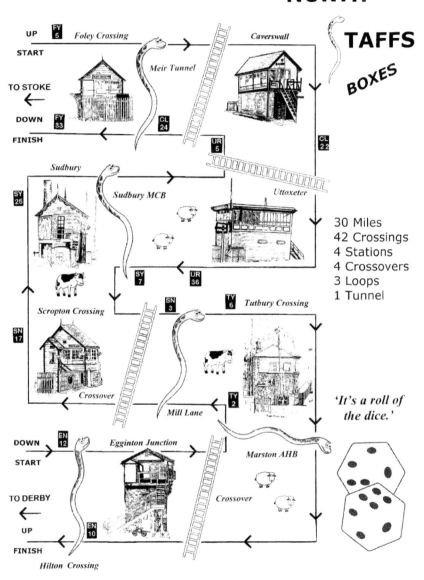

THE NORTH TAFFS BOXES

UP FY 5   Foley Crossing   Caverswall

START

Meir Tunnel

TO STOKE ←

DOWN FY 33   CL 24   CL 22

FINISH

UR 5

Sudbury   SY 25

Sudbury MCB   Uttoxeter

30 Miles
42 Crossings
4 Stations
4 Crossovers
3 Loops
1 Tunnel

SY 7   UR 36

SN 3   TY 6   Tutbury Crossing

Scropton Crossing   SN 17

Crossover   TY 2

Mill Lane

'It's a roll of the dice.'

DOWN EN 12   Egginton Junction   Marston AHB

START

TO DERBY ←

Crossover

UP EN 10

FINISH

Hilton Crossing

6

FOREWORD

By Bryn Davies – Support Engineer (Porterbrook).

Where to start? Having never written a foreword before, I have been procrastinating of late, awaiting inspiration. The author, our very own Tim Helme, advised me to keep it light, humorous and honest. He also hinted that it had to be polite, so I'm now back to square one. Having known Tim for a few years I suppose I'd better start from the beginning.

Whilst out and about with the camera around the North Staffordshire Line one day, I came across a signal box situated down a narrow country lane within the village of Scropton. As I wandered down this lane towards the box, the now familiar sight of the two home signals slowly came into view from behind the trees. To the left, a pair of weathered white gates and, to the right, the gentle curve of the line towards Sudbury. Facing me, in all its miniature glory, was Scropton Crossing Signal Box, from its smartly painted brickwork to the ornate finials upon its roof: a well-kept box with a charm all of its own, hidden away in an isolated corner of England.

It is all too easy to become lost in the tranquil surroundings as the wind gently blows and the birds sing from the trees – until a signal bell sounds in the box. Sadly, this is where the illusion ends. The door of the box swings open and the signalman comes down the little wooden steps towards the gates. Clad in orange, he quickly swings the gates shut and locks them before making his way back into the box. After a few more bell chimes, and several unnerving metallic crashes, there is an eerie pause before the local passenger train storms through, usually in the form of a Class 153, struggling to keep time with its tiny screaming diesel engine. Soon after, the gates are swiftly re-opened and the calm returns.

Having both worked at Derby Etches Park, Tim and I soon got into easy conversation and have remained in touch ever since. Well, someone has to keep an eye on him and make sure he's kept up-to-date with current affairs and the modern world – more on that in later chapters...

By Richard King – Train Driver.

How many people, when travelling by train, actually look out of the window and watch the world go by? In the main, passengers seem unable to draw themselves away from their own little world, tapping away on their laptops and mobile phones, or engrossed in the latest novel. Those who take the opportunity to look up for a few moments are greeted by the treasure of unspoilt countryside and the best and worst of the back yards of Britain flying by in a blur.

On rare occasions they may catch a glimpse of a little piece of Victorian Britain – the humble signal box, going about its business largely unnoticed in a world far removed from the technologies in use on the passing trains. A world where a bell and tapper are still the primary means of communication, and signals are operated manually, using levers, pulleys and cables, not by the push of a button or click of a mouse. Operated by men and women who, quite possibly may be the last generation of manual signallers (even the title 'Signalman' is obsolete now!), using their own initiative, common sense and straight talking, to keep the trains moving on a modern railway where the above traits are now largely frowned upon.

Train On Line is the story of one such signalman, whose personal account makes an interesting comparison between living in the modern world and working in an environment harking back 150 years.

PREFACE

Although this is essentially a railway book, I wanted it to be more than just a typical account of day-to-day operations, so the reader will have to forgive my temporary deviations from the loco cab and signal box whilst I attempt to take in a wider landscape. Whereas *Derby Trainman* dealt with the last gasp of British Rail, this book, I hope, will provide an insight into what it was like to live and work in the mechanical signal boxes, which truly are the last bastions of the old railway. I think there is a nice symmetry in there somewhere – or synchronicity, as Carl Jung might have termed it. Actually, there is a surprising amount of symmetry throughout the book, although I never quite realized it until I'd finished writing.

The title 'Train On Line' refers to the indication on a block instrument, which is used by a signaller in Absolute Block signalling. There is a brief description of this method in the Appendix, which I have endeavoured to make as painless as possible, although I doubt my success in this undertaking. (The more I tried to simplify it, the more impenetrable it seemed to become.) Nevertheless, 'train on line' means that a section of track is occupied, either by accident or design, or a train has entered the section for which the relevant signaller is now wholly responsible for and committed to – locked and loaded as an American might say.

I was originally going to entitle this book 'My Life in Wooden Boxes' because, looking back, I seem to have spent an inordinate amount of time in one sort or another. It has been said that the wooden shed has always been the traditional male retreat, but it's not one that I've actively sought. It would appear to be one that has actively sought me instead. If I leave aside the early years of wooden cot and playpen and jump straight to my teens, I suppose my first experience of this wooden box lifestyle was with Her Majesty's Forces (some would have thought Her Majesty's pleasure more appropriate), although fortunately for me, the wood was quickly upgraded to reinforced concrete with barbed wire and sandbag trimming. Upon joining British Rail as a trainman, I frequently rode in wooden brakevans, the ever-changing scenery mostly compensating for the distinct lack of comfort. After redundancy from the railway I spent several years as a groundsman based in a wooden stable block, whilst also undertaking part-time jobs that occasionally involved working in a wooden boathouse and a park keepers' hut. I then fully embraced the lifestyle when I rejoined the railway as a signalman, working a variety of manual signal boxes, all wooden but perched upon brick plinths (except for Tutbury Crossing, which was predominantly brick). In the end I shall no doubt spend some time in the smallest wooden box of all, but before then, I hope to have retired to a suitably appointed beach hut – although a static caravan seems increasing likely.

I have worked at many different places in a variety of roles, but the railway has always felt a constant – it gets in your blood somehow. During my twelve-year exile between trainman and signalman it was always there in the background, even when I had no intention of ever returning to the industry. This was certainly true at the end of *Derby Trainman*, but its epilogue proved surprisingly prophetic.

I'd also like to take this opportunity to confirm that I can still lay a claim to being the 'Derby Trainman' because even though I was based on the North Staffordshire Line, all the signal boxes I worked were still in Derbyshire – Sudbury only just! Alrewas, on the South Staffordshire Line, was the only box I worked that was actually in Staffordshire. There were of course other North Staffs boxes, namely Uttoxeter, Caverswall and Foley, but travelling expenses versus benefit gained made them uneconomical for me to work, and as a result, this book only covers Alrewas and the North Staffs boxes as far as Sudbury.

I have strived to keep the signalling events in chronological order, but if the reader experiences a certain 'jumping about' during the first few chapters relating to my time as a relief signalman, then perhaps that is no bad thing. Hopefully (but unintentionally) the back and forth nature of the early narrative will provide an accurate representation of what life could sometimes be like for a relief signaller. Also, it may be beneficial for the reader to have a reasonable knowledge of 1970s-1990s popular culture....

Finally, the modern railway embraced the neutral title of Signaller and inflicted it upon me, but I've always considered 'signaller', in this case, to be better applied to a mixed group. Working in a box on your own you are either a Signalman or a Signalwoman – only a Signaller if you're not sure. Therefore, throughout this book I will use the correct titles in the correct context. For example, out of about 30 signallers and crossing keepers, there were only three signalwomen when I started on the North Staffs. This briefly rose to five then dropped back to one (and remained so until 2020), but I'm fairly sure this had nothing to do with me. Readers will note that I also use the term 'manual signaller' (one who pulls levers, as opposed to pushing buttons or clicking a mouse) throughout the book too. I appreciate the insertion of 'manual' now contradicts the neutral title of 'signaller', but this was merely serendipitous.

(Readers may also like to note that most of this book was written at Scropton Crossing Signal Box between the years 2014 and 2018.)

Tim Helme, Derby.

1. RECONCILIATION

Perhaps my reconciliation with the railway began in January 2006. I had just released *Derby Trainman* and suddenly found myself on the publicity circuit. It was great, but slightly embarrassing to appear in all the local newspapers and do a talk for Radio Derby, as well as other public speaking engagements. Most unexpected was being reacquainted with many former colleagues and reminiscing about old BR/Derby 4 Shed days. In some ways it felt like those days had never ended. I was pleased that the book had been so well received, not just by them, but also by rail enthusiasts, local historians and others who'd simply enjoyed reading it. I got swept up in all the nostalgia and was further buoyed by researching, writing and editing other railway books, as well as the odd article. Although I was beginning my twelfth year in exile, and had done many different jobs in that time, I was still a railwayman at heart. At times I had forgotten that, but *Derby Trainman* reaffirmed it for me.

At that time, I was a HGV owner/operator and partner in a groundwork company. I was working extremely hard for very little reward and becoming increasingly disillusioned with it all. But that was something I'd found since redundancy from BR; whatever job I ended up on I always seemed to work twice as hard for less money. Not long after the book release I sustained a back injury at work and it became difficult to cope with the physical demands of my job, so I decided to end my self-employment and grudgingly take some part-time work whilst I recovered. I also had a couple of sessions with a member of the Spanish Inquisition (although it said Chiropractor above the door) and after being strapped, stretched and tipped upside down on a table several times, I made good progress over the next couple of months and began applying for full-time positions again. That's when I noticed a job advert to become a Signaller with Network Rail and decided to apply.

In March I was invited to attend Rail House in Manchester for aptitude testing...again. Only this time it was for signalling, not driving. It was hard to believe all that had taken place over seventeen years ago. I completed the psychometrics and was then called for an interview two weeks later. By that time, I knew the box vacancy was at Edale on the Hope Valley Line, and although still in Derbyshire, it was a good trek for me, especially during the winter months. What I hadn't realized was that, to become a signalman, I would have to undertake an eight-week residential course at either Leeds or Watford training centre, which was difficult to contemplate at the time. My lack of enthusiasm must have shown through during the interview, and once my daily commute to the box had been considered, I was no longer the top candidate. Another chap who was interviewing against me lived in Buxton and, quite rightly, was offered the position.

I headed home, changing at Stoke-on-Trent, to rattle along the North Staffs back to Derby. As we pulled into Tutbury & Hatton I could see the signalman replacing levers, raising the barriers and talking on the telephone all at the same time. It looked far too complicated to me and I doubted I could ever do the job anyway, especially tugging levers with my back still in the recovery stage. I'd also managed to avoid what sounded like a rather daunting residential course, and so returned to scanning the job section in the local newspaper and thought no more about becoming a signalman.

Five months later I was still languishing in part-time, mostly mundane clerical work, which really did not suit me. It was then I noticed another signaller vacancy advertised. As I'd already successfully completed the psychometrics, I decided there was nothing to lose and reapplied. It would seem that nostalgia, money, circumstances, aptitude and fate had all conspired to redirect me back to my true calling of railwayman.

Seven months after my Manchester interview I was invited to attend another one at the Railway Technical Centre (RTC) in Derby. No one seemed sure where the vacancy was, but Scropton General Purpose Relief (GPR) was mentioned, and with this box being only about fifteen miles away from home, it was a much more convenient location for me than trekking into the High Peak. Two managers, who were doing the good cop/bad cop routine, interviewed me. They both seemed to exceed their remit because the bad one gave me a hard time, presumably to see how I acted under pressure, whilst the good one kept leaning back and mouthing the answers to me in true pantomime style. I found out much later, through the railway grapevine, that a friend of a friend of an ex-colleague had put a good word in for me – it's a small railway world after all. Unfortunately, I've never been much of a lip reader, and as my railway knowledge was at least a decade out of date, I didn't think I had performed very well at all. Nevertheless, I was subsequently offered the job, and this time, having had seven months to digest the prospect of an eight-week residential course, I accepted.

Starting with Network Rail at the end of November 2006 was very much a case of hurry up and wait. Within a week of the job offer I underwent a hastily arranged medical, signed the written contract and then gave notice to my current employer. It all happened very fast and I started on Wednesday 29, with full expectation of commencing signalling school at Watford on the following Monday. Unfortunately, my enrolment had been put back a week, and as they weren't sure what to do with me, I was given a high visibility orange coat and told to visit some of the North Staffs boxes to fill in the time. None of the signallers would be expecting me and there would be no introductions, except the ones I made myself. I was left to my own devices. I was also a little vague on the exact locations of some of the places I had to visit. I knew where they were from a railway point of view but finding them by road was an entirely different matter; much like a relief train crew trying to find the ballast jobs of old.

I did feel conscious of just turning up and intruding on the duty signallers, but I eventually established that my Local Operations Manager (LOM) was on annual leave, which explained why I'd been left to fend for myself. Initially I found the lack of any managerial guidance odd but reflected that being able to manage your own time, workload, and more importantly, yourself, has always been a major part of railway life, particularly in the line of work I was about to enter. I was pleased to find this hadn't changed much during my exile.

Egginton Junction was the logical place to start and I remembered the former station building was situated near Hilton Crossing, but could see no sign of the signal box upon my arrival. I passed over the crossing a couple of times, but because of the treacherous bends and limited clearance there, I had to keep my eyes on the road and was unable to look either side. Had I done so, I would have spotted the box about 200 metres on the Down trackside. I suppose I could have checked with the crossing keeper at Hilton but decided to press on into Hatton, where I knew the next box to be situated at Tutbury & Hatton station, and therefore slightly easier to access. Well it would have been except for the locked gate preventing access to the box steps from the platform. I eventually managed to attract the attention of the duty signalman and, after explaining the nature of my visit, stayed chatting with him for a couple of hours before returning home. During our chat I was surprised to learn there was no night shift on the North Staffs now, particularly after flogging up and down there at all hours in trainman days. One thing that hadn't changed though was the strong whiff of coffee from the Nestles factory next door and, with the wind in the right direction you could get a decent caffeine buzz just by sitting in the box.

The following day I headed out to Scropton, making several passes through the pleasant little village before eventually finding the box tucked away down a farm track, just off the main road. At the time I had no idea this box would play such a large part in my future, but it's fair to say I liked the place immediately. There had been a box in this locale since 1884 and it didn't look like much had changed: perhaps that's why I liked it so much. The environment and method of working reminded me of old BR days and it was an environment I felt comfortable in. I did wonder how I'd ever be able to work the box myself though after watching the duty signalman hammering the bells, crashing the levers and grappling with the gates. It all looked extremely complex, but it was early days for me.

I particularly liked the large rear-view mirror attached to the wall, which enabled the signallers, who usually sat with their backs to the crossing, to keep a watchful eye on the approach road for any management arriving unexpectedly. It served as an ideal early warning and the box occupant would usually have time to suspend any questionable activities before an interloper reached the box steps. (Numerous examples of questionable activities can be found throughout this book.) I also noticed the wooden door threshold, the central part of which had been compressed into a 'U' shape by the many feet on it over the years. There were similar indentations on the frame kickboard, particularly in front of the distant signal levers, which obviously denoted years of heavy cable pulls.

After a couple of hours, I took my leave of Scropton and turned left into Leathersley Lane, with the intention of spending the afternoon at Sudbury and hopefully crossing another box off my itinerary. First however, I pulled into one of the lay-bys for a quick sandwich and to wait for the next Derby-Crewe service to go by. I rejoined the road shortly after its passage, but in my peripheral vision, I became aware of a light loco Class 37 keeping pace with me. When I arrived at Sudbury, it was stood at the home/section signal, awaiting acceptance by Uttoxeter. Up to that point I'd only seen trains zip up and down, never held, so, upon ascending the box steps, I found it slightly unsettling to have a loco so close, grumbling and throbbing impatiently, its exhausts flaring like the nostrils of an angry bull at a gate. However, once the initial shock faded, it felt good to be up close and personal to the locos again.

The first thing I noticed about Sudbury, apart from the impressive horseshoe 'tache on the great stocky bear of a signalman who greeted me, was its highly polished brassware. The block bells, sink tap, doorknob, hasp and staple, and even the padlock were burnished to a high standard. Either the residents were very house proud, or they had a lot of time to kill, or both. I returned to Scropton on Friday then had the weekend off.

I finally managed to cross the threshold at Egginton the following Monday, but only after the crossing keeper at Hilton had unlocked the access gate and allowed me through. Ever since I've been self-employed, I've always had a white van of some description, and coupled with my new orange coat, I must have looked sufficiently managerial, and therefore highly suspicious. As I drove along the private road towards the box I could see the crossing keeper on the phone, no doubt warning the signaller of my impending arrival. I imagined he'd be saying something like "There's someone heading your way. I'm not sure who he is, but he looks dodgy." The story of my life really! I was probably already a minor celebrity anyway, because ever since I began this odyssey, the omnibus line connecting the boxes would no doubt be red-hot (or at least lukewarm) with news about this stranger in a white van.

Without exception, the signal box interiors all seemed to be a cross between a working museum and the Bagpuss & Co. shop, with some of the occupants disturbingly similar in manner and appearance to the characters found in the latter establishment; a dishevelled rag doll in a wicker chair, a jovial biscuit tin hogging toad (sans banjo), a brusque and bespectacled professorial type, and of course, the inevitable saggy old cloth cat, who was baggy and a bit loose at the seams. Instead of woollen toys circa 1970, these were woollen signallers circa 2006, and much like the previously mentioned shop, these characters appeared to do very little apart from accumulate strange items, tell tall stories, disagree amongst themselves then inevitably fall asleep. I think most signallers (me eventually included) fell into one or more of the above character composites. There was also a distinctive musty, oily, paraffin aroma whenever you entered, although come to think of it, that may have been the duty signaller. Nevertheless, the boxes and their inhabitants certainly brought back memories of old 4 Shed days and, during these visits, I did feel as though reconciliation had been achieved and that I'd returned 'home' in many ways.

For the next two days I resided at Scropton, partly because the resident signalmen there seemed amenable to my presence, and partly because it was supposed to be my 'home station' after all. I still had no idea what it was all about, but they let me pull a few levers and attempted to explain the process to me. I called in at the RTC on Thursday to collect my rule books, three of them to be precise, and with a combined spine width of eight inches, they made *War and Peace* look like a pamphlet in comparison. I gave the Scropton signalmen a break on Friday and went to Egginton to leaf through my rule books and try to grasp the immensity of what I'd taken on.

On Sunday 10 December I departed for Watford. I'd received very little guidance about travel arrangements, but I think it was expected that I'd go by train. Owing to weekend engineering works however, this would mean a mammoth five-hour journey, some of it by bus, with three changes en-route. No sane person would willingly put themselves through such torture, so I opted for the more sensible and slightly less stressful journey in my van, and in so doing, would claim mileage expenses, along with a slight vagueness about any other travel arrangements. I set off at 18:00, checking in at the Watford Travelodge just over two hours later. This would now be my primary residence Sunday evenings to Friday afternoons inclusive for the next few weeks. After checking in I made the short walk from hotel to training centre, just to familiarize myself with the route for the morning.

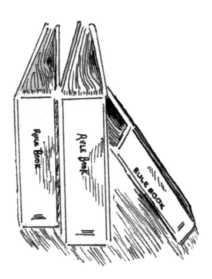

2. BACK TO SCHOOL

It was to be an all-male course and there were twelve of us seated in the classroom at 09:00 on Monday, poised and ready to begin unravelling the mysteries of railway signalling. Everyone introduced themselves in turn and gave a little of their background before joining the railway. I was not going to mention my previous railway experience, mainly because it was such a long time ago and I decided it would be better to start from scratch. However, I eventually had to come out of the closet (or lineside equipment cabinet in this case) and admit I'd been a former trainman. From that point onwards, the instructor would begin virtually every session by pointing to me and saying, "Tim will know all about this." Unfortunately, I didn't because my knowledge was twelve years out of date. I also had very little idea about what happened in a signal box, having spent most of my time in a loco cab, so I eventually had to say, "I used to pass signal boxes every day, but only had cause to go in one once."

"Oh, what was that for?"

"To sign the Train Register Book and remind the signalman of my presence, old Rule 55 I believe."

"Bloody hell, what were you on, Stephenson's *Rocket*?"

Cue much guffawing in the classroom. In future, whenever the broad, sweeping statement 'Tim will know all about this' was proclaimed, it now included the additional 'when he was on Stephenson's *Rocket*' or 'when he was helping Brunel hammer a few rivets into the Royal Albert Bridge'. There were endless combinations. I think my favourite was 'when they used to wear stovepipe hats'. I didn't know why the instructor bothered to go so far back into history; he could have just said 'when they still had slam door stock and used brakevans', which would have been perfectly true in my case, only not as funny I suppose. What *was* funny was that most of the class would eventually end up working boxes and using equipment and methods that were over 120 years old, perilously close to the historical context in question, but none of them had quite grasped that fact yet.

Few of my previous occupations have ever equalled the railway for its humour or plethora of colourful characters and I was pleased to find this was another aspect that was largely unchanged, even in these ultra politically correct times. If a comedian were to sit and listen to a group of railwaymen for any length of time, they would quickly amass enough comedy gold for life, although it may take a while to perfect the dry, deadpan, matter-of-fact delivery that makes it so successful. A good sense of humour is a necessity for railway work and my classmates and I would no doubt be requiring one in the coming weeks. They seemed a good bunch and we bonded quickly in the classroom environment, but I did wonder how some would cope because it looked like most of us had left school a long time ago, or to make use of the current vernacular, 'when they still had desks with inkwells in them'. Judging by the content of our rule books, this was going to be a serious and sustained assault on the old grey matter, not to mention an exam at the end of most weeks.

It was now the Railway Group Standard Rule Book and we would need to be conversant with all 30 plus of its modules. Some of them carried an English Crystal Clarity mark from the Plain English Campaign, which I didn't set too much store by. Having flipped through a few pages before school, if this was plain English, the modules that didn't yet carry the mark were surely to be dreaded. The contradictory nature of the old BR Rule Book was well known, but the new one seemed to contain a lot of repeat instructions, and much more cross-referencing of modules. Nevertheless, most of these rules had been written in blood and were the direct result of the many accidents and disasters that had occurred ever since the first wagon had been set upon rails. Not only was it a code of practice, it was also a history book, and to paraphrase George Santayana, who incidentally may have made a decent signalman: 'Those who don't learn the lessons from history are destined to repeat them'.

Having said that, like numerous people before me, I've always believed rules are for the guidance of the wise and the obedience of fools, nowhere more so than the railway. Although the emergency regulations and safe systems of work are fully adhered to, common sense still has to be employed, especially by the lone worker, even though the use of such is often dismissed, and even vehemently opposed sometimes, and therefore rarely applied nowadays. There can never really be a carte blanche rule book because people interpret rules differently and every signalling location is different. (At the time there were twelve different types of level crossing on the network alone.) Special, local or modified operating instructions always take precedence over the Rule Book anyway. They must, otherwise certain tasks cannot be carried out and some parts of the railway would cease to function. But also, more importantly, life itself doesn't follow a rule book.

The last time I'd ploughed my way through the Rule Book from beginning to end was in 1990 during my trainman course at Toton. The Baron, an old freight guard, had read it to a dozing half dozen of us, page by page, rather like a daily six-hour episode of *Jackanory*, but without any suspension of disbelief or accompanying fulfilment. Like *Jackanory* ('when televisions were in wooden cabinets and had three channels'), I often thought the Rule Book would have been better presented if guest speakers were to deliver its content. Richard Burton or Patrick Stewart would have been natural choices, although I would have liked to hear Brian Blessed take a crack at it too. I could just imagine him booming out all the occasions when a train may pass a signal at danger. But judging by the frequent looks of incomprehension on the faces of my classmates, it may as well have been Klunk from Vulture Squadron delivering the content – the pilot/inventor with the speech impediment from *Dastardly and Muttley in their Flying Machines*, for those without a fully rounded 1970s upbringing.

At least with the Baron, we'd been based in the middle of Toton yard, albeit choking on coal dust and diesel fumes, but if we wanted to view something in real life, we only had to look out of the window or take a short walk into the sidings. No safe work zones, minimal orange gear, just get out there and get your hands dirty. Now we were based in a sterile office building on an industrial estate in Watford, far removed from the railway, although we did have a model railway and a lever frame simulator to play with. The lever frame didn't quite replicate the pulls you'd receive on a proper frame, and because it had no interlocking, you could clear signals that ordinarily you wouldn't be able to in real life. After the first go there was little point in using it again, and having previously operated the frame at Scropton, it just became a pointless distraction as far as I was concerned. I didn't find the model railway to be a useful aid as the only thing that vaguely corresponded to real life was the plastic Humpty Dumpty figure being used as the signalman. Fortunately, our instructor didn't put a lot of emphasis on these things either, but he allowed us to play with the toys in our spare time. Also, for reasons that remain unclear to me, blackboards had turned into white boards, then ultimately into smart boards. Our instructor often used one to show us little animated trains moving from left to right, or alternatively, from right to left across the screen, which of course, was a startling revelation and furthered our understanding no end.

As it turned out, the first week mainly consisted of corporate induction, although we eventually had a full day just on railway communications, which was an entirely new development as far as I was concerned. Signallers had lead responsibility for all safety critical communications, except where an Electrical Control Operator was involved, and messages had to include the phonetic alphabet where applicable. To reach a clear understanding, you also had to ensure the other person repeated back the message you'd just given. I don't know how we ever operated the railway before all this, and it occurred to me that the more the powers-that-be had tried to master communications, the bigger mess they'd made of it. I also found that, during my exile, Train Protection Warning System (TPWS) had been introduced, and since I'd last used one solely for prank calls in Chaddesden Sidings, cab phones had now morphed into Global Systems Mobile-Radio (GSM-R). Two things Tim definitely didn't know about because he'd probably been too busy polishing Stephenson's brass funnel, or some other suitably anachronistic task.

The importance of communication seemed particularly topical since I'd still had no contact with my LOM, and the road map to Watford, which Human Resources had furnished me with, stated the wrong junction off the M25 for the training centre. (Incidentally, I have yet to encounter a human resources department that is either human or resourceful.) Either way, I'm glad I didn't go by train because, weekend engineering works notwithstanding, the station they suggested I get off at had been closed for over a year. I found out from Dave, one of my classmates who lived in Long Eaton (about ten miles away from Derby), that HR had sent him to London for his medical. I told him they'd originally tried to send me to Bristol, but I'd dug my heels in for somewhere local. Consequently, I ended up having my medical in Long Eaton, about two streets away from his house! I eventually came to realize that proper meaningful communication only really existed amongst front line operators; it didn't seem to happen at all within the rest of the rail industry. HR was by far the biggest offender and communication – or rather the lack of it – is a theme that is revisited often throughout this book. I gave Dave a lift home at the end of the first week and we took it in turns thereafter.

Ordinarily the course was scheduled to last nine weeks, but only eight of those would be residential. Week five was supposed to be spent in our normal place of work gaining experience, but as Christmas was looming and the school would break for two weeks, our box experience would occur then. For me, this would mean another seven days over the holiday period trudging around the North Staffs harassing the duty signallers. It also meant that on our return to Watford in the New Year, the first six weeks of 2007 would be spent wholly in the classroom. Over all, our eight weeks in Watford would be composed of seven weeks learning the Absolute Block (AB) method of signalling, and for those who required it (which apparently, I did), a one-week Track Circuit Block (TCB) conversion course.

Perhaps one of the most difficult things to write about, and certainly to make sound interesting, is a person's daily occupational routine. For that reason I don't want to delve too deeply into AB signalling, but I think a 'simplified' overview would be beneficial, partly because it is a marvellously antiquated method that deserves documenting, and which one day may only exist in the sphere of preserved railways, but more importantly, because it might help to explain what was actually happening in the background whilst I was putting together all these anecdotes and writing this book. It's probably easier to explain quantum theory than Absolute Block, but once a basic truth or principle has been grasped, the rest may slot into place of its own accord. Therefore, in quantum theory, waves can behave as particles and particles can behave as waves. In Absolute Block, under normal circumstances, the idea is to prevent more than one train being in a block section on the same line at the same time.

In the early days of railways, men called 'policemen' (some were originally sworn constables) were positioned at specific points along the track to control train movements using a method called Time Interval Working. The clue is in the name and this involved one train following another after a certain amount of time had elapsed. The major flaw with this method was that if the first train broke down or stopped for any reason, the following train could, and often did, crash into the back of it. Absolute Block evolved with the advent of the telegraph, which allowed dedicated signalmen, who eventually replaced the policemen, to communicate with each other using a block instrument. The obvious information being exchanged through these block instruments (i.e., a block indicator and a bell), would be that a train had passed safely, a specific section of track was again clear, and that another train could now be accepted, hence *absolute* block. Incidentally, a signalman was still referred to as a 'Bobby' (amongst other names!) many years later, but twenty-first century safety critical communications put an end to that quaint practice. Absolute Block became mandatory on passenger carrying lines in 1889 and the method has remained largely unchanged, although the rules continue to evolve, usually after every accident or major operating incident. Surprisingly, Time Interval Working wasn't removed from the Rule Book until 1991, but the railway has always been slow at catching up.

Now you have the basic principle of railway signalling, feel free to skip the more detailed explanation in the Appendix about how this is achieved, unless of course you happen to be reading in bed, in which case carry on! Either way, do not worry if enlightenment eludes you. In the subject of Absolute Block, enlightenment only really comes after practical experience in an actual signal box, and for some, not even then. But perhaps this was why the AB course was seven weeks long...

The block instruments at Sudbury – note the highly polished block bells. *Author*.

Actually, the AB course was so long because signalling trains is only one part of the job. There are other facets that people don't often realize, such as controlling movements over level crossings, first line management of faults, failures, accidents and emergencies, shunt moves, overseeing engineering possessions and keeping maintenance crews safe on the track.

Like abbreviations, the railway also loves its paperwork, so along with the thirty odd Rule Book modules, there were about twenty different report forms I had to become reacquainted with, as well as the weekly and periodic operating notices, Sectional Appendix (or Sexual Appendage as it was often known), Level Crossing Occurrence Book, and the all-important Train Register Book (TRB), not forgetting the phonetic alphabet and over fifty different bell codes to memorize as well. It's not just about lowering level crossing barriers and frustrating motorists, which to be fair, is the only part of the job most people really see. Whenever you encounter the railway, whether as a fare paying passenger, motorist or even a trespasser, there will be someone in a box looking after your welfare and keeping you safe whilst you pass through their section.

During the second week we started turning pages of the Rule Book with increasing intensity, and as our days were spent in the classroom and part of our evenings spent writing up notes and revising, I was concerned about not getting enough fresh air, having previously been used to more outdoor labours. There was also a danger of overindulging in the Travelodge bar, and thus, life beginning to imitate art, i.e., me starting to resemble the plastic signalman from the model railway, so I determined to get some exercise. Being a typically tight railwayman and not wanting this enterprise to cost me anything, I decided to walk the couple of miles to the Harlequin Shopping Centre every evening, as its opening hours had been extended for Christmas. I was wrong about this enterprise not costing me anything because I grudgingly updated my predominantly Primark wardrobe. No matter the ensemble though, I still looked like an extra from *Minder*.

At the end of the second week we had our first exam. I didn't feel as though it had given me any problems, except that it took an interminably long time for the papers to be marked and for us to receive our results before homeward departure. It was Friday afternoon and, Christmas notwithstanding, there were, of course, major road works on the M25 and M1, so Dave and I were understandably anxious to be underway. We decided to sally forth without our results, but once we'd hit the M1 our instructor phoned to say that we'd both passed.

During the Christmas break I made Scropton my temporary residence and was allowed to work the box under the supervision of the duty signalman, putting what little theory I'd learned in two weeks into some sort of practice. I operated the gates and signals and began to gain confidence tapping out the bell codes whilst they made the necessary entries in the TRB. For the first time I felt the full weight of the job, especially when it came to authorizing motorists to cross at Mill Lane user worked crossing (UWC), which was about 200 metres away and supervised by Scropton. It suddenly felt a huge responsibility, even when there were no trains on the block, and initially, I was very reluctant to even answer the phone concentrator, often prompting the duty signaller to shoulder the burden.

Authorizing people to cross was done at least ten times a day, every day, and although I eventually came to take it in my stride, I considered it to be one of the hidden stresses of the job and always remained very wary whenever the phone concentrator bleeped. The resultant rise in blood pressure aside, perhaps that was the best way to be. Mill Lane was about the only thing that could trip you up at Scropton, and I vowed to always remain on my toes.

It also became depressingly clear to me how far I still had to go before I could call myself a Signalman. Assuming I got through the next six weeks of school unscathed, I would then have to undergo a ruling with my LOM, followed by an approval conducted by Her Majesty's Signalling Inspectorate (HMRI), before hopefully being passed competent on the rules. After that, I still had to learn a signal box, then a further box after that before I could finally obtain my official grade of Scropton GPR Signalman. It seemed a long road stretching before me. Speaking of long roads, I had still never met my LOM during those days at the box and wondered if he was still on annual leave. If so, I could only assume it was one those all-inclusive 80 day round trips with Phileas Fogg.

We returned to Watford on 7 January 2007 and gradually got back into the classroom routine again. The pace at which we were devouring Rule Book modules had been stepped up and I felt the old grey matter beginning to bulge against the cranium. I wasn't sure if it was newly acquired knowledge being stored or an imminent critical mass, although I very much suspected the latter. The main theme throughout was AB signalling and we continued to plod through its many facets such as restricted acceptance, blocking back, obstruction of the line, train passed without tail lamps, train proceeding without authority, train divided and train failure. We only had a couple of hours learning single line working whereas a full day had been spent on communications. I found this odd, but I suppose people were always (allegedly) communicating and single line working was rarely employed nowadays. (If one track has become obstructed, single line working allows trains to be run on an adjacent unobstructed track in *either* direction.)

If anything, it was the basic mode of signalling that initially confused me. According to the Rule Book, in a situation where there are three signal boxes, A, B and C and you are the signaller at box B, you accept a train from box A, and then after you have received 'train entering section', you offer it on to box C. But every box has its own Signal Box Special Instructions (SBSI) and I'd been using Scropton's, thinking that was the norm. There, you accept a train from box A and immediately offer it on to box C (providing it's a class 1, 2, or 5 train on the Down). Upon receiving 'train entering section' from box A, you then send 'train approaching' (1-2-1) to box C (but only for class 1 or 2 trains on the Down). On the Up line, you accept and offer immediately and send 1-2-1 for every train. No wonder the grey matter was about to bubble over! It also reinforces what I mentioned earlier about how the Rule Book cannot be absolute. If it were, there would be no need for SBSIs. What might be an exceptional circumstance in one location could perhaps be common practice in another.

You could always rely on the railway to provide a few decent mnemonics, acronyms and abbreviations as *aide-mémoires* though. TOSBIN was a good one, which stood for Train Out (Of) Section Block Indicator Normal. But by far the best and I thought the most imaginative mnemonic related to the sending of 6 bells, better known to signallers as Obstruction Danger. There were several occasions when 6 had to be sent, other than for an emergency, and TITS RA RA was a good way to remember them, if a train arrives at your signal box and the following criteria has not previously been met:

Train entering section not   Received.
Is line clear? (train bell code description) not   Acknowledged.
Train without authority in right direction not   Received.
Shunting into forward section not   Acknowledged.

I also thought the phonetic alphabet would have made a good riddle or crossword question too: What has a Greek start, a rousing encouragement, five male names, is triangular shaped, repeats the fifth letter, has two ballroom dances, is a good walk spoiled, offers bed and board, was part of the Empire, includes a Shakespearian play, has metric weight, is the capital of Peru, is an autumnal month, has paternal qualities, is a Canadian province, a Ford car, wears professional dress, is an intoxicating drink, has a revealing sweep of radiation, and a restless native after an American? (Alpha, Bravo, Charlie, Delta, Echo, Foxtrot, Golf, Hotel, India, Juliet, Kilo, Lima, Mike, November, Oscar, Papa, Quebec, Romeo, Sierra, Tango, Uniform, Victor, Whiskey, X-ray, Yankee, Zulu).

The Rule Book section that dealt with a loco running round its train appeared to cause much confusion amongst the class, which wasn't surprising considering there were three separate bell codes to learn, one for each stage of the process. Also, the loco that left the train might not be the same loco that picked it up and may even come from a different direction. As can be imagined, this revelation caused much scratching of (now fully enlarged) heads.

"Come on Tim, you must have done this move before," bemoaned the instructor, without feeling the need to refer to any historical references this time.

"Yes, thousands of times (I even wrote an explanatory paragraph in DTM about it), but I was always on the ground, never in a signal box."

I understood the procedure perfectly, but how a signaller achieved it, other than move points and clear signals was a total mystery to me. I was still grappling with the fact that a signalman wasn't called a 'Bobby' anymore, or more to the point, that a signalman wasn't even called a signalman anymore.

After all the effort of re-branding everyone a signaller, I never understood why the railway continued to use the nonsensical title of

Pilotman. Person In Lieu Of Token described the role exactly, regardless of gender. The 'man' part is completely unnecessary, as no doubt some women would agree. (A 'Pilot' is used during single line working.) British Rail had a similar problem with the Trainman Concept. As there weren't many trainwomen on the job at the time, the written generic title was always Train(wo)man. The addition of brackets made it positively clunky, but this was British Rail in the late 1980s after all. I have no idea what the modern neutral title would have been as Trainer is misleading and Trainperson lacks imagination. In a similar vein, I have yet to discover what the neutral title for 'white van man' might be too. I have heard other motorists refer to us as suicide jockeys on occasion (obviously those mad courier drivers giving us a bad name), so that might cover it. I do recall someone telling me that a yardman/travelling shunter had been re-designated as a Shunt Captain...Ahoy maties! The old 4 Shed boys would have loved that one. I can just imagine some of them assuming the names of the crew from *Captain Pugwash* (the urban myth version) so as not to feel left out. There were already innumerable candidates for the roles of Master Bates, Seaman Staines and Roger the Cabin Boy.

I know Royal Mail had a similar problem in the 1990s when they started calling a person who delivered the mail a Post Person, but it didn't last very long. I never heard anyone call their Postman or woman a Post Person, unless they specifically wanted their letters shredded. (What's wrong with Postie anyway?) The only group I can immediately recall who had any success with this was the fire service. The title of Firefighter fitted the bill perfectly, regardless of gender. These wacky titles are all relative anyway. I remember one chap at Toton who was designated Environmental Manager...he swept the mess room and closed all the windows. In later years, I came across a woman in HR who had the ludicrous title of Talent Manager yet had absolutely none herself.

Although AB remained the constant theme we continually studied and cross-referenced the other pertinent modules such as General Signalling Regulations, incident management, shunting and detained trains, engineering work and possessions (not the supernatural kind I hasten to add), Level Crossing Regulations and wrong direction movements. We also had to be conversant with the duties of drivers, platform and shunting staff. We learnt and committed ten bell codes to memory each week and these were constantly practised during our break times and the short walk between training centre and Travelodge. Dave and I would sometimes have an impromptu revision session during our journey to Watford on Sunday evenings, but never on Friday afternoons. We just wanted to get home, particularly after the stress of waiting around for our exam results.

We upset the instructor before one exam when he asked us to name equipment you'd find in a signal box. He went around the room, but people were scratching their heads and saying obscure things like chair or mop bucket, no one said the obvious like levers or block instruments, much to his increasing irritation. The question had taken us by surprise because we'd been expecting something more complex like trying to talk our way out of a failed train scenario.   The question was so simple and commonplace it had bamboozled us, and we couldn't effectively answer it, not to his satisfaction anyway.   He wasn't pleased and said that we'd better get our act together, before marching out of the room.   I then realized this was a common training tactic.   I suspect he went for a cuppa and put his feet up in the office, and then he'd send a colleague in to gee us up a bit.   Sure enough the spare instructor came in shaking his head and saying things like "You lot have really upset him, what have you done?" and so forth.   From then on, I couldn't help smiling, partly because of the absurd answers that had been given, but mostly because it reminded me of a time, nearly twenty years before in the Forces, when my squad hadn't been up to standard during an element of field training.   Corporal Cole, one of the instructors, did a similar thing, only a lot less diplomatically.

Corporal Cole never seemed to be attached to a specific squad; he just appeared out of thin air to offer gentle words of advice and encouragement, convincingly disguised as threats and insults.   I came to realize that all recruit training corporals, including physical training instructors (PTI), were the result of some secret MoD cloning project.   They were all tough, lean and mean, with eyes in the back of their head and the ability to talk *at* you, not *to* you, from the side of their mouth.   This probably explained the strange enunciated speech they all seemed to have, as a common phrase was always '*Yew* is being *idol*,' never 'You are being idle'.   They were also gifted with superhuman hearing and endurance.   Some models may have sported a 1980s porn star 'tache, but they were all clones just the same.   The PTI models often came off the assembly line slightly cross-eyed, due to what I can only assume was a groin strain in the original prototype.   It also explained how they could be looking straight ahead yet still managed to see things way back in their periphery.   It wasn't just insects that had compound eyes.   I assumed Corporal Cole was a hybrid model because not only did he have the crossed-eyes, it was also rumoured that he'd been the UK Forces speed marching champion at one time or another.   He was probably only in his mid-twenties but already had curvature of the spine from carrying heavy packs and speed marching everywhere.   He looked like a bipedal ant and everything he did was at a fast pace, which was most unsettling.

On the occasion in question his face was already contorting, and he began by saying "You..." but was so disgusted to even address us that there was a pause whilst his face contorted some more as he stalked up and down the front rank burning everyone with his intense glare.   Next, he would get as far as saying "You people..." He just couldn't bring himself to call us men, let alone soldiers.   Then there would be more stalking and glaring before he finally seemed able to choke down his disgust and complete his sentence, "You people better start getting your act together because I'm watching you."   He made the 'you' sound like you as an individual rather than you as a group, and with his slight cross-eyed glare it felt as though he was looking directly at you too.   But that was all a man as fearsome as Corporal Cole needed to say.   He really did have the power to make our lives a misery and the last thing you wanted was him watching you. He let the words sink in then stalked off stage right. Another corporal then entered stage left, not a clone this time, but a general duties corporal. He sauntered in, shaking his head and sucking on his back teeth. "It doesn't look good lads; you'd better start sharpening up a bit," he said, nodding in the direction of the recently departed Corporal Cole. Back then there was always the constant fear of being put back a squad if you weren't up to standard, or 'new bed space, new friends' as it was often called – a harsh reality of recruit training that's not mentioned before you sign on the dotted line.

For most of us at signaling school, if we didn't pass the exams, there was no back squad, no job and we'd be back on the street, so we felt the pressure well and truly upon us throughout our time at Watford. We were spared the trauma of an exam at the end of the third week but were clobbered with one at the end of every week thereafter, with the fifth and sixth week seeming the most intense. Week seven seemed to pass quickly but included some heavy sessions, and we had the final AB exam on Thursday, so that we could mount an assault on Watford's drinking establishments later that evening, leaving a bleary-eyed Friday for the remaining admin and certificate presentation.

In comparison, the TCB conversion course during week eight felt a bit of an anti-climax. That module only contained a quarter of the pages that the AB module did, primarily because large areas of the network were operated by power signal boxes (PSB) or integrated electronic control centres (IECC), and train movements were controlled by track circuits, instead of lots of little signal boxes tapping out bells and using arcane methods to move them about. (It is quite amusing to find that TCB itself is now somewhat of an antiquated system!) As a relief signalman, I needed this part of the course to work at Egginton Junction and Alrewas, which were fringe boxes, with Track Circuit Block to Derby PSB one way and Absolute Block to Tutbury and Lichfield Trent Valley respectively, the other. Resident signallers worked their own box, whereas relief signallers covered their periods of absence and were trained to work numerous boxes, which would be my eventual fate upon return to the North Staffs. Just to add to the confusion, some AB boxes also contained the odd track circuit, but these generally only applied to a small area and made little difference to the overall method of signalling. Scropton, for example, had one track circuit, which was only about 100 metres long.

From a total lack of enthusiasm to an eventual grudging acceptance of having to undertake a lengthy residential course I found, to my surprise, that I very much enjoyed my time in Watford, and in a perverse sort of way, I knew I would quite miss it. I wouldn't miss the Sunday evening departures, the motorway commute or the stress of waiting around for exam results, but I would miss the laughs, jokes and camaraderie; something to remember in the years to come when working a signal box alone, as most of us were now destined to do.

Upon successful completion of signalling school on Friday 16 February, and having received no other instructions, I reported to Scropton the following Monday morning. The duty signalman let me work the box and I began to reacquaint myself with its many fickle ways. Presently, a Network Rail car pulled up and a stern-faced orange-coated chap got out and strode purposefully towards the box. The duty signalman noticeably stiffened, much like a person does when spotting a police car in their rear-view mirror whilst driving.

"Watch out, here's the boss."

Finally, I was going to meet my elusive LOM. However, it wasn't quite the great meeting of minds that I'd envisaged. He had no idea who I was, or that the Scropton GPR vacancy had even been filled. I told him I'd just completed signalling school where good communication had been one of the first lessons. He didn't look too impressed and even less so when I presented him with my travel expenses form.

"You were meant to go by train."

"Oh, was I? I didn't know," I lied, launching into the selective vagueness act I'd been rehearsing for several weeks (unfortunately it wasn't always an act with me). It wasn't an encouraging start and he told me to forget everything about Scropton and go and learn Tutbury. There were obviously a lot of internal politics that I was not yet fully cognisant with, but no matter, I had obtained a good grounding at Scropton and was interested to see how it related to Tutbury. First though, I would need a proper, official induction day, where all the paperwork would be correctly shuffled, and the boxes ticked (visited too in the case of the North Staffs ones), which apparently should have been carried out a mere ten weeks ago. Perhaps that's why he looked so unhappy, although the duty signalman assured me that he always looked like that.

Part of the reason for my move to Tutbury was because of another trainee. Sloth had preceded me from Leeds signalling school by a month, and whilst I was finishing at Watford, he had somehow managed to be passed competent on his rules, passed to work Tutbury, and was now ready to learn Scropton; and two trainees were not allowed in a box at the same time. With gangly arms and legs and a permanently tired look on his face, Sloth had the appearance of having just dropped from a branch to which he'd previously been clinging fast asleep. I could imagine him being interviewed for Nick Park's *Creature Comforts* as a plasticine sloth, hanging from the rafters of a signal box and explaining why it was difficult to remain awake and signal trains, all in a monotonous Brummie accent.

I didn't call him Sloth out of any malice, not from the outset anyway. It was only when I found out that his lax attitude and poor performance matched his physical appearance that it sort of stuck. As he preceded me to most boxes, I would often get tarred with the same brush until I could prove myself otherwise. Even when I'd got a couple of boxes under my belt I still couldn't get rid of him because he was either next door or we were taking each other off duty. He was always at great pains to tell me how he'd given up a fantastic paying job to come and do this, but the question lurking in my mind was why? The only conclusion I could come up with was that he'd got the push from this previously fantastic paying job. I knew he was a wrong 'un and it didn't bode well.

After my official induction on Tuesday I reported to Tutbury to meet one of its resident signalmen who would be training me for the next couple of weeks. Unfortunately, he wasn't there and was taking a few days holiday, no doubt to recover from training Sloth. So far, the communication had been outstanding, and once again I had to plod around the North Staffs, alternating between Tutbury and Sudbury. It wasn't until Friday when I finally managed to meet my trainer and do part of a shift at Tutbury.

An illustration of an old North Staffordshire Railway lever collar/reminder appliance. Hardly a high-tech piece of equipment, but it did the job (see page 31).

3. TUTBURY TRIALS

Tutbury Crossing, August 2005. *David Pritchard.*

Tutbury Crossing was a compact but attractive little box, which was kept scrupulously clean by its two resident signalmen, although clinically clean may perhaps have better described it. I was beginning to wonder if I should have worn gloves and plastic bags on my boots, or at least one of those jaunty hats they wear in food preparation factories, as I crossed its threshold. The place would have made a regimental sergeant major's moustache quiver with delight, except for the eclectic assortment of tat and plastic troll doll/action figures adorning some of its walls and ledges. At first, I thought a few of the plastic characters from the Watford model railway had followed me here and it looked as though some overzealous Womble had been picking stuff up off the track and displaying it in the box – but then again, I'd yet to meet all the staff. I tried to avoid these largely unwanted insights into a person's character, but even Doctor Watson, with his questionable skills in deductive reasoning, would have been able to form a reasonably accurate assessment of a box resident's character and lifestyle based on the bric-a-brac within. In most boxes there appeared to be a sort of 'my style, my madness' theme going on.

In keeping with the intimate box environment at Tutbury was a nice little lever frame, consisting of a distant and a combined home/section lever for each direction, as well as two spares and a release lever. All Tutbury's signals were semaphores, but the distant signals were motorized for an easier pull. I smiled the first time I used the frame because I'd used ground frames that were bigger. Particularly Avenue Ground Frame, near Chesterfield, which in trainman days had consisted of three release levers and three co-acting point levers, where I had performed complicated shunt moves and run ballast trains round. But back then I hadn't needed to concern myself with all the signalling regulations and I could just get on with it, much as I'd tried to explain to my instructor at Watford.

Tutbury's bijou (and spotless) frame, August 2006. *Helen Chadfield.*

Now however, I did have to concern myself with such matters and suddenly found myself under pressure as the first morning trains in either direction often arrived at once. The mode of signalling was as per Rule Book and, having received 'train entering section' (2) on the Down, or 'train approaching' (1-2-1) on the Up, the barriers could be lowered, and the relevant signals cleared. The only difference was that 1-2-1 had to be sent for non-stopping trains on the Up, as specified in the special instructions. There was a lot to think about with two trains at once, and you could always tell a trainee fresh from school; he was the one nervously pacing up and down and wearing a hole in the freshly vacuumed carpet. For some reason I kept expecting my cheerful LOM to turn up right in the middle of it, just in time to see me implode from all the multi-tasking, particularly as the box also supervised four UWCs. However, only one of these (Weer Lane) was used with any sort of regularity.

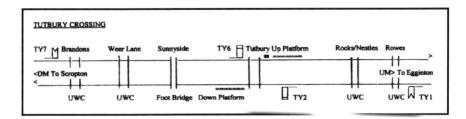

I was under the watchful eye of my trainer throughout, but he told me that he didn't really consider himself a proper signalman. He wasn't working a junction box, there were no sidings or trains to regulate, and he was just sending one down and one up. That was easy for him to say; the rut I'd created in his carpet was now an inch deep! In years past there would have been much more to deal with, even at a simple crossing box, such as trains passing with carriage doors open, paraffin tail lamps blown out, hot axle boxes, divided trains – all proper signalling. My instructor would have loved this discussion, plenty of anachronistic references to squeeze in here. Now the time was just filled with corporate flannel and extra paperwork that none of the old signalmen would have had time for, both professionally or personally.

Nevertheless, the pace of work suited me just fine, provided I remembered to answer the correct block bell when it rang. Each bell was cast in a slightly different shape to give a higher or lower tone when struck. Although there was a discernible 'ding' to each one, it took a while to become accustomed to the slight differences, especially if you'd had your back to them or been unable to observe the hammer strike when 'call attention' was received. A quick flick of each bell would resolve any uncertainty and the correct one could then be answered. The process of elimination was easy, it could only be Egginton one side or Scropton the other.

There were also weekly track inspections and periodic maintenance to consider, which always involved the completion of a line blockage form before granting permission to maintenance staff to carry out their on-track duties. (This process was originally called a T2, after its specific Rule Book module, but was eventually renamed simply as a line blockage.) Obviously, these blockages were granted during suitable gaps between trains and the signaller would place a lever collar/reminder appliance on the relevant protecting signal lever and request the box in advance to turn their commutator to 'train on line' as further protection. It was often a juggling act getting staff on and off the track in between trains or granting a block on one line whilst still running trains on the other, but their lives were in your hands and good communication, concentration and box knowledge was vital.

When not keeping a beady eye on me, my trainer kept a beady eye on any passing females, either walking to and from the adjacent supermarket or passing in cars. This is something every heterosexual male is programmed to do, regardless of age and marital status. It had always been one of the perks of HGV driving for me and I was amused to find the practice alive and well in the signal box. My old HGV instructor used to call it 'pesting'. If you actively engaged women in pubs or nightclubs it was 'trapping', if it was just a look, nod, smile or wink, that was 'pesting'. Women, on the other hand, may have had another term for it. But before those of us who hold a deep respect and life-long appreciation of the female form are castigated or accused of a 'hate crime', let me make it clear that this was merely admiration from afar and one of the many box activities. In fact, a study was conducted some years later that determined adult men spent, on average, more than eleven months of their lives eyeing-up the ladies. Apparently, we gaze at up to ten women every day, spending roughly 43 minutes admiring them. I don't think enough manual signalmen were canvassed; the data seems a little tame to me.

We'd been told how to open and close boxes at signalling school (5-5-5 to open and 7-5-5 to close), but I'd never actually seen it in real life. Whenever I mentioned to any duty signaller that I'd like to come first thing in the morning or stay until the last train at night to observe the process, they always looked shocked and tried to dissuade me from any such notions. Most seemed very defensive about their early mornings and downright evasive about their late evenings. It was all very mysterious. I suppose it was because the process was so straightforward they couldn't understand why you'd want to observe it, and because they were seeing enough of you in the day, they didn't want their morning and evening routines disrupted as well. I began to suspect some were conducting black masses or weird Masonic ceremonies on the side. I never did get to see the process during training and when my time came to do it for real, there was no mystery and I just did it.

In between signalling and 'pesting', my trainer and I discussed the hours of duty on the North Staffs. Early turn was 06:30-14:16 and late turn was 14:16-22:02 weekdays, with a 06:10 start on Saturdays. Sunday was a late turn only from 13:55-22:25, and the boxes were open every day apart from Christmas Day and Boxing Day. The afternoon shift start time could sometimes be as much as an hour earlier, particularly on a Saturday, owing to old traditions – mainly involving sport or beer, but usually both – which most of the current signalmen still maintained, even though sports coverage was now unlimited and licensing hours unrestricted.

"There are nights you know," my trainer suddenly exclaimed.

"Yes, I know," I replied, rather unenthusiastically, aware that engineering arrangements sometimes meant night shifts, usually covered by the relief signallers."

"It's just that one trainee was refusing to do nights." He looked to see if I was about to make the same refusal. I'd refuse them if I could because they were certainly not my favourite shift, but I had accepted them as part of the job a long time ago.

I reflected that at least fifteen years had passed since I'd last been on a night shift at Tutbury. On that occasion I'd been seated in the back cab of a pair of Class 20s that were heading an engineering train. So as not to foul the road crossing we'd been positioned right in front of the box, and there we stood for the entire shift. I can't even remember when we got relief, but to steal a perfect line from Nicholas Monsarrat's *The Cruel Sea*, it was '...at some dead hour before the cock crew and ghosts must walk no more.' I only remember that it was an extremely miserable shift, as most ballast jobs were, but it must have been equally miserable for the signalman, having two noisy locos out front and choking on their diesel fumes. I did wonder if it had been my trainer on duty all those years ago but was suddenly jolted back to the present by a 'ding' of a bell. A neighbour was calling my attention and, until I flicked each bell, I wouldn't know for sure which one.

Of course, having women to 'pest' meant that members of the general and travelling public were at large too, and they regularly pestered the signaller. Tutbury's downside was ironically its Up side station platform situated next to the box, which instantly made its hapless occupant the first point of contact for all enquiries and complaints. However, unless the enquiry or complaint related directly to the Derby-Crewe-Derby service, the enquirer or complainant may have had more success speaking to the checkout assistant in the nearby supermarket. My trainer introduced me to the loudspeaker system that would have to be used to make the necessary station announcements regarding delayed or cancelled trains. Perhaps I was being a trifle pessimistic but I rather suspected that after using this equipment to relay such messages, I might as well just pin a target on my back.

Until I worked a signal box I never fully realized how reckless (stupid is probably a better word) people were upon encountering level crossing barriers which were about to lower. Instead of acting as a warning to motorists and pedestrians to stop, the red flashing road lights and audible alarm just seemed to encourage some of them to put an extra spurt on. Even as the barriers were visibly lowering, people were still determined to go under them no matter what. I tended to think that these road users were descended from the sort of people who continually laid siege to castles centuries ago. No matter how many times they had boiling oil and flaming arrows rained upon them, they kept coming. I kept a mental note whilst I was training, and on average, a signaller at Tutbury was getting at least two close calls a shift. By close calls I mean car aerials, roofs (and occasionally heads!) making contact with the barrier skirts. I was initially shocked but quickly became relaxed about it. These people had made the conscious decision to cross, despite the warnings, so I continued with the lowering sequence regardless. Obviously, I would stop if it were going to damage the barriers or cause me to fill in any paperwork; I just wanted to try to shock them into some awareness as to the stupidity of their actions. I came to realize this was largely a fool's quest, but I cannot deny that the thought of raining boiling oil or flaming arrows upon these transgressors was a curiously satisfying one.

As the main road through Hatton was narrow in places, and there were two busy junctions directly behind the box (one for the supermarket and one for the Nestles factory), traffic would often back up across the level crossing. Many motorists obeyed the solid white lines either side and didn't encroach on the crossing, but not all. I would often start the lowering sequence only to look down and find a rather worried motorist about to be trapped on the tracks. It was one sure way of grabbing their attention though, or rather them desperately trying to grab yours. There were also the occasional blue-lighted ambulances dashing to Burton Hospital – usually when the barriers had just been lowered – and these would obviously pass the standing traffic to wait at the front of the queue. If no signals had been cleared it was possible to raise the barriers, show them a green hand signal (flag or lamp) and get them across. You then had to quickly lower the barriers again before anyone else tried to have a go. If the signals had been cleared the ambulance could only jump the queue and wait, in which case the signaller would feel largely hopeless until the train passed clear. Some motorists must have thought us callous, but once the signals had been cleared, there was no going back. The consequences of returning the signals to danger to raise the barriers could be catastrophic, particularly with a combined home/section signal and a non-stopping train. It would certainly negate the noble objective you were originally trying to achieve.

As may be gathered from above, Tutbury's barriers had no approach locking and could be raised before a train had passed. This was one of the contributing factors in the terrible incident at Moreton-on-Lugg in 2010. Although that incident happened in Herefordshire, its impact was felt around the network, but it wasn't until after the inquest in 2013 that Tutbury's barriers had approach locking fitted: another rule tragically written in blood.

Towards the end of March, I felt my time at Tutbury beginning to drag a little. I had hoped for a ruling with my LOM before then and began to wonder if I'd been forgotten again. I'd interspersed my time with several visits to Scropton and, thanks to my colleagues, my rules knowledge had been adequately honed, but I knew the edge would dull if left too long. At the beginning of April, I got to caution my first train. Although I didn't know it then, my first time using flags to caution a train would also be my last. With cab phone to signal box communication becoming the preferred method, the requirement for a signaller to use flags and engage in face-to-face communication was removed from the Rule Book shortly afterwards.

On this occasion Marston automatic half barrier (AHB) level crossing, which lies between Egginton and Tutbury, had developed a fault, and although Egginton supervised the crossing, Tutbury had to caution Up trains if there was a problem there. The procedure was simple enough, once the next Up train was at (or nearly at) a stand at Tutbury's combined home/section signal, clear the signal slowly, display a red flag to the driver for the train to stop at the box, give the necessary verbal instructions, then display a green flag for their authority to proceed…all very Victorian. If I'd known it was going to be my last time using flags, I'd have worn a waistcoat, pocket watch, stovepipe hat and stuck on some whiskery sideburns. If I ever end up on the railway again in my next evolution, it won't be a case of Stephenson's *Rocket* anymore; it will be 'when they used flags to signal trains' and I will be able to say "Yep, done that!"

On 10 April I was finally summoned to the RTC for my ruling with the LOM, and it was brutal! He grilled me for seven hours straight on the first day, then five hours the following day. I think he was trying to exact some revenge for my Watford travelling expenses, although there was a rumour circulating that he'd originally been a member of the Stasi but had been kicked out for being overzealous. Nevertheless, I talked my way through it to his satisfaction and was then sent for my approval by HMRI a week later. The inspector quizzed me for a couple of hours before passing me competent. Now I just had to get a signal box under my belt, but first I took a week's pre-arranged leave. I was pleased to have finally got through this part of the process, but all signallers had to undergo the Signallers' Continuous Assessment Programme (SCAP), which was a rules assessment designed to keep knowledge up to date. Like household bills, these assessments arrived quarterly and were welcomed in much the same manner. It also meant that from now until the end of my career I would never be free from rules tests.

After my leave I briefly rejoined my trainer at Tutbury until the LOM arrived on 2 May to pass me out. He gave my long-suffering colleague an early day then watched me work the box for a few hours, occasionally firing the odd question in my direction. There were no surprises and I felt reasonably comfortable throughout. The real test would come the following morning when I would do my first shift alone. That morning soon came, and I felt like Atlas as I ascended the box steps. I too felt the weight of the world upon my shoulders, but I had the additional burden of many butterflies in my stomach. There is trepidation on that first day, as there is doing anything for the first time that is initially out of your comfort zone. Along with this trepidation however, comes a curious sense of exhilaration and freedom. After months of training, you are suddenly let loose to face the final test alone.

The box key was kept on a ledge above the door, or rather tossed to the back of this ledge by the last person out, very often rendering it out of reach to the next person in. For all Tutbury's interior cleanliness, grasping around that ledge just brought down dusty detritus on your head, and sometimes an incongruous little metal hand shovel that seemed to serve no discernible purpose, but was always left in the most inconvenient places. I didn't know how some of my vertically challenged colleagues carried on, but I deduced from the small crumpled metal wastepaper bin nearby that it was regularly upended and stood on to facilitate key retrieval.

After gaining entry, I reasoned that if I could just signal the first two trains without incident, then everything would be fine, and so it came to pass. That was until seven Network Rail vans pulled up in the supermarket car park at 09:00 and twenty Permanent Way (PWay) blokes began digging up my level crossing! I spent the next four hours arranging line blockages and blocking back inside my home signal in both directions between trains, which doesn't sound too terrible when written here, but was a very intense first shift. Blocking back inside the home signal is done when the clearing point (safety margin) beyond a home signal needs to be obstructed – in this case, by the blokes digging up the level crossing. After sending the appropriate bell code, you purposely switch your block indicator to 'train on line' to lock the signals of the box in rear. Taking a line blockage on the other line results in a similar action, only it is the signaller in advance who switches their block indicator to lock your signals. Along with reminders placed on the relevant signal levers and commutators, these actions help to prevent a train from being inadvertently signalled on the obstructed lines. But even with all these safeguards, it still rests with the signaller to implement them and maintain concentration. It became quite a plate-spinning act getting the workers on and off safely between trains and was certainly a baptism of fire for me. They say everyone remembers their first day working a signal box on their own; well I certainly had cause to.

That first shift alone was not dissimilar to how I used to feel as an agency truck driver in the mid 1990s, the apprehension intensifying as I waited around for the dreaded phone call that would launch me into the unknown. When it came, as it often did about 10:30 – after the better part of the morning had been wasted – I would arrive at the haulage company not knowing what sort of vehicle I would be driving, what load I'd be carrying, or even where I'd be going. (In my case, it could be anything from 7.5 to 38 tonnes, frozen chickens to hazardous chemicals and anywhere in the UK – or conceivably anywhere in Europe for that matter – although I tended to avoid overnight runs, eventually specializing mainly in Class 2 tipper work.) Also, there was no sat nav back then, so a professional driver would have to carry a wide selection of maps with them, if they wanted to survive the day. Other than the address of the company that you were being dispatched to, it was a waste of time trying to elicit further information from the agency about what you might be facing because they always assured you that it was local multi-drop work, just to get you to turn up. On reporting to the company however, you'd invariably find it was six drops in central London, or something equally hellish. (You could be reasonably assured of getting the jobs and/or vehicles that no one else wanted, simply because an agency driver would not be required otherwise.) But whereas I'd had nearly five months learning to be a signalman, I'd only ever had seven actual days learning to drive a heavy goods vehicle. Obtaining my licence was perhaps the easiest part because, after that, it was automatically assumed that I also had intimate knowledge of the motorway network, different types of trailers, methods of load and restraint, drivers' hours and many other facets of HGV driving that went largely unmentioned during the L-test. One of my first driving jobs also involved operating a lorry-mounted crane – something else I'd never been trained on – which had considerably more levers than Tutbury box. It was more like playing a piano, as I gingerly tickled and stroked its keyboard-like arrangement of levers. Unfortunately, no sweet music was forthcoming as the crane jib shook, shuddered and rotated in every direction but the one I wanted. However, taking the plunge and muddling through enough of those fearful agency jobs was the only way of gaining the experience. You could study all the rule books you liked. There was simply no substitute for standing up and doing it. So it would be with signalling – or almost any occupation for that matter – but, like agency HGV driving (and perhaps a pilot doing their first solo flight and a bomb disposal operative on the 'longest walk'), I am hard-pressed to think of many other jobs where you took that gut wrenching plunge entirely alone.

4. SCROPTON SWINGER

If you wanted to conjure up an image of a classic mechanical signal box, Scropton Crossing may well have been it. It was a box straight out of the AB training manual too, with cable pull semaphores in both directions, a crossover and manually operated crossing gates. If you weren't swinging on its levers, you were swinging on its gates! I remembered Scropton from my old trainman days, particularly the very distinctive bell tower of St. Paul's Church. When passing this point on all those mundane test jobs from Crewe, it still seemed a long way to go before reaching Derby, signing off duty and hoisting that first pint. I never dreamed that one day I'd end up in the signal box.

With Scropton Brook and the River Dove running close by, the area was prone to heavy fog and flooding at certain times of the year, which I had definite cause to remember. I was once receiving some driving instruction on a Class 150 unit and we were returning to Derby in thick fog. I got checked at Scropton's Up Distant and started braking, bringing the unit nicely under control, my eyes glued to the windscreen looking for a pinprick of red light. I was probably only doing about 5mph, when suddenly the home signal loomed out of the impenetrable greyness and I had to quickly put the brake into emergency to avoid passing it at danger. Consequently, it wasn't a very graceful stop and I ended up with my nose pressed against the windscreen, which was a small price to pay for stopping on the right side of the signal. It seemed strange to be standing in the box, pressing my nose against the window and seeing the back of that signal now.

During my many stints at Scropton over the past few months I'd got to know the resident signalmen quite well. They seemed an unlikely pair because one was young and relatively carefree, whereas the other was well into his sixties and fastidious. It didn't help that Old 'un was an ex-Guardsman (should that be Guardsperson?) and there seemed to be a preponderance of little yellow Post-it notes everywhere, mainly addressed to the relief signallers reminding them to clean up after themselves. I was convinced he'd stick one on me if I stood still long enough. Some of these missives started with the heading 'Polite Notice' and descended into impolite consequences should the notice not be adhered to. I was often tempted to stick one up with the 'Polite Notice' heading, then 'Thank you for reading me' underneath. You couldn't get a politer notice than that. Completely against the rules, Young 'un had a TV set wedged in his locker and regularly subjected himself to the inhuman torture of daytime television. I now fully appreciated the value of the large rear-view mirror as an early warning device. If any management showed up unexpectedly, he would quickly switch off and close his locker door before they ascended the box steps. Unfortunately, there were certain giveaways of recent TV usage, such as the aerial cable sometimes poking through his locker door, and always that residual heat and aroma of burnt dust that only an old cabinet TV in a confined space can produce. Therefore, everyone knew what he was up to, but these things were tolerated so long as the goodwill wasn't abused.

Scropton's frame consisted of a distant, home and section lever for each direction, plus three levers for the co-acting crossover and corresponding ground signals. There were also two wicket gate levers, the release lever and four spares. All the signals were cable pulls, with the Up distant 1400 yards and the Down distant 998 yards away from their home signals. Two good tugs by any stretch of the imagination or stretch of a cable in this case. As well as Mill Lane, Scropton also supervised (the rarely used) Archers UWC. I quickly eased back into the signalling routine and enjoyed the semi-rural surroundings and low-tech way of working but remained wary of Mill Lane. Going up and down for the crossing gates provided a nice bit of exercise too, particularly since a car pulled up virtually every time I closed them to road traffic. The gates would be closed roughly a minute after accepting a train on the Down and between three and four minutes after accepting on the Up.

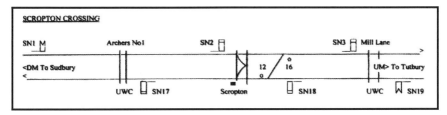

Common but non-serious mistakes for a trainee consisted of accepting a certain class of Down train without first offering it (as specified in Scropton's SBSI in Chapter 2) and trying to offer a train whilst one was still in the advance section. These errors occurred simply because trainees often stood too close to the block shelf and automatically responded to the bells without first checking the indicators. Picking something to lean on that was far enough away cured this over exuberance. Fortunately, the TRB writing slope was at the perfect height and angle for just such a purpose and I eventually trained myself to adopt the position, when it didn't interfere with Young 'un's TV viewing of course.

There was still the occasional confusion regarding which bell was which, but again, easily remedied by giving each one a flick to determine who'd 'dinged' you. It could only be Tutbury or Sudbury, but answering the wrong bell wasn't necessarily the end of the world because most of the trains at Scropton were accepted and immediately offered, so if you had hit the wrong bell, you could just offer the train on then immediately accept instead, all quite seamlessly. After a while, most trainees started to resemble Quasimodo, pacing up and down the box with their hands over their ears shouting, "The bells, the bells!" That was until they encountered the release lever sticking out of the frame. Unlike the useful nature of the TRB slope, the release lever was at the perfect height and angle for crunching a signalman's testicles. I cannot class this as a common and non-serious mistake because it was achingly serious, and a wise man tended to avoid a repeat of it. However, bent double in the aftermath, the resemblance to Quasimodo became more apparent. I'm not saying the pain was prolonged, but it was still possible to mimic the falsetto parts of Jackie Wilson's 'Your Love Keeps Lifting Me (Higher and Higher)' ten minutes later.

The author on duty, September 2007. The flat roofed porch was altered to a more sympathetic pitched slate one after refurbishment in 2009. Scropton's frame – note the knacker-cracker release lever waiting to claim its next victim. *Philip Helme/Author.*

The distant signals occasionally suffered from dirty contacts and the relevant repeater in the box would show 'WRONG', even though the signal arm had dropped, and the lever was back in the frame. After the passage of each train, you had to ensure the repeater showed 'ON' after replacing the distant lever and before putting the section signal back, otherwise the frame would lock and you would be unable to give a 'line clear' for the next train. If this happened you had to go through the entire signalling sequence again, jerking the distant lever back and forth until its repeater needle decided to drop to 'ON'.

Remembering to check the repeater each time was a difficult habit to get into, what with observing the approaching train, sending the appropriate bell signals, checking tail lamps, making TRB entries and replacing the signals in the correct order. Simply put, there were many distractions and it was easily missed. Young 'un probably had the worst record for it, but instead of going through the signalling sequence again, he would go outside and vigorously tug up and down on the relevant cable until the needle dropped. It looked far too exhausting to me and it was not a method I adopted initially, as the first time I tried it, I grasped the wrong cable and spent several minutes pulling my guts out to no avail, much to Young 'un's amusement. In those early days, I found it just as easy to close the gates, ask the relevant advance box for a 'line clear' to unlock the signals then just pulled and replaced them again.

Nevertheless, I failed to check once when the LOM was doing a box visit. The train had passed, and I'd put all the signals back, feeling quite pleased with myself...until I noticed the repeater showing 'WRONG'. Pride forbade me from mentioning this fact, so I leant against the indicator as inconspicuously as possible and tried to attract Young 'un's attention by jerking my head towards the lever. He eventually understood my meaning and nipped outside to do some frantic upright rowing whilst I distracted the LOM with my usual pointless small talk. I don't think I was very successful, particularly since the cable could be heard whizzing through its pulleys, much like a lawnmower pull cord. Eventually the needle dropped, and I was able to give Young 'un a surreptitious thumbs-up, whereupon he staggered back into the box red-faced and out of breath. I'm sure we covered it well and the LOM was none the wiser.

After two official training days I decided to try to get passed out for Scropton. Although I'd spent a lot of time at the box, I still didn't feel supremely confident but wanted to get it over with, as I would only gain the necessary confidence when I was working it on my own. The LOM turned up on 15 May but wasn't keen to pass me out because he thought I hadn't been training the box long enough. He was obviously unaware that, before Tutbury, I'd spent most of my time here. He tried to catch me out on largely irrelevant questions like where certain notices and manuals were kept in the box. Unbeknown to me, Old 'un had moved the Sectional Appendix from the shelf and put it under the TRB slope during one of his cleaning frenzies, but after a fevered search I eventually laid my hand upon it. (He could have at least left a trail of Post-it notes to follow.) The LOM then hammered me on failed train and single line working scenarios. To be fair I was a bit ropey to start with and he wasn't happy – he rarely was – but I eventually redeemed myself on the rules and he grudgingly passed me competent after three hours of torture, during which we'd virtually dismantled then reconstructed the box.

I couldn't work the box the following day because I had to cover a few shifts at Tutbury, so it wasn't until two days after passing out that I finally got to do a shift on my own at Scropton. Downwind of the Nestles factory, the intense coffee aroma coupled with fresh manure spread on the fields rivalled any smelling salts I'd ever encountered. Individually these smells were enough but combined they were a real slap in the face and I was instantly jolted to my senses as I arrived for an early shift. I was dreading it really, but after signalling the first couple of trains I felt much more at ease. I switched to a late shift the following day, and in between signalling trains, I watched the birds, the farmer ploughing his field, and the sunset. It was very pleasant, I would even say idyllic.

Scropton Crossing, August 2007. *Helen Chadfield.*

I've been fortunate to have several German shepherd dogs in my life. When I joined the Forces, I opted to train as a dog handler, even though completion of the course meant an immediate posting to Northern Ireland and a place very much at the operational forefront. I didn't mind. I'd be working with German shepherd dogs all the time, and although some days I may falter, my fearless and loyal partner never would. I knew a canine companion would give me strength and carry me through, and this remained my philosophy regarding German shepherd dogs long after my time in the Forces had ended.

In 2001, almost ten years since my last GSD, I got another one from the local shelter. He didn't even have a name, and no one knew how old he was. Before arriving at the shelter, he'd been wandering the streets and it was obvious he'd been mistreated. I named him Ben and estimated him to be about two years old. To be honest he was a holy terror. He didn't like anyone or anything and I had to keep him carefully segregated. There were many days when I wanted to return him, but I persevered and eventually there came a point when we finally accepted one another. From then on, it became difficult to imagine life without him and he eventually became a fine companion.

I was working as a groundsman at the time, often within a small team, so it was difficult to have him with me regularly. After becoming a signalman, I'd already sized up the possible locations where he could accompany me, so after passing out for Scropton, he did his first early shift with me two weeks later. I had to return him to the van before each train because he was too much of a distraction whilst I was signalling. He also took a dislike to the clanking levers and wanted to attack them every time I tried to pull them.

In the past, I imagine most signalmen kept dogs or other pets in the box, but in these current times, no doubt the practice would be frowned upon. I didn't make it obvious and always returned him to the van if unexpected visitors turned up. I had to anyway because of his temperament. I couldn't really disguise the fact I'd got a dog because, like Young 'un's TV, there were certain giveaways, such as my van rocking violently from side to side, accompanied by a dreadful cacophony of metallic barking from within. Therefore, Ben was known about but tolerated. I think cats were the popular choice at signal boxes anyway, primarily to keep the rodent population in check. I knew a stray cat (Sunshine) had been adopted at Foley Signal Box, so I didn't feel quite so guilty about bringing Ben. Although I suspected Sunshine was far easier to accommodate.

Ben also accompanied me on my first night shift in July. Scropton was an intermediate box during an engineering possession and I was primarily there to operate the crossover and get an on-track machine (OTM) from one line to the other, which I did about 01:30, once I'd extricated the point lever from his jaws! As no signals are operated within a possession, I used a Bardic hand lamp to let the OTM driver know when he'd passed clear and when the points had been set, whilst my canine companion glowered at him through the window. A satisfying bit of shunting in the early hours and, thirteen years previously, I would have been doing similar work, only I would have been in a loco cab, not a signal box.

5. BIG SWITCHES AND COLOUR LIGHTS

After passing out for Scropton I was sent straight to learn Sudbury, so armed with a suitably sized tin of Brasso, I went off to disrupt the tranquillity of the resident signalmen there. I would have preferred to gain more experience in the two boxes I already signed rather than learn a new one, but I continued to alternate shifts between Tutbury and Scropton and train on my spare days.

Sudbury was another classic looking signal box, but compared with Scropton, I always found it a little claustrophobic bordered by houses on two sides. Although it worked AB in both directions (Uttoxeter one way, Scropton the other), there were no semaphores. Its signals were all two aspect colour lights, and with no cable resistance, the levers were essentially just big light switches. This didn't detract from the overall signalling experience though as most trains zipped past at 70mph and there was the busy A515 road crossing to contend with too. In fact, the constant rumble of traffic over it tended to dull my senses after a while, or at least what little I had left of them.

The frame was similar in size to Scropton's but contained fewer operational levers than Tutbury. Apart from a distant and a combined home/section lever for each direction, the rest were spares. A barrier console was situated in the corner overlooking the crossing, and once the barriers had been lowered, a 'crossing clear' button had to be pressed to release the signal levers from the frame, hence no release lever. The lowering sequence would be initiated upon receipt of 'train entering section' on the Down and about five minutes after receiving it on the Up. The box also supervised two UWCs and Dovefields, which was a miniature red and green light crossing. Langridge UWC appeared on the diagram, but Sudbury had no jurisdiction over it.

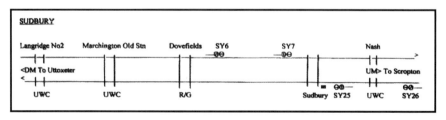

As the Derby-Crewe-Derby services often crossed in front of the box, it was sometimes possible to 'buy one, get one free', i.e., lower the barriers for the first train and keep them down for the second. You tended to start sweating a little if you'd misjudged it because, like Tutbury, you were right in the firing line for disgruntled motorists. There was an annunciator, which sounded in the box when an Up train was approaching but its initiator was set too close to the distant signal, and by the time the signaller had started the lowering sequence, the driver would be preparing to shut off power at the still cautionary distant. Immediately the barriers were down and the 'crossing clear' button pressed, the signaller would yank the levers from the frame giving green lights all the way, which must have been very frustrating for the driver. All this hassle simply because the initiator couldn't be re-positioned an additional 50 metres away from the distant signal.

Most signallers would try to estimate the Up train arrivals, but you could almost guarantee that if you left the barriers down it would be an additional two minutes before the train arrived, or the second you raised the barriers the annunciator would sound signifying its imminent arrival. I found it amusing that in this modern age of technology, it still came down to a signaller's best guess as to when the Up train might arrive, but I suppose that was true at most crossing boxes. One of the resident signalmen had an egg timer device which, after completing its five-minute countdown, would rattle violently along the block shelf like a pair of joke false teeth then, in a fit of fury, throw itself to the floor, continuing to make forward progress until its spring finally wound down. You would then tentatively approach it like a suspicious package, prodding it with the mop handle to see if it was really dead, whereupon it would suddenly flare up and chatter a couple more times, causing you to recoil in shock. But even with all this 'high-tech' equipment, it still came down to a 'guesstimation' based on the assumption that a driver had been able to maintain line speed through the section and your neighbour at Uttoxeter had sent accurate bells.

As it was such a long section between Sudbury and Uttoxeter I had to get used to accepting a train on the Up then sitting down for ten minutes before receiving 'train entering section', which was a little different from my bell hanging tendencies at Scropton. After receiving 'section' the angry egg timer would be initiated for another suicidal five-minute countdown. In the interim, one of the residents would usually produce a couple of teabags and declare a brew but using the box water supply could sometimes be a little tricky. I hated to put fingerprints all over the burnished brass of the cold tap, and the geyser seemed to have a mind of its own. Several meaty turns of its tap would elicit only the barest of trickles, but the slightest provocation after that would release a jet of water of such velocity that it would hit the sink, bounce back out and generously soak the fly area of my trousers. Although this was a highly embarrassing stain to have in company, it was of entirely no consequence when alone in the box. A signaller could strut around with total abandon, safe in the knowledge that no one would be pointing and consequently sniggering behind their back – barring unexpected visitors of course. That's what I liked about box life; any embarrassments could generally be kept to oneself. The second Sudbury resident always kept a pair of binoculars close to hand, which he claimed were for bird watching. I doubted he could see the supermarket car park at Hatton, if bird watching was his euphemism for 'pesting', but they were actually a good idea being as it was a long stretch of straight track in both directions. It was certainly a much drier pastime than fiddling with the geyser's hair-trigger anyway.

After Tutbury, it seemed most of the barrier dodgers made their way to Sudbury because many of the motorists displayed the same level of recklessness, only at much higher speeds. The first time I initiated the lowering sequence I had to hit the emergency stop because of a car roof scraping under the barrier skirts. The resident signalman seemed a little hurt that I'd halted the sequence for what he considered a very minor contact.

"They can see the flashing lights, hear the audible alarm, and the lowering barrier rather gives it away. Cause as much damage as possible to their cars without upsetting your equipment or the running of trains," he advised.

That had been my way of thinking ever since Tutbury and I was glad it coincided with an experienced opinion. I just hadn't adapted to the higher speed they were coming at me yet.

There also seemed to be a preponderance of traction engines in the area and, like the ambulances at Tutbury, these warranted special treatment. As they required a generous braking distance, particularly if you were about to drop the barriers in front of them, their drivers would sensibly 'whistle up' before reaching the point of no return, and you would display either a red or green hand signal. Although trains had priority, I never really wanted to risk displaying a red hand signal to a traction engine, just in case their stopping distance had been underestimated. They would occasionally appear at weekends and Bank Holidays and could be heard huffing, chuffing and clanking along the road well in advance, allowing enough time to grab your green flag and wave them across.

One of the crossings that Sudbury supervised was Marchington Old Station Crossing and I always had a little smile to myself whenever I remembered an incident there in the early 1990s. One of my trainman colleagues was undergoing driver training and road learning Crewe at the same time. After Tutbury, the next station stop is Uttoxeter, but for some reason my colleague decided to stop at Marchington, which was fairly understandable considering both its platforms remained intact and were in surprisingly good order, even though the station closed in 1958. I suppose it was quite an historic moment; the first passenger train to stop there in over 30 years, although the instructor was a little horrified, particularly since the guard nearly released the train doors thinking it was the next scheduled stop.

Box training continued to mid-June, but as there was only so much to learn, I was just hanging around waiting to be passed out. As no one seemed in a rush to do this I decided to switch to Egginton Junction and start training there. I would have preferred to get Sudbury out of the way first, but my LOM had apparently disappeared again. I put all my Sudbury knowledge to one side and started acquiring Egginton's but on my second morning there I received a call from the deputy LOM telling me that he was at Sudbury and would pass me out. I didn't know if I was coming or going but plodded back there to work the remainder of the shift. I was passed competent for Sudbury on 19 June; even though I thought I was still at Egginton most of the time. I did a shift on my own the following day, but after all the ups and downs, it came as a blessed relief. It had felt an age trying to get passed for Sudbury, when it had just been over a month since passing out at Scropton. But perhaps it was more the road travelled rather than the time passed.

It was certainly an age (sixteen months to be precise), *and* a road well-travelled, before I returned to Egginton. With Sudbury under my belt, I was now considered a useful relief and able to plug key gaps in the roster. Therefore, further box training was put on hold and I was left to ply my trade on the relief circuit unfettered.

It wasn't long before I got my first night shift at Sudbury, which on this occasion, would be an intermediate box within an engineering possession. My one action for the entire shift would be to lower the barriers and show a green Bardic to a ballast train coming at some indeterminate time in the early hours from Uttoxeter. As it was a midweek possession, and I had previously been covering the late shift, I found it difficult to make the sudden switch to nights and therefore had to forego any sleep during the preceding day. It would also require a further sixteen hours of forced wakefulness after the shift, to maintain any semblance of a 'normal' sleep pattern and complete my remaining late shifts for the week. This would put yet another dent in my already battered circadian rhythm. Not that much rhythm remained. I think my internal band had packed up a long time ago but could still occasionally be persuaded to play for tips – usually strong black coffee and certain junk foods. After taking duty at 22:00, I brought Ben up to the box and bedded him down. As nothing else would be happening for several hours, I decided to stretch out on the floor next to him, with the box Bardic, pre-set to a green shade, grasped firmly in my hand.

After what seemed only minutes of me conducting a supine examination of the back of my eyelids, I was rather ungraciously yanked from the blissful embrace of Morpheus by the strident blast of the annunciator and ultimately deposited back onto the hard floor of the signal box. Although I was unable to account for its passage, the time now read 02:26, and the ballast train, my raison d'être, was approaching. I felt a bit like that character in the film *Kelly's Heroes*, whose one responsibility had been to provide an artillery barrage at 03:00 and who had been bribed with a gold bar to do so. He had fallen asleep with an alarm clock in one hand and his gold bar in the other. Upon hearing the alarm, he simply shouted "Fire!" first into his gold bar, then into a field telephone, before promptly resuming his slumbers. My actions were not totally dissimilar to his upon being subjected to the clamorous fanfare of the annunciator. I lifted the Bardic to my ear, thinking someone was trying to phone me, but then realization dawned, and I sprang to my feet, pressed the barrier lower button and displayed my green light to the driver. He then flashed the loco's headlights in acknowledgement and continued in a leisurely manner over the crossing. After the last wagon had rumbled clear I raised the barriers and flopped back down on the floor again. Unfortunately, sleep remained elusive for the rest of the shift, mainly because a rather puzzled German shepherd dog was keeping me under gimlet scrutiny for any further frantic and unscripted actions.

6. (DON'T) TAKE A LEAF OUT OF MY BOOK

It was a relief to finally be a Relief (signalman that is) and signing for Scropton had officially made me one. I now had Tutbury, Scropton and Sudbury all in a nice row, a bit like a set of Monopoly properties. And not unlike the board game, I continued to pass Go, avoid Jail, take the odd Chance and sometimes get sent back three spaces, particularly if Sloth was working next door. I also had a brush with the 'Community Chest' at Tutbury, but more on that later.

Working a different box each day meant having the right box head on each day too, and the worst thing a signaller can do to a driver, other than set them on a collision course or instruct a motorist to cross their path, is to put a signal back to danger in front of them. It would sometimes be necessary to do this in an emergency but could so easily be done in error too. This would become apparent after working Sudbury for a couple of days then switching to Scropton. At Sudbury, once a train had passed the box, you knew it had passed the combined home/section signal and could immediately return it to danger. But at Scropton, particularly on the Up, once a train had passed the box, it still had at least another 400 yards to travel before passing the section signal, so you could end up putting the signal back too early if you still had your Sudbury head on. I likened it to driving an artic all day then going home in your car. There would be lots of over steering, exaggerated clutch movements and constant checking of wing mirrors for a trailer, simply because you still had your big truck head on. Worzel Gummidge perhaps would have made a good relief signaller with his interchangeable heads, but I fear his peers may have ostracized him because of his superior social skills and dress sense.

All boxes on the North Staffs were eventually furnished with a computer that had Train Running System (TRUST) installed on it. Before the arrival of this system signallers were essentially prisoners of their block bells and were not able to stray too far from them for too long. With TRUST, a signaller could now reasonably determine what trains were heading their way, and more importantly, when. A meal, toilet break, or questionable activity could be comfortably attended to between trains and a signaller would now rarely be caught out with any unexpected bells. I say 'comfortably' with a slight tongue in cheek because, like trainman days, there were no official breaks in a single-manned box and you simply had to attend to any personal needs between trains. This doesn't sound too bad if you perhaps got a 40-minute lull each hour, but unfortunately, most boxes were still at the mercy of a least one level crossing telephone and a signaller could be up and down like a fiddler's elbow whilst trying to eat or digest their meal. This was especially true at Scropton at mealtimes or when visiting the blue-boxed outdoor latrine. The second a sandwich touched lips or cheeks touched porcelain, Mill Lane Crossing phone would bleep. This happened with uncanny regularity and I began to suspect that users were observing me through one of those 'penny in the slot' pier telescopes permanently trained on the box. I could imagine them saying "Right, he's just sat down, phone him now."

Most of my questionable activities involved Ben, who had begun to accompany me to the various boxes, usually on lates and nights. He eventually visited all the boxes I worked, but only ever crossed Tutbury's threshold once. That was because there was nowhere to easily secure him should an unexpected visitor turn up, but also because the residents would have instantly detected a single dog hair and I would have never heard the end of it. They didn't like the relief staff being in their box, let alone one with a dog, so there would be endless inquests, letters to MPs and an in-depth laboratory analysis of any offending hair. I always felt this was a little unfair, particularly since Ben was a lot cleaner in his habits and actually shed less hair than some of the relief.

To illustrate the level of zeal displayed at Tutbury, I was once accused of not emptying the waste bin there after a late shift. When I arrived for duty the following afternoon, both my accuser and I spent several wordless seconds peering into said bin, which had been conveniently placed on the table as Exhibit A for my edification. I was at a loss to understand the full nature of the resident's concern and, at length, admitted as much "There's nothing in there, apart from that single foil top from a milk carton."

"Exactly!" was his serious, but perceptibly triumphant reply.

I respected the zeal for the most part, but never understood it fully, partly because a half full mug of water had been sitting atop the gas fire at Tutbury, no doubt for years, judging by the unsightly green encrustation around its rim. When questioned, all the relief seemed equally baffled as to its purpose, with some even a little apprehensive about the permanency of this unusual fixture. Most however, accepted that it was some benign experiment being conducted by the residents, but to what end, no one was sure. I never asked either resident outright for two reasons. Firstly, I knew I would be extremely disappointed by any mundane explanation, and secondly, I was afraid that I might have to call some psychiatric institute on their behalf, and quite possibly the World Health Organization too, if the explanation turned out to be anything other than mundane. The mug may have had something to do with adding moisture to the air whilst the gas fire was in operation, but why it couldn't be washed out and put away during summer then re-filled and returned to its position in winter eluded me.

Tutbury's enthusiasm even stretched to the four-page roster that was faxed (latterly emailed) to the boxes each week. On their copy, one of the residents devoted much of his time to meticulously colouring in each line of work with different highlighter pens – and all this before adult colouring books became fashionable. When I first encountered all these colourful patchwork sheets of artistry, I thought he might have been involved in some kind of postal Tetris competition (possibly a bit like postal chess, but much, much slower). The different colours however, denoted who was working overtime, or who was engaged in duties other than normal shifts, and that any subtle but potentially dubious manipulation of the rosters had been identified and sufficiently colour coded for all to see. (Some signallers scrutinized these pages the way a rabbi might scrutinize the Torah.) Diligent as this enterprise was, I couldn't see the point really, unless it was to show we workaholics the error of our ways, but I suppose it gave the resident twenty minutes of pleasant colouring each week. It may have been my imagination, but I could have sworn there was a unique colour code for Sloth – Day-Glo red I think it was.

The author adopts the classic signalman's lean at Sudbury, June 2007. *Philip Helme.*

It was very easy to tell who was working next door to you by the sound of their bells. Not only could you ascertain their identity, you could often gauge their mood too. Bells could be fast, slow, weary, sarcastic, impatient, frantic, uncertain, angry, amusing, and on rare occasions, non-existent. The latter could happen if neighbours were late on duty, attending to an urgent call of nature, fallen asleep between trains or some hitherto unknown disaster had befallen them. Two real life examples in this last category were one collapsing from ill health and another being relieved from duty by a manager – who then, inexplicably, didn't know how to work the box! Some signallers rattled out bells so fast the block bell was in danger of flying off the instrument, others were so slow you could fill in the TRB in the time it took to receive the code. In those circumstances, the signaller in between often acted like an electrical transformer, stepping the bells up or down accordingly as they passed them on. Sometimes Scropton's Up block bell hammer would miss a beat, which was rather like having a typewriter with the E key missing, but the odd thing was that however the bells were received, there was an almost overwhelming tendency to acknowledge them in the same manner.

Another way of ascertaining the identity and mood of your neighbours, other than their bell delivery, was how they responded to yours. Some signallers would take ages to answer your 'call attention' and you would wonder where they had gone. Most boxes weren't that big, so why the delay? I think some hoped to remain in a reclined position for as long as possible and would have put a rubber glove on the end of the mop handle to answer the bells if they could. Some would leave a long pause before acknowledging a bell code and you would wonder if they'd received it. Some would call your attention then leave a long pause before they sent you a bell code and you'd stand there drumming your fingers waiting. It was the equivalent of someone knocking on your door and you shouting, "Come in!" only for nothing to happen. It was infuriating for someone like me who was a bit of a bell hanger, ever ready, super-efficient and unfailingly modest – which of course is exactly why they did it.

In the normal method of Absolute Block signalling, 'train on line' is the second movement of the block instrument. This all sounds very musical, but I doubt many AB signallers consider themselves musicians. However, if the loose definition of a musician is to manipulate an instrument to make a sound, then the same could be applied to an AB signaller. The block instrument is also manipulated to make a sound, but unfortunately it only has one key (bell tapper) and one tone (bell), which makes it very monotonous – literally and musically. Nevertheless, it was the music that moved trains.

As 7-5-5 (box closing) equated to seventeen beats, the first few bars of a simple melody could be tapped out between participating signallers on a late shift. I managed to send 'Happy Birthday To You', 'Here Comes the Bride' on the eve of a signalwoman's wedding, and even 'Jingle Bells' one Christmas, but unless it was a well-known melody, anything else would be guesswork for the person on the receiving end. As it was easy to get carried away or lose count, I would sometimes finish with the uncomplicated 'We Will Rock You', which unfortunately didn't sound as good having only one note to play with. Also, after five bars, you had two beats left over, which really ruined the ending. Mostly however, I just sent 7-5-5 like a clockwork toy winding down; fast to start then progressively slower towards the end, which pretty much summed me up on a late shift really. It was always best to check you had a suitable partner next door before engaging in any virtuoso bell ringing performances though. A rapid fire of bells could come as quite a shock to the unsuspecting and unimaginative types amongst us.

As well as block bells, the omnibus (or circuit) phone was the other form of communication amongst the boxes on the North Staffs. Our system was in fact the next model up from the one Alexander Graham Bell used in 1876 when he uttered those immortal, but largely forgettable words to his assistant (who happened to be in the next room), "Mr. Watson, come here. I want to see you." Admittedly, his model had better voice clarity than ours (two tin cans connected by a length of string had better voice clarity than ours), but ours had slightly better coverage. It worked, after a fashion, from Egginton to Uttoxeter (four rooms away in this case). It was also a party line, which meant several users could be on at once.

Along with the handset there were four bell-push type buttons (red, green, white, black). Only the black button was used on our circuit, and to contact another box, it would be pushed according to the relevant code for that box. (Again with the bell codes I hear you cry – well, they were the 1880s version of a text message.) Scropton's code was one dash and three dots, which happened to be the letter B in Morse code, although that had no relevance as far as I knew. However, I was vaguely intrigued as to the other box letters and decoded them once during an idle moment (one of many) between trains. Sadly, they did not elaborate some great truth, like a railway equivalent of the Da Vinci code – or even form a rude word when put together – they just seemed to be a random series of letters, the type of which might make for a rather dull game of Scrabble. (For those interested – although I can't think why – from Egginton to Foley the sequence went thus: X, G, B, F, I, S, H.) But perhaps Signal & Telecom (S&T) were having a laugh after all. If the intent was to attribute x varieties of Great British fish to North Staffs signalling personalities, may I offer Trout, Bullhead, Chub, Grey Mullet, Carp, Pout and Flounder for starters. I already had categories 2 and 4 single-handedly covered, as well as a borderline 3.

The Morse type bells were only used when a signaller wished to contact a box other than an immediate neighbour, as a brisk 1-2 on the relevant block bell would alert those signallers either side that they were required on the circuit. Apart from giving the occasional early warning of a LOM visit, the omnibus was primarily used to initiate or cancel line blockages and engineering possessions, or discuss train movements during faults, failures and other exceptional circumstances. As previously mentioned, there were only two shifts on the North Staffs (earlies and lates), with one shift generally observing a vow of silence, whilst the other seemed to consist of frustrated talk show hosts desperate to interview guests. As a relief, jumping between these shifts, you were either blowing the dust off the phone and meekly enquiring "Is anybody there?" or holding the handset with a cloth as it positively glowed from all the party line chatter. On the talkative shift, the omnibus was the source of all knowledge, although the veracity of this knowledge was highly questionable since almost all of it was based on gossip, rumour and downright fabrication – much like any other source of information I suppose. Sometimes a perceptible click could be heard on the line, which meant another user had come onto the circuit. If no introduction was forthcoming, you had to be careful about engaging in any knowledge sharing as the person being gossiped about could surreptitiously be listening in. The identity of a mystery listener could usually be determined from the roster, in which case, the omnibus would suddenly become the ideal tool for psychological warfare and the passing of false information, the scale of which GCHQ would be quite envious.

The thing about having neighbours was that if they had a signalling problem, it could also become your problem since you both had a part share of the section in between. This would usually involve having to caution a train through the section on behalf of your neighbour. Similarly, a neighbour's bad workmanship could also reflect on you. I was never quite sure what I'd done to deserve it, but I regularly had Sloth working next door to me and, for reasons known only to himself, he had developed his own method of signalling which didn't correspond to anything in the Rule Book. In fact, it was contrary to everything in the Rule Book.

His downward spiral began innocently enough and had started to manifest itself within the first couple of months of us both passing out as relief signalmen. He had somehow managed to convince himself that it was all right to offer another train whilst one was still in the advance section. The block indicator would clearly be at 'train on line', but he'd still call the attention of the box in advance and try to offer another one. Everyone slips up occasionally, but he seemed to be doing it with worrying regularity. The best piece of advice I'd been given for this situation was to walk away from the block; which is exactly what I did. As we were both new and inexperienced, there was a danger of compounding his error and ending up with two trains in one section. I would still answer his 'call attention' because there was a slim possibility he was trying to send a bell code other than a train, but in his case, for slim read skeletal. After three attempts to offer another train, the phone would ring and there would be that mournful *Creature Comforts* voice on the other end.

"Why aren't you accepting this train?"

"Because I've still got one in section."

"It's all right, you can accept another one."

"No, you can't. That sort of defeats the principle of Absolute Block."

"Oh."

The phone would go dead and there would be a brief pause, then just as I thought it might have sunk in, 'ding', he'd be calling my attention again.

I could accept the occasional lapse in concentration, but he was doing it all the time, and worse, he didn't seem to know he was doing anything wrong. I began to wonder if he'd been taught Time Interval Working at school instead of Absolute Block. I also think he'd brainwashed himself that delaying trains for any reason was wrong and they had to be kept moving at all costs. My greatest fear was that if he couldn't clear a signal for any reason, then he'd tell the driver to pass it at danger without first ascertaining *why* he was unable to clear it. This alone was enough to unnerve me, but things were about to get much, much worse.

My next brush with Sloth occurred whilst I was working at Tutbury and he was next door at Scropton. He had just arranged a line blockage with me and given permission for a maintenance team to go onto the track. I thought it a little unusual because I knew from TRUST that the next train was close. It was always better to wait for a longer gap between trains, but it wasn't unknown for maintenance teams to snatch odd minutes here and there. I felt reasonably confident that even Sloth couldn't mess this up, being as it was *he* who had initiated the line blockage and I'd locked his signals by turning my commutator to 'train on line'. As there was little for me to do until he gave the block up, I took a break from wearing a hole in Tutbury's carpet with my anxious pacing and sat down, to nervously eye the block instrument instead.

Three minutes later I received a 'ding' from him. I shook my head. Surely he wasn't going to offer me a train? I stood up and answered him with a due sense of dread. Four bells rattled straight back at me. He was trying to run an express passenger train through a line blockage he'd taken less than five minutes ago. I was stunned and could only stare at the block in disbelief. Twenty seconds passed, and I received another 'ding', which I again answered, receiving yet another four bells. I sat back down. This was unreal. Another twenty seconds passed and there was a further 'ding'. I didn't even bother responding this time. Then the phone rang.

"Why aren't you accepting this train?"
I could only stare at the handset blankly. For some reason Corporal Cole popped into my head and I thought how he might have dealt with this situation. He too would have been initially speechless, but then would have immediately speed marched down the track to Scropton and kicked Sloth's backside all around the box. It was a tempting thought, but hardly realistic in the circumstances, plus we're supposed to live in more enlightened times now. Enlightened perhaps, progressive no!

"Try to think what you did less than five minutes ago," I finally managed to say.
There was a long pause and I could hear the overweight hamster in his head, huffing and puffing on its exercise wheel trying to keep up.

"What have you just arranged with me?" I urged.
There was a further pause as the hamster managed to complete one revolution of its wheel.

"Oh, I'd better get those blokes off the track."
I had just prevented Sloth from killing several members of staff and should have returned home after that shift feeling elated, but there was no elation, only confusion and anger. I was angry because the job was stressful enough without having to work next door to a maniac who was actively trying to kill people, and I was confused because I was unsure how next to proceed. I believed it was something that could be sorted in-house, but as the newest recruit, I should not be in this position. I quite favoured the Corporal Cole approach and would have taken great delight in twisting Sloth's stupid head off its largely useless body. Forget interchangeable heads, I could replace Sloth's with a pineapple or a potted plant; anything would be infinitely more useful than what was currently sitting atop those shoulders. In the event, I canvassed more experienced signallers and the consensus was that I should speak to him, although some did express an interest in the head twisting option. When I felt calm enough I phoned him and desperately tried to ascertain if he had any understanding of how

catastrophic his actions could have been, but exactly 2.6 seconds into hearing that dreary voice I knew I was on a loser. If he'd said to me "Sorry Tim, I know what I did wrong and it won't happen again" I would have accepted that, but there was no understanding. The hamster was dead on its wheel.

It's difficult to convey how nerve-racking it was to have Sloth as a regular neighbour and the stress oft contributed to my ashen countenance. I've always looked older than my years. When I was fourteen, I looked forty, but I attributed this to having three paper rounds and a Saturday job of 'wringer out' for a one-armed window cleaner. Well, maybe the last bit isn't strictly true, but I'd had part-time jobs since the age of ten, all of which inevitably took their toll – that and small cigars anyway. At the old-style newsagent/tobacconist I used to deliver for they were easy enough to acquire and I always told my boss I was picking them up for my bedridden father. Well, as I started my round at 06:30, he was still bedridden. As a kid, I could see the practical uses of cigar smoking; I mean you never knew when you might have to light the fuse on a stick of dynamite or blow smoke in a rival's face. However, I really saw myself as Hannibal Smith, the cigar-chomping white-haired master tactician with the ill-fitting belted safari jacket and the confident 'I love it when a plan comes together' catchphrase. Now, thanks to Sloth, I was almost living the dream. I already had the ill-fitting clothing, and my white hair was becoming increasingly abundant, at least in the parts where it hadn't yet fallen out, but instead of my plans coming together, Sloth was constantly picking them apart.

Although George Peppard (and Clint Eastwood in the spaghetti westerns) had a lot to answer for, developing a penchant for small cigars in my early teens was just a natural, if somewhat unhealthy extension of always having to carry matches or a lighter around. Leaving aside my schoolboy flirtation with pyromania, I used to do a lot of camping and backwoods cooking, then, in the Forces, I always seemed to be dwelling in fields or cold, wet mountainous parts of the country. Later, in BR days, there would often be paraffin lamps or brakevan stoves that required the application of a naked flame – brakevan stoves especially, if you required hot sustenance or just simple warmth during a shift. (I also used to take a candle for illumination...oh, the deprivation!) Therefore, cigars just became an enjoyable accompaniment to the necessary ignition equipment and smoking the occasional one briefly helped take my mind off the cold, misery or boredom that so often accompanied the above circumstances, and more importantly, helped to relax and de-stress me. I had curtailed my patronage of Henri Wintermans before rejoining the railway, but quickly re-established the relationship after the stress of my first solo shift in a signal box – then with chain-smoking gusto whenever Sloth was nearby.

Ten days had passed since the line blockage incident, during which time I had remained relatively Sloth free. I'd not had to suffer him working next door, but merely trailed a shift behind him as we alternated between Tutbury and Scropton. I arrived at Scropton for a late shift and casually reviewed the last page of the TRB, as any good, and nosy, signaller should. I went back as far as my late shift entries from two days ago, noting Sloth's early shift entries immediately below mine, but something wasn't right. I studied my entries on the Up page carefully. Everything was there correctly, all the trains I'd signalled, all the timings, even my signatures when signing on and off duty – but something still wasn't right. It took several minutes before I realized it wasn't my writing, but how could that be possible? It took even longer to work out what he'd done. Well, it didn't really it just took a long time to believe he'd done it. For some reason, he'd loosened the staples, removed a complete four-sided double page from the TRB (a legal document), then proceeded to forge my Up entries on the next blank leaf. I was astounded. I am writing this many years later and remain astounded. It also worried me that someone without any obvious brain activity could be so creative. It was all very unsettling.

I initially thought he'd done it to cover up his line blockage debacle, but too much time had elapsed, and I had already checked those entries anyway. Strangely enough they made no mention of him trying to run a train through a group of unsuspecting human beings. I gathered from the gossip on the omnibus line that he'd recently put a signal back to danger in front of a driver at Scropton, but whatever he was trying to cover up, I was now involved, simply because my entries had been on the same page. There were 30 plus staff on this line, why did he have to keep picking on me? I phoned the duty Mobile Operations Manager (MOM) for some off the record guidance. He came straight out; no doubt to relieve me of duty because the story was so incredible he must have thought me under the influence of something stronger than tea. Even when he arrived at the box, he kept looking over his shoulder, fully expecting Jeremy Beadle to pop up and tell him it was all a gag, but after much page turning, handwriting samples and head scratching, the TRB was withdrawn for further analysis. Something this bizarre could not be kept off the record, for my own sake really.

I had just started a late shift at Tutbury the following Monday when a glummer than usual LOM appeared in the doorway, carrying the now much thumbed TRB. He threw the book at me, literally, as he entered.

"Explain this," he demanded.

I caught the TRB and told him what I thought had happened.

"Pretty much what the MOM and I thought, but with nearly fifty years' combined signalling experience between us we've never encountered anything like this before."

Yep, Sloth was unique all right. Well I certainly hoped he was. The thought of any more like him working in a safety critical role frankly terrified me.

"What happens now?" I asked, already suspecting the penalty for tampering with an official document.

"I'm going to sack him."

Sloth was 'invited' to attend a meeting that week, but because he admitted altering the pages straight away, HR overrode the LOM's decision to sack him. This was unprecedented. Giving out inaccurate joining instructions to new employees was one thing; overriding a front line manager's decision on what was clearly a case of instant dismissal was another, but it was my first real introduction to the dreadful HR monster and its abuses of power.

Sloth had told the LOM that he'd spilt an energy drink on the TRB, and therefore, had no option but to remove the pages. A spurious claim I thought, considering the only energy drink that could keep Sloth alert and vital would have to be administered intravenously throughout his entire shift. The weary LOM decreed that Sloth would have to be re-educated, but short of attaching electrodes to his testicles or some other form of pain assisted learning, I really couldn't think how he might accomplish this. Sloth made no apology for dragging me into it, and subsequently sent me to Coventry. That didn't quite make up for his lack of contrition, but I was grateful nonetheless. Unfortunately, this non-speaking routine of his also included the exchange of pertinent box information during shift changeovers, but most people were wise to him now and were extra vigilant whenever he was in the vicinity. It was business as usual because Sloth had never exchanged pertinent box information before this incident anyway. One signalman who took him off duty once was amazed to find a rail defect in the section and a temporary speed restriction in place, but Sloth had never said a word. The only consolation for me was that he'd picked on someone else that time.

When not unwittingly involved in Sloth's lunacy, I continued to hone my craft on the relief circuit, with Tutbury, surprisingly, often providing the best lessons. Just one week of late shifts in August 2007 saw an armed robbery at Hatton Post Office and police officers swarming all over the tracks, then the following day I dealt with a trespasser/potential suicide at Sunnyside Bridge. I don't know if the two events were connected, but perhaps the criminal had mistaken Hatton for Hatton Garden and was a little depressed with his swag of three postal orders and a 1976 presentation set of Christmas issue stamps. Also, if a name like Sunnyside can't dissuade someone from taking their own life, it's a poor show. Mind you I fear its name is slightly misleading as Rusty Drab side may suit it better. After much wild gesticulation and legs being swung over the parapet, the chap eventually got fed up and disappeared, possibly more depressed than before since the police presence was somewhat lacking for this event. British Transport Police (BTP) did phone back with an incident number three months later though.

Sunnyside Bridge doesn't really live up to its name, but 153357 provides a vivid splash of colour as it passes underneath en-route to Crewe, March 2012. *Bryn Davies*. (After an ecological survey, specifically for newts, the bridge was revamped in 2020, after it was found that no newts used it.)

As alluded to at the beginning of the chapter, my encounter with the 'community chest' came the following day. I'd just completed an entry in the TRB and was enjoying a contemplative lean on the writing slope when my eyes casually drifted into 'pesting' mode, as so often occurred in this position at Tutbury. A young woman was riding past on a bicycle at the time and I just happened to catch her eye. Much to my surprise, she abruptly stopped and gave me a thumbs-up, as if we were old friends. I had no idea who she was, even with all my extensive 'pesting' over the past few months but returned the gesture just to be civil. Within three seconds she'd propped the bicycle against the box and was up the steps and trying to unzip my trousers...it was that fast! I hadn't realized the inhabitants of Tutbury & Hatton were so friendly, but it quickly became clear that I'd inadvertently engaged the services of the local prostitute simply by returning an innocent hand signal. This was an entirely unexpected development and I wondered if I'd perhaps missed a session at signalling school. I certainly couldn't recall anything in the Rule Book about this situation, which was a little disappointing as the Rule Book contained information and advice about everything. It even used to contain a passage about personal safety stating that 'You must not lie down between the rails', but I reasoned if a person was having difficulty with such fundamentals, perhaps a career on the railway wasn't really for them. (The

Rule Book did contain several clauses about Permissive Working, but unfortunately these related solely to the practice of allowing more than one train at a time to be on the same line in a section, and were therefore entirely useless in my current predicament.)

What followed were scenes reminiscent of a Carry On film, with me as Kenneth Williams desperately trying to dissuade an over-amorous Hattie Jacques, although it must be said that Hattie would have been a much more attractive prospect than what was currently pursuing me around the box. This woman evidently hadn't seen my van bumper sticker that read 'Signalmen tug their own levers' and my usual platitudes about being a tight railwayman didn't seem to discourage her either. In the end I turned my back on her and resumed my leaning position on the TRB slope, hoping she'd take the hint and leave. She didn't, and sat partially under the slope facing me, but I continued to ignore her. That was until I heard the unmistakable sound of my zip fly being pulled down. We'd now graduated from Carry On to *Police Academy* and I was Commandant Lassard in front of the podium. I could just imagine my LOM walking in now. Whatever crimes Sloth had committed, and believe me they were many, none would compare to this. Also, that this unseemly act would potentially take place near the Tutbury residents' perfectly plumped cushions was unthinkable, although not entirely without some degree of personal amusement value. With much relief (not provided by her I hasten to add) I eventually managed to guide her to the door, shove her across the threshold and quickly drop the dead lock. It was unprecedented – the signalman at Tutbury had been 'pested' *and* 'trapped' all in one go! When I spoke to my neighbours on the omnibus line later, it was suggested that I put a red shade on the Bardic lamp and display it in the window whenever I was on duty there.

7. UP THE JUNCTION

I continued to work my little collection of boxes, with spare days devoted to acquiring new ones. Egginton Junction was next on my list, and of all the boxes I'd visited, it was the least accessible, which was one of the things I liked about it. As previously mentioned, there was little chance of unlocking the gate and proceeding down the drive without the crossing keeper at Hilton or the signaller becoming aware of you – or so I thought.

In due course I was officially dispatched there to start training and elected to arrive early on my first day, so I could finish around lunchtime. There was no movement or challenge issued from Hilton as I unlocked the gate and continued down the drive, parking up at the box. I suffered what I thought to be the first stages of altitude sickness as I climbed the mountainous box steps but reflected that at least the metallic ring of my footsteps would alert the duty signalman to my presence and not unduly upset him upon my eventual arrival. Visitors in general were not encouraged and a trainee would be a particularly unwelcome prospect, certainly one at this early hour.

Egginton Junction Signal Box, February 2008. *Richard King.*

All was dark when I reached the top landing and stood gasping at the door. I knocked but there was no sign of life. Peering through the window I could just discern a pair of stockinged feet sticking out from the end of a high-backed bench affair. I knocked again but the feet didn't even twitch. I tried the door handle but the occupant, whom I presumed to be the owner of the feet, had sensibly locked it. Having now fully recovered from my ascent I banged on the door, whereupon the feet flew into the air and crashed down again, their momentum causing an attached bulky torso to be catapulted forward into view, shedding its newspaper blanket in the process. A large hairy figure hauled itself up, wearily rubbed its eyes and wobbled to the door. The face displayed that now familiar look of dismay and resentment that most of the shift would have to be spent with company, and conversation may even have to be engaged in. This seemed to be a common facial expression of a box occupant when visitors arrived unannounced.

The high-backed bench arrangement turned out to be the wooden lockers belonging to the resident signallers. An angled piece of wood had been attached at one end, with a foam cover laid on top, to form a rudimentary chaise longue. (Tutbury had a similar set up but theirs was less obtrusive.) Comfort was important, and the ingenuity displayed by railwaymen in providing this comfort never ceased to amaze me. In some boxes the variety and abundance of cushions alone would have made a sultan's palace look slightly sparse.

The 'Junction' part of Egginton was a misnomer now, but at one time, its frame had contained 47 levers. It must have been quite an experience to work the box when the Great Northern and North Staffs traffic was all heading your way. It now only contained a distant, home and section lever for each direction, plus four spares, a point lever and, unusually, one ground signal lever for Up to Down only. There was also a release lever for Hilton Crossing. The signal levers operated a mixture of colour lights and cable pull semaphores. On the Up was a colour light distant, a semaphore home and a colour light section signal. The Down consisted of a colour light distant and home, then a semaphore section signal. As well as Hilton and Marston, the box also supervised three UWCs. Derby PSB supervised Egginton AHB, but Egginton controlled the protecting signal for it on the Up.

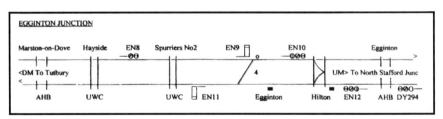

It was also a fringe box, which meant working AB to Tutbury and TCB to Derby. This, of course, was the reason for my TCB conversion during the final week of signalling school. Instead of two block instruments on the shelf there was only one for Tutbury and a train describer (TD) monitor for Derby. The headcode of a train from the Tutbury direction would be interposed by means of a keyboard and would move along the monitor screen as the train activated track circuits on its way to Derby. Similarly, a headcode would 'bleep in' from the Derby direction, which would then be offered to Tutbury by the normal mode of AB signalling. A case of a real live train disappearing onto a monitor screen as it passed the box on the Up, and an on screen moving headcode materializing into a real live train as it approached the box on the Down.

As detailed in the Signal Box Special Instructions, bell codes would be sent to the crossing keeper at Hilton to warn him of an approaching train and prompt him to close the gates to road traffic; 5 bells for a Down train and 2 for an Up train. The crossing keeper would then send 1-2 to indicate the gates were shut and give the release, whereupon the signaller could clear the relevant signals. The speed the gates were closed varied according to who was on duty at the time. One resident crossing keeper was like a greyhound out of a trap upon receipt of the bells, whilst another would be more akin to a tortoise going to investigate a lettuce leaf on the crossing, so the signaller would have to gauge the bells accordingly for a train not to be checked.

Sometimes it was like having a real life equivalent of Sudbury's angry egg timer, as the crossing keeper would ring up if you were slow giving back the release after the passage of a train, or if you had misjudged your timings and road traffic had been held too long. One even used to ring up and complain about having to close the gates for certain types of trains, clearly forgetting that this was his actual job and the signaller had no say in the matter anyway. He didn't seem to mind the Derby-Crewe-Derby services, but either his pride became somehow bruised having to close the gates for anything he perceived to be inferior to this, or he was involved in some other great work of importance in his cabin so that any extra trains were just an annoying distraction. I didn't know what this other great work could be, but having seen the size of the crossing cabin, it couldn't have been much. There was barely enough room to accommodate a cat in there, let alone swing one. But perhaps a lick of the cat may have been beneficial in his case – and I *do* mean the one with nine tails, as opposed to the one with nine lives.

All the boxes I'd worked up to now had a standalone blue box toilet, but Egginton still had a toilet attached to it. For good and obvious reason, it was known as the 'long drop' and was a bit like one of those toilets you often saw stuck, somewhat precariously and very much as an afterthought, to the sides of downmarket seaside guest houses in the 1970s, so they can boast all rooms as en-suite. Hilton Crossing had a blue box toilet, the dimensions of which were more generous than the crossing cabin it served, but as the cubicle had never been seated properly upon installation, it tended to wobble at the most inconvenient and delicate moments. No wonder both resident crossing keepers seemed to be of permanent nervous disposition.

Egginton also marked my first dealings with TPWS (This system automatically applies a train's brakes if it passes at danger any signal fitted with it), but I couldn't understand why it was fitted to the Down Home signal. If a train were to pass this signal at danger, an event known as a SPAD, it would wipe out Hilton's gates and anyone unfortunate enough to be near them before being brought to a stand. I wondered if it had been fitted to the wrong signal, as it would have perhaps been better on the Up Home. The outcome for Hilton would be similar, but there was a more generous stopping distance on the Up. I figured the Greyhound would have been all right in this situation, but the Tortoise would have to be a little livelier.

The thing about Egginton, compared with the other boxes I worked, was that the section signal levers for the Up and Down were next to each other in the frame. Sometimes, in these bleary-eyed early mornings, if you were 'off' for both lines, it was very easy to grasp the wrong lever and inadvertently put back in front of a train. If I felt myself in this semi-awake condition (and I often did), I would put reminders over the relevant levers until I'd satisfied myself the correct train had passed the correct signal. Although you still had to be quick with Hilton's release otherwise the Greyhound would be phoning and moaning.

Whenever trains were in section I always maintained a close watch on Hilton Crossing. One of its approaches was particularly hazardous and it wasn't uncommon to hear the squeal of brakes from a speeding car having just encountered queuing traffic on the blind bend. Other than shunting the first car onto the crossing, its only escape route would be down the embankment and onto the track, so I always kept near the signal levers, ready to put back in an emergency. However, if the train had already passed the distant signal, this course of action would yield no better results than TPWS.

My training continued sporadically throughout August and September, before developing into the usual frustration of waiting around to be passed out. The LOM finally appeared in mid-October and the first question he asked was what steps I would take if an aircraft were to crash on the tracks. "And don't say bloody big ones in the opposite direction," he added quickly. This sounded a totally implausible scenario, until I realized what he was getting at. There was an airfield at the back of the box and trainee pilots often practised directly overhead, using the railway as a point of reference. This was great: not only was I grimacing every time I heard a squeal of car brakes, now I'd get a facial tick each time a light aircraft passed over, particularly if they were practising stall procedures, (always that regulated propeller beat followed by a spluttering then a brief but eerie silence before the dreaded Stuka dive bomber scream). Nevertheless, I was passed competent to work Egginton on 18 October and was supposed to be passed competent to work Hilton at the same time, but as I'd devoted all my time to learning the box, I managed to avoid this 'honour' for a further nine months.

It was the following week when I got to do my first solo shift at Egginton. I liked that the box key was kept under an old BR mop bucket by the door for safekeeping. I suppose it was as good a place as any. It was the most accessible key for the most inaccessible box on the North Staffs, but oddly enough, the most secure too. Perhaps the line of thinking was that if a relief signaller never touched the mop bucket, no self-respecting thief would either. This theory was proven correct when thieves, who never considered the key to be at their feet, once smashed their way through the door.

This enhanced key security was all very well, except for when a bleary-eyed signalman (i.e., me) would try to retrieve it on an early shift. Any fumbling with the bucket at this point would cause the key to slip through the metal grille floor and drop 30 feet into the weeds below. This in turn, led to an angry descent, a feverish search in the dark, then an eventual triumphant but weary ascent of those mountainous steps again. Don't ask me how, but I managed to do this twice on one occasion. Consequently, I felt relaxed about cancelling my membership of the local step aerobics class shortly after.

I had two consecutive early shifts at Egginton and they were both busy with plenty of extra trains to play with. I observed a fantastic sunrise as well as some classic autumn weather. I don't know whether it was the spaciousness of the box or being so high up (and perhaps suffering the initial stages of hypoxia) that gave me a confidence boost, but I always felt comfortable working at Egginton – and it wasn't just the chaise longue!

Incidentally, a driver who once visited the box was incredulous when he saw it. "It's no wonder you're slow getting that back 'un off (distant signal), too busy stretched out on that chaise!" he exclaimed. From that point on it was forever known as the 'chaise' between me and him and word soon got around the local mess rooms. It became a common utterance by certain members of train crew for any delay, real or imagined, in the North Staffs area.

8. WHAT A RELIEF!

It wasn't long before Sloth reared his ugly head again. His 're-education' had involved him being seconded to Egginton to cover a resident's long-term sickness which, as misguided ideas go, was a little like allowing Willy Wonka to re-introduce tours around his factory for school children. As HR was so keen to keep him, they should have absorbed him into their department where I'm sure his gross incompetence would have been an asset and improved their function no end. He certainly couldn't make things any worse and may even have been slightly under qualified for the role. Nevertheless, I was at Tutbury and he was next door to me again, presumably using pages from Egginton's TRB to make paper aeroplanes.

The trouble with Tutbury box was that it was too small to effectively pace about and really work off some nervous tension, which was what I desperately needed to do. Two decent strides and that was it lengthways, although diagonally from barrier control pedestal to door offered a little more leeway. I'd already covered this distance in a two second mad dive to drop the dead lock as Hattie had cycled past earlier and tried to gain entry again. However, she wasn't the source of my tension. Sloth was far too close for comfort and his presence was hanging over the section like a big black cloud, which unbeknown to me, was about to unload.

We were about halfway through an early shift and I'd just accepted the next Up train. After receiving 1-2-1 from Scropton, I duly lowered Tutbury barriers and was about to pull some levers when the telephone rang. If it had been anyone other than Sloth next door, I would have happily cleared my signals and then answered the phone, but I felt a cold hand grip me and, fortunately for all concerned, left my signals un-pulled and answered the phone with a due sense of dread. I knew it was him before I'd even picked up the receiver, so it came as no surprise to hear that horrible adenoidal voice on the other end.

"Marston AHB is on local control."

"When did this happen?"

"About forty minutes ago."

"Why didn't you tell me forty minutes ago? I was just about to signal a bloody train into the section!"

Local control meant there was a problem with the barriers at Marston and a crossing attendant was in place to operate them by hand. It was the Egginton signaller's responsibility to make all the arrangements and tell Tutbury to caution trains on the Up the moment local control had been taken. It was also Egginton's responsibility to inform the attendant whenever there was a train approaching in *either* direction and instruct them to lower the barriers. The attendant would then display a green hand signal to the driver, which was his authority to pass over the crossing. If I'd cleared my signals before answering the telephone I would have sent a train through an open crossing at line speed, which would have collided with anything on the crossing at the time, including possibly the attendant.

"Have you told the attendant the Up train is on its way?" I enquired, rhetorically more than anything else.

"That's your job."

"No, it's your job! Read Egginton's special instructions, and while you're at it, give me the attendant's mobile number."

There was no way I was going to trust Sloth with any arrangements, so for the duration of the crossing failure, the rather bemused attendant received an additional call from me to warn him of approaching Up trains, which I suppose was better than him ending up maimed or dead.

What worried me most about this incident was that it would have been me who had cleared the protecting signal and allowed that train to proceed, not Sloth. I would have felt morally responsible if anything had happened, even though it was his duty to pass on the information in a timely manner. Equally worrying was that voice recorders had been installed at all locations, but had not yet been commissioned, so chillingly, it would have been my word against his. If anything had happened though, I would have made damn sure HR were made answerable.

I made it quite clear that I wasn't prepared to work alongside Sloth any more, but because of a lack of any *real* evidence of his wrongdoings, and the difficulty in arranging shifts, this wasn't always possible. I knew from the gossip on the omnibus line that towards the end of 2007 he had fallen into the second of the two SPAD traps, as previously mentioned. The first had been at Scropton where he'd put back too early on the Up, the second was inevitably at Egginton. He was 'off' in both directions and put the wrong signal back in front of a Down train. He got away with it of course, but an experienced signalman next door at Tutbury knew exactly what he'd done by the timings.

As well as passing out for Egginton, October 2007 turned out to be a busy month for me. Once again it was Tutbury providing some good solid signalling experience as I opened the box at 05:30 one morning for the RHTT (Rail Head Treatment Train). Unfortunately, Egginton didn't open on time and the train was held at North Stafford Junction until someone arrived to take duty. The RHTT ran under a special bell code of 3-4-2, which I always remembered as 'Put (3) Sand (4) On (2)' – not quite in the same league as TITS RA RA, but it was a useful *aide-mémoire* nonetheless. When belled quickly it sounded like something you'd hear being stamped or clapped out at a football match. The RHTT applied a substance called Sandite to the rail head, which helped to prevent train wheels slipping on the autumn leaves, but this was eventually replaced by a high-pressure jet of water containing a chemical called Citrusol, which was blasted onto the rail head to clear any leaf contamination. Both lines were supposed to be treated before the first trains ran, hence the early start, but as Egginton was late opening on this occasion, the objective was no longer achievable. That pretty much set the tone for the rest of the day as far as I was concerned.

As soon as I'd got the delayed RHTT out of the way, one of my track circuits failed, possibly as a direct result of whatever substance had just been sprayed near it. I then had the first two passenger trains roughly arriving together and had to instruct the driver of the Up train to examine the line. After that, I think virtually every Up train on the network was sent my way and I had them all queuing. First the RHTT made a return visit, then a freight train, immediately followed by a light loco, and all in between the usual passenger services. I was glad Sloth wasn't next door at Scropton – it would have been carnage. I spent the morning cautioning trains and didn't sit down until 11:00. Typically, the fault was rectified before my relief showed up, so he couldn't understand what all the fuss was about. It was hectic but a good experience: not bad for my first time instructing a driver to examine the line anyway.

Having to use the loudspeaker system at Tutbury to inform waiting passengers of delayed trains was bad enough but using it to inform them about ones which had been cancelled altogether was tantamount to standing in no-man's-land and firing a flare. The difference between the two announcements was that a signaller could remain in full view whilst making the first one, but it was preferable to be seated on the floor out of sight whilst making the second one. The apparatus in the box consisted of a push-to-talk handset and I often had to resist the urge to revert to Citizens Band (CB) radio speak when using it: "Breaker, breaker, that's a negatory on the eastbound and down. Catch it on the flip-flop good buddies. I'm gone, bye, bye." (Rough translation: Attention please, the next train to Derby is cancelled. There will be another train tomorrow. This is where my responsibility ends, so don't bother asking me any questions, thank you – few realize the linguistic versatility of CB speak). There was also a button that sounded the jaunty 'bing-bong' before any announcement, and curiously, another button that sounded a klaxon type alarm. As the klaxon only ever really seemed to be used in underground armament factories, U-boat pens and other Nazi installations, I couldn't really foresee an occasion when it would be needed here. Thus, I used it with much vigour whenever I had an announcement to make. Who wants the insufferable 'bing-bong' when you can have a strident klaxon followed by a voiceover from the Rubber Duck? (Or the Ey up mi duck, as it was in Derbyshire.) After such announcements, the passengers would be like a small group of zombies on the platform, all wandering and shuffling about aimlessly, but then they'd spot you in the box and start gravitating towards you, groaning and moaning with their arms outstretched. I would answer anyone who shouted "Hello" or "Excuse me" but would ignore the ones who shouted "Oi" or whistled for you like a dog. All I could really do was direct them to the bus timetable anyway because a manual box signaller was always the last to be taken into a train operator's confidence. On those occasions the box fax machine would suddenly burst into life and constantly spew forth totally irrelevant instructions and out-of-date information. That was until it suffered one of its frequent but catastrophic paper jams and spent the remainder of its operation squealing mournfully at you.

I covered an early shift at Scropton the following week, which became nearly as hectic. The driver of the first Down train reported that Mill Lane crossing gates had been left open, so I had to caution the first Up train. Unfortunately, the RHTT had been delayed again and had not yet treated the Up line, so possibly because of leaf contamination, the first Up train (in this case a Class 156 unit) slid all the way from the distant signal and very nearly passed the home signal at danger. The driver was a little shaken and staggered into the box claiming exceptional rail head conditions, so I took extra time to complete the paperwork whilst giving him chance to regain his nerve. I knew exactly how he felt, and it brought back memories of my fog bound experience. Although he was in no position to appreciate it, I wondered what he'd say if he knew the Scropton Signalman had been in a similar predicament fifteen years earlier. This must surely be a unique happenstance, certainly in North Staffs railway history anyway. Eventually, he felt ready to proceed and it seemed a bit of an anti-climax to ask him to stop at Mill Lane and close the gates for me, which was the reason I'd stopped him in the first place.

The next train to follow was of course the delayed RHTT, which unwittingly exacted a small measure of revenge upon one of the Mill Lane Crossing users. Just as it passed the box in full spraying mode, Mill Lane Crossing phone started bleeping, which I immediately answered.

"Hello, can I cross...bloody hell!"

The line seemed to go dead, although in the background I could hear a tremendous whoosh and what sounded like two buckets of water being thrown over someone. I don't know how close he'd been standing when it passed, but it took several reassurances from me, when he eventually spoke again, that it was now safe to cross.

The RHTT, consisting of two Class 66 locos (top & tail) with five tank wagons and a generator in between, always began its tour of duty spotless, but by the end, roughly ten weeks later, it was filthy. So much so, that the driver had only the extent of the windscreen wiper sweep to see through: essentially just a slit, which I imagine was like driving an armoured personnel carrier.

I finished the month with another night shift at Scropton, this time operating the crossover for a rail grinding machine to make several passes between the Up and Down. The sparks it emitted made for an impressive firework display, but as it was 01:43 on a Sunday there were few people around to be impressed, apart from Ben and me – and he was rarely impressed by anything. I also doubted the success of the operation, as the crossover was never quite the same afterwards. Over the next few years it was continually booked in and out of use and I cite that day as when its problems first began. Well, that and the increased traffic over the crossing, which caused the road surface to be pressed onto the point rodding rendering it virtually immovable.

At the beginning of 2008, the Nestles factory in Hatton began some major extension work on its site, so for most of February, the Tutbury signallers had a hand signalman to keep them company in the box. (I can use this title with impunity because it was always a man in this case.) Whilst crane jibs swung large metal girders next to, and sometimes over the tracks, the hand signalman acted as a physical reminder for the signaller during the many line blockages required. I found myself much in demand the following month, undertaking numerous night shifts at Tutbury, Scropton and Sudbury for engineering possessions. It wasn't my favoured shift when I was a trainman, and little had changed now I was a signalman, but at least it kept me away from Sloth for the most part.

His final act with me came in April when I was at Sudbury and he at Scropton. He had no idea how to react when a train passed without tail lamps, which after a year of operational signalling, was incredible, even for him. Unbeknown to me, he'd applied for a signalling vacancy in the West Midlands and miraculously had been accepted, so by the end of the month, he was gone. What a relief – in both senses!

Scropton Crossing looks a little tatty in February 2008 and was certainly ready for its refurbishment the following year, but the Up Home shows a good 'off' for the Liverpool-Ratcliffe. *Philip Helme.*

I expected some tragedy to befall us on the North Staffs at some time, but I always thought Sloth would be involved. A month after he'd gone however, someone decided to park their car on the tracks at Marston AHB and commit suicide. I only missed it by a couple of hours, having just completed an early shift at Tutbury on the day in question, with the subsequent devastation unfolding around 16:00. I found all this out upon arrival at Egginton the following morning, closely followed by two Gestapoesque characters from HMRI. Fortunately, I'd been warned of their impending arrival by the Greyhound at Hilton and managed to secure Ben safely in the van. They spent an hour examining level crossing records, then one looked at me over his glasses the way Himmler might have done when he was questioning someone. "It sounds like there's a big dog somewhere close by."

"Yes, I think they keep one at the old station house." I lied.

Fortunately, I'd parked the van on the far side of the box and they couldn't see it rocking violently from side to side.

At the end of the month, Ben and I returned to Egginton for a night shift, which turned out to be quite an involved one for us, especially since no crossing keeper had been booked to operate Hilton gates during the possession. I used the crossover several times to enable a tamping machine to access both lines, then being the enthusiastic railway team that we were, Ben and I took an 02:00 stroll to Hilton to operate the crossing gates as the work progressed there. I was still not officially passed to operate Hilton at this stage, but if someone with my crossing gate experience (the Denby Branch – formerly seven hand-operated crossings – and Scropton Crossing) couldn't handle it, then it was a poor show. It felt a bit like working Denby North Crossing, as the tamper made its slow progress towards the gates whilst I tried to judge its arrival. Not that there was much road traffic to worry about, although we did have a close call with an early morning motorist who, when speeding around the corner, did not expect to encounter closed gates and a large immovable tamper across his path at 04:00.

After about half a dozen shunts, Ben and I walked back to the box, whereupon the possession was given up. As I'd agreed to work 12 hours on this occasion, I was still there to signal the first passenger trains of the morning, and to end this varied shift, the first Down train stopped at the box to report sheep on the line. I would have sent my Teutonic companion with the alleged shepherding skills if I thought he could have been trusted, and then between us, we'd have fulfilled all the missing roles for this shift.

That was essentially the nature of relief work, to fill in the gaps. Sometimes you could find yourself doing four hours in one box, then four hours in another, or a full shift in one box, then four hours somewhere else, up to a maximum of 12 hours. Unlike a resident, you could never really set your stall out, and all your rule books and provisions would have to be constantly lugged from place to place. It was a nomadic lifestyle, but I enjoyed the variety, not just in the work, but also in the boxes themselves. It was interesting to note that all the boxes served the same purpose but were all totally different; Egginton had a crossover and a crossing keeper, Tutbury had a station, Scropton had signaller-worked gates and a crossover, Sudbury had colour light signals. Each box had an individual personality, mood and feel too. From the ground up, they were also an unwitting historical record of structural materials. Firstly concrete, masonry and timber then the seemingly indestructible 1880s cast iron to the 1950s Bakelite and moulded composites of the modern age.

What I initially found odd about being a relief was that I could be working next door to a resident one day, and then working the other side the following day. It was of little consequence to the resident, but as a relief, it seemed strange to be signalling trains or arranging a line blockage one side, then doing the exact same thing the following day in a different location and under slightly different circumstances, but still dealing with the same person next door. Line blockages weren't particularly relished because it meant someone would eventually be coming along to disturb your routine. Usually, it was nothing more than the weekly track inspection, but occasionally it was possible to end up with multiple line blockages in the same time slot. I once had four separate line blockages at Sudbury – two of my own and one from each of my neighbours – which was very intense and took longer for me to complete all the paperwork each time than it took for them to do the work on the track.

Towards the end of 2008 I got to use Egginton's crossover again, not in a possession this time, but for an unexpected operating occurrence. A Down passenger train had failed in Tutbury platform and required assistance from the rear. Unfortunately, a light loco was following immediately behind, which was unable to provide this assistance, so I crossed the loco onto the Up line, got the assisting train past, then put the loco back behind it; a nice little signalling exercise which helped pass the shift. A few years later I met a driver at an industry seminar who, when he found out I was a signalman on the North Staffs, proceeded to tell me a story about being shunted to the back of the queue at Egginton. "Yes, I know," I replied, "It was me that did it to you." It's a small railway world.

Actually, it's a *very* small railway world. Forget six degrees of separation; it's more like two among front line railway staff. Everybody knows somebody who knows somebody, no matter which part of the country they happen to come from or currently be in.

9. FULL CIRCLES OR JUST MERRY-GO-ROUNDS?

(Reflections of a Relief Signalman)

My first trainman job at Derby in 1990 was to act as secondman on an engineering train that had been tasked to assist in the lifting of the old Mickleover Test Track accessed via Egginton Junction. At the time there were several derelict Class 45s stored opposite the box, and once the signalman had swung the points over, we propelled our wagons past these forlorn looking locos and onto the former Great Northern Railway route. Within the sidings there was also a connection to the MoD compound at Hilton. Although I couldn't realize it at the time, I would eventually come full circle with this location because, after redundancy from the railway in 1994, I worked for a groundwork company who were contracted to lay stone on part of the old track bed, and in 2008, I was back again, only this time as a relief signalman.

The connection from the main line to the sidings was severed shortly after the test track had been lifted, whereupon it eventually became the Great Northern Greenway. Surveying the scene from the signal box window I noted that the sidings had been left in situ, although they were now completely overgrown, and a housing estate had been built around the former MoD land. I reflected that, not only had I worked one of the very last trains on the test track – albeit whilst simultaneously removing it – I'd also helped create the greenway and had even delivered some of the building materials used on the housing estate when I was driving for a local haulier. Not content with this potted history and these dubious claims to fame, I once flew over it all in a light aircraft chartered from Derby Airfield at the back of the box (a £25 flight experience, where I had been allowed to take the controls), but oddly enough, I never got around to walking the greenway until years later. Suffice to say that I've viewed the area from a variety of different angles, as well as play a small part in its history – both endeavours that were continuing from my lofty perch in the signal box. In the future, I will of course expect English Heritage to attach one of those blue plaques to a suitable structure in my honour, if any suitable structures remain that is. (See *Derby Trainman 2ⁿᵈ Edition & Lost Lines.*)

My first couple of shifts after passing out at Egginton were very much how I imagine working a colliery box might have been like in the 1980s. Slotted in between the Derby-Crewe-Derby passenger services was a light loco Class 56 that was being used for road learning purposes. I knew this by the number of bodies squeezed into each of its cabs and the frequency with which it went back and forth during my shift. It felt very nostalgic, and also provided some good signalling experience during those green days of mine. Just when I thought all the freight companies had fully embraced the Class 66, it was pleasantly surprising to see all these old locos running about in their weird and wonderful colour schemes. Although I retained a soft spot for the big liveried BR blue Class 56s of the 1980s (pulling full circle merry-go-round trains of course), I had no desire to be riding in the cab of one again. The noise and vibration under full load were quite horrendous (36,000 components all simultaneously trying to unscrew themselves, as someone once said), and I was content to observe this one from the comfort of the signal box.

The author is but a silhouette in Egginton Junction's history, February 2008. *Richard King.*

It wasn't just me coming full circle; the locos were at it too, and at one time or another, I was graced with a revenue earning representative from virtually every old BR class of diesel locomotive. However, I did read somewhere that it was because of EU rules on diesel emissions. The modern locos somehow didn't meet these requirements, so all the old locos, which were apparently exempt from these rules, were being pressed back into service. Surely, I'm not the only one who found this completely absurd? Nevertheless, even though there was no requirement to do so, I'd adopted the old BR signalman habit of writing the class of each light loco that came past in the TRB remarks column, although I confess to having to scratch my head a little whenever a re-invented Class 47/57, or some of the modern loco classes appeared.

It wasn't long before I was reacquainted with the Grangemouth-Sinfin aviation fuel tanks. Signalling that train, or the return empties, never seemed to lose its novelty, even after having done the job on the ground many times as a trainman; well, the last bit from Derby Station Yard to Sinfin Central or vice versa anyway. I had prepared it, driven it, and was now signalling it. Whenever it came rattling past the box I was always reminded of the time when, as a young trainman in 1992, I was dispatched with a driver to assist the booked crew who, we were informed by our supervisor, were having undisclosed 'difficulties' on the branch. What he really meant was 'I have no idea what's going on, but it sounds bad, that's why I'm sending you'.

We departed 4 Shed light loco and cautiously headed along the branch, to be met eventually with a scene of utter devastation Virtually the whole train was derailed and all the tank wagons (fortunately empty) were leaning at unnatural angles. What we had here was a classic case of 'wheel to ballast interface', but as management speak had yet to be invented it was more simply known as being 'off the road'. However, this looked largely catastrophic whichever way you phrased it. Whilst propelling towards No3 ground frame, the hapless trainman had forgotten to set the trap points. It was a pity because he was a decent chap, and in a previous career, a decade earlier (perhaps even ten years ago to this very day), he'd diffused land mines around Port Stanley. A job, which my driver rightly concluded, he had obviously taken much more care over than this one – although disrespecting land mines or 100 tonne aviation fuel tankers seemed to yield similar results as far as we could see. It wasn't long before the orange clergy were in attendance though – lots of blokes in HV all wringing their hands and saying "Christ!"

56105 heads the Sinfin Tanks (empties) in their 2013 evolution, passing Marston-on-Dove AHB, August 2013. *Bryn Davies.*

A year later, just before redundancy from BR, I found myself back in Sinfin once again. At the end of 1993 I did my HGV 1 (LGV C+E) training in an old eight speed Mercedes tractor unit coupled to a flatbed trailer, and as the test centre was at Sinfin, most of my training was conducted around Derby city centre and its environs. The traffic and streets were difficult and claustrophobic then, so I wouldn't even like to contemplate doing it now. I'm not sure how my instructor stood it, but he (mostly) remained calm amid this terror. At that time any qualified artic driver could slap a pair of L-plates on a wagon and become an instructor, but I'd been fortunate to study under this experienced and long established one. We often headed out into south Derbyshire and had lunch at the Salt Box Cafe, just up the road from Tutbury Signal Box, as well as practising trailer coupling/uncoupling and reversing manoeuvres at an old airfield in Foston.

After redundancy from BR and passing my test I got intermittent work through an agency and, oddly enough, my first ever Class 1 (artic) job was to Stud Farm quarry and my first ever Class 2 (rigid) job was to Denby opencast – both former trainman haunts. By 1995 I had a semi-regular position at a paint warehouse in Burton and ended up with the south Derbys/Staffs run, regularly passing all the signal boxes as far as Uttoxeter, as well as Alrewas and Lichfield. I often got caught at Sudbury's barriers and would watch the signalman going through the motions, with no idea that eleven years later, I would be working the box and stopping the very same truck.

I also had a brief stint at Ind Coope/Allied Burton Breweries working as a yard shunter. Using an old, battered and often reluctant Seddon Atkinson tractor unit, I would shunt tankers and trailers around the yards and prepare units and trailers for MoT. The reason I mention this job is because it provided yet another sojourn in a wooden shed, although it contained no home comforts and was merely a place to loiter in between the many trailer pick ups and drop offs. Apart from looking like Windy Miller from *Camberwick Green*, winding all those trailer legs up and down, it was a nice little job while it lasted. Unfortunately, my time on it was cut rather short when someone got a little careless with a tub of engine de-greaser and a jet wash hose, causing me to plummet into an inspection pit, cracking two ribs on the way down.

Before this unexpected and calamitous dive, I witnessed a rare event at the brewery when a young chap, who'd just completed his apprenticeship as a cooper (barrel maker), had to endure an initiation ceremony. I didn't know how long his apprenticeship had been, or what precisely the initiation ritual entailed, apart from him being partially stripped, drenched with copious amounts of beer then getting rolled around the yard in a barrel (possibly one he'd made earlier), but it looked extremely humiliating, and therefore a great deal of fun. This has nothing to do with full circles, apart from his around the yard in a barrel, but surely there can't be many coopers about, or even the inclination and training to be one nowadays.

It was easy to dip in and out of the decades whilst sitting in my various signal boxes. On cheerless days, my mind would contract on itself, but during long summer afternoons, when there was that particular slant of sunlight on the levers, it was free to roam. Sweltering in the greenhouse-like conditions of a signal box was no different to sweltering in the greenhouse-like conditions of a truck cab. (No air-con in either at the time, unless you count an open window.) Looking out from Tutbury's window, the street scene hadn't changed much, but a decade before; it could have been me in any one of the innumerable trucks that rumbled past.

Seldom, in either my personal or professional life up to this point, had I spent any appreciable time gazing out of a window, but this is mostly what a manual box signaller does, whether they are always consciously aware of it or not. After signalling trains, it must surely rank as the next most common box activity. Whether done to provide early warning of possible management incursions, 'pesting' purposes, sheer nosiness or simply just to observe the sunrise or sunset, it was now my stock-in-trade too.

But through these observations came a deeper connection with nature and my surrounding world: a definite intimacy, almost as if nature were conducting these things for my viewing pleasure alone. From a partial eclipse of the sun to a full blood moon, from fearsome black clouds boiling into a storm in one window to a shimmering full arc rainbow in another. Sometimes the view resembled the front of a 1930s radiogram, with that classic Art Deco sunburst motif, perfectly framed in glorious colour. At other times, a fierce wind would be blowing at ground level, powerful enough to bend trees, but above this maelstrom hung great fortress piles of clouds that seemingly would never move again. Even a single elegant poppy in the unruly undergrowth had the power to make me return its smile. This is how the writer, John Stewart Collis, thought he would prefer to catch sight of Beauty '...through the corner of my eye, while immersed in something else, while not seeking her at all'. After sharing a similarly elevated viewpoint to his (the top of a hayrick in his case, albeit 70 years ago), I must agree. Perhaps we both just caught the briefest of glimpses. At Sudbury in late autumn once, I watched the sunrise through the east window, and then during a 12-hour shift, watched it set through the west window. A common experience you might think. Not for me. I'd never sat in one place long enough to witness the entire event from start to finish; the sun seemingly revolved around me – from the temporal to the eternal, the circle of life: surely the ultimate full circle.

I wasn't the only former trainman to return to the railway, my brother Phil rejoined as a driver in 2007. If anyone had told us in 1994 that we'd both end up back on the job, we would have thought them quite mad, particularly after the shameful way we'd been treated when BR was in self-destruct mode. Between the two of us, he truly came full circle, but we never imagined that I would end up as a signalman and he a driver, or moreover, that I would be signalling him on the North Staffs whilst he drove the Derby-Crewe-Derby service.

Driver P. Helme passes Scropton Crossing, en-route to Derby, February 2013. *Bryn Davies.*

July 2008 marked my first visit to the newly opened Rail Operating Centre (ROC) in Derby, a place, it was envisaged, where most London Midland signalling operations would eventually be based. It was officially called the East Midlands Control Centre (EMCC), but most people tended to refer to it as the Early Learning Centre, or perhaps more appropriately, the Death Star. I was not an honoured guest on this (or any subsequent) occasion and had merely been summoned to this charmless building for my quarterly rules assessment. I often wondered why all these new structures had to be nondescript grey boxes, and why some of the old railway architectural styles couldn't be employed in their design, particularly since most of our railway heritage was going to be absorbed by such places. This included the North Staffs manual signal boxes, whose areas of responsibility would end up spread across several monitor screens and their signals operated by the click of mouse. But I suppose that was the point; sweep away all the old and replace it with the new.

Seven years later, I encountered yet another full circle (or merry-go-round), finding myself back in Chaddesden Sidings again. Instead of loose shunting battered ballast wagons with equally battered BR locos or dashing in with spoil then dashing back out with ballast during my tipper driving days – much like Stanley Baker in the film *Hell Drivers* – I now found myself in the modern but characterless surroundings of the recently built Mercia House for the occasional safety briefing. There had originally been ample space at the Death Star, but after a couple of years of what I perceived to be a grudging accommodation of us, the rooms seemed to get smaller and smaller, until we were eventually squeezed out altogether and shunted around various broom cupboards within the RTC before being exiled to Chaddesden Sidings. (We were eventually re-admitted to the Death Star in 2016.)

Network Rail had a 'Future Vision' of creating twelve ROCs, which would eventually control signalling for the entire country. It was a bold and ambitious plan, but one I doubted would ever come to full fruition, at least not in my lifetime anyway. Few would dispute that Absolute Block is an antiquated method, and its continued use in the modern railway was perhaps an embarrassment to some in higher management but rendering all the mechanical signal boxes obsolete seemed like a backward step to me. Not because I'm overly sentimental for the method of working, or indeed, the way of life, but there's a reason this system has lasted so long. It was a Victorian solution for enabling a Victorian railway system to work, a system which we inherited, and to some extent, are stuck with. Of course, the Victorian railway in turn, was set by the geography of this great country. I think level crossings will always be a problem, or rather, the often-unpredictable actions of people who encounter them, but in each crossing box there is already the most up-to-date bit of technology; a human signaller – although some might say 'human' and 'signaller' are mutually exclusive. Also, with numerous signallers spread over a wide area, there is always someone on the ground, which, from a safety and response point of view, must be better than miles and miles of track remotely supervised from a central location. Therefore, ROCs do not fully meet all the requirements for the efficient operation of our railway system. There are also still a lot of boxes tucked away in awkward places, which would not be cost effective to remove, so perhaps mechanical signal boxes will never really go away. A hundred years hence, *they* may even come full circle, but we'll all be in little wooden boxes ourselves by then.

10. ACROSS THE BORDER

My first cross-border operation into Staffordshire occurred in mid-January 2008 and was specifically a fact-finding mission to gather intelligence on Alrewas Signal Box and its two crossings, Roddige and Fine Lane. I had already decided to learn no further than Sudbury on the North Staffs purely for economic reasons, but Alrewas, on the South Staffs, was within my remit and there was a good potential for overtime, even though the journey seemed to rapidly shrink the contents of my fuel tank. It was no further than Sudbury really, it just felt longer and more tedious having to skirt halfway around Burton-upon-Trent to reach it.

Alrewas box was spacious and surprisingly modern inside, although I gathered this was due to an unscheduled refurbishment because of some fire damage a couple of years previously. I didn't really want to quiz the duty signalman about the specifics of this incident too much because he was forever twitching and mumbling to himself and fiddling in his coat pockets. I decided that if he suddenly produced a box of Swan Vestas or a Zippo I was out of there! I did have to admire his sun lounger in the window though. In every box I'd visited I'd been constantly surprised and amused by the various seating arrangements within, but I'd never encountered a sun lounger before. The sheer audacity of it! But why go through all the needless expenditure and upheaval of installing a conservatory at home when the signal box was a natural one already? Nevertheless, it was a bold statement to make, one that seemed to be along the lines of 'This is *my* box, and I don't care'. I also considered the wearing of carpet slippers by any box occupant to make a similar statement.

Like Egginton, Alrewas was a fringe box, but unlike Egginton, it had no levers to pull. There was only a simple panel with one switch for the set of points at the end of the single line, and two signal switches, equating to a distant and a section colour light signal for each direction. Working TCB to Derby and AB to Lichfield Trent Valley Junction, there was of course the requisite TD monitor and block instrument respectively. The barriers were the same as Tutbury's, but as the road was a dead-end that only served a few small businesses, traffic was minimal. Nevertheless, not unlike Scropton, whenever the lowering sequence was initiated, a vehicle would invariably show up. There was also a 2-1-5 bell code for the Lichfield direction, which was essentially the normal 2 for 'train entering section' with the 1-5 added, to remind the signaller there that a train was destined not for Birmingham, but rather the Trent Valley and ultimately the West

Coast Main Line.   Lichfield supervised Brookhay AHB, but Alrewas controlled the protecting signal for it on the Up.

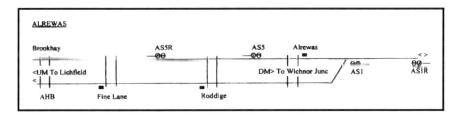

The pace of work at Alrewas meant the sun lounger, or other chairs with reclining capabilities, could be put to good use, because on average the box would be lucky to see ten trains in any 24-hour period. It was surprising to find a standard three-shift system in operation with that sort of workload, but apart from a brief break over the weekend, the box was manned constantly, primarily as a diversionary route to and from Birmingham. (Saturday and Sunday shift times varied depending on service requirements.) Night shifts notwithstanding, it looked as though it would suit Ben and me very well. Boredom seemed to be the main obstacle to overcome and I made a mental note to renew my library card, obtain a few magazine subscriptions and perhaps bring a cocktail shaker to complement the sun lounger.

The main customers were Virgin Voyagers shuttling between their Central Rivers depot (or Muddy Waters as it was more commonly known) just around the corner at Wichnor Junction, and their start point of Birmingham New Street. A brace of them would appear between 06:00 and 07:00, all eager and ready to start work, returning all worn and weary looking between 22:30 and 00:30. The night shift may then see two further trains in the form of freightliners (usually Felixstowe-Trafford Park) at 02:00 and 04:00 respectively. The late shift would occasionally get to signal a couple of freight trains, a light loco or a test train, but that was about as exciting as things got really, unless diversions were in place. In that case, practically everything would get sent via Alrewas and it would become very hectic very quickly. It was a box of extremes, ranging from two trains a shift in normal circumstances, to forty trains a shift if diversions were in place. Forty odd trains doesn't sound a lot, but when they were all queuing at the bottleneck and it was taking about ten minutes to deal with each one, plus level crossing use too, it could be quite a juggling act.

I did sign the South Staffordshire Line as a trainman, but usually spent most of my time at the other end of it, accessing places such as Brierley Hill, Round Oak, Wednesbury and, of course, the rather daunting Bescot Yard, all via Sutton Park. I only worked the Alrewas end (cross city route) on rare occasions i.e., special workings and the previously mentioned diversions.

The Alrewas signaller supervised Roddige and Fine Lane, which were both crossing keeper controlled with their gates closed to road traffic. Under normal circumstances, the signaller was just a glorified telephonist, with each shift predominantly spent authorizing crossing keepers to open their gates for motorists, then confirming they were closed again before transcribing all this dazzling information into the TRB. From the outset, I felt this to be an odd way of working because, owing to the usual infrequency of trains, it would have been far better (and safer) to leave the gates open for motorists, and then have the signaller confirm the route in its entirety whenever a train was due. This seemed a natural and more logical sequence of events to me, and one that could help reduce the margin for error that sometimes existed in respect of gate status during the long periods of boredom.

Having crossing gates closed to road traffic had been standard practice since railways began, but none of those stovepipe-hatted gentlemen could have foreseen the rise of the motor vehicle, let alone the volume of today's traffic, even at obscure backwoods crossings such as these. Obviously, it was just horses and carts in those days, then early motor vehicles, and finally the impatient mobile phone wielding drivers of today, but at many crossings, the ratio of cars to trains had now completely reversed. Unfortunately, the railway method of working had not kept pace with this development. Even as late as 2007, Scropton's special instructions still dictated that 'gates should normally be kept closed to the road', but the increased traffic had rendered this method totally unworkable. Scropton's special instructions were altered to 'normally kept open to the road' that same year, but I believe it required an Act of Parliament to enable this 'simple' change. Ideally the same initiative was required at Alrewas.

I didn't know why Roddige and Fine Lane were so popular anyway. Situated down rough unlit farm tracks with treacherous soft verges that steered you into deep drainage ditches either side, there was nothing much out there and it always felt like a little pocket of *Deliverance* country to me. It was at times like this I wished I'd learnt to play a musical instrument, specifically the banjo, because I would surely need one to duel with some of the residents – resident crossing keepers that is! This feeling was exacerbated with neither location having running water, and only Roddige having electricity. Fine Lane relied on bottled gas for its heat and light, and, because there was no water supply, both places harboured the dreaded blue chemical toilet. I never understood why these things were always blue, even the harsh smelling liquid that was used to hand pump/flush them. No doubt on some psychological level, the blue colour represented that misleading sense of fresh water, but in my opinion, it would have been far better if everything in those dreadful cubicles was brown or yellow in colour. Using one was always an unedifying experience, and if it wasn't for the importance of maintaining hygienic standards (largely non-existent at both these locations anyway), I would have made use of the hedgerow every time. But even with this supposed deprivation, I liked the isolation and solitude of the crossings. There was little to recommend Roddige, but Fine Lane lived up to its name, offering a very pleasant countryside aspect with a nice wide-ranging view. (It wasn't until September 2019 that Roddige, Fine Lane and Hilton had their cabins upgraded.)

I was determined not to sign as competent for Alrewas until I'd signalled a train in each direction, which was a rather modest goal to set oneself, and one which was taken for granted at almost every other location but was to prove exceeding difficult to accomplish here. My initial visit in January had yielded no trains, but my sun lounging colleague had seemed to imply that if I were to appear during the early hours of my next training day, I might get lucky and see one. I duly returned one morning in February at 02:00 but was thwarted by a points failure at Wichnor Junction. Even a train officially booked to come this way would not now be doing so. At the end of February, I turned up at 04:30 and finally got to signal four trains in a row, which was quite an achievement under the circumstances. Unfortunately, they were all Voyagers heading towards Lichfield and I still hadn't managed to signal one towards Derby. I tried again one evening in March at 18:30, only to send another one trundling off in the Lichfield direction. This was turning out to be a real quest.

Training days were sporadic, but as usual, no one was in a hurry to pass me out anyway. This was an observable phenomenon in real time, particularly since spring had now turned into summer. The box had been managing on two residents for a while, with relief signallers covering the vacant third shift, but it wasn't until one of these remaining residents entered a period of long-term sickness (possibly sunstroke) that there was a mad rush to pass me out. This had to take place when it was known a train would turn up, so the LOM could actually see me signal something. I dreaded to think how long it would take before one of his visits coincided with one of mine, not to mention the added difficulty of getting a train to turn up too, but I could just imagine him organizing two of the MOMs to ride past, feverishly pumping one of those old seesaw trolleys if all else failed. It took a few attempts, but I finally managed to signal a train in the Derby direction, albeit on the day I was passing out, and was passed competent to work Alrewas and both the crossings on 28 July. The following day I worked my first early shift and signalled a train in each direction straight away, after which, there was nothing for the remainder of the shift. Unbelievable! Not being cognisant with the reservation procedure, I also brought my beach towel and laid it on the sun lounger, just in case.

I got passed for Hilton Crossing that same week, and that was it. That was about as far as I could economically go as a Scropton GPR living in Derby. There was a whisper about going to learn Moira, Mantle Lane and Bardon Hill signal boxes, which were all on my old haunt of the Leicester/Burton Line. I was tempted, but this was like coming too much of a full circle for me. I'd already spent the better part of my trainman career practically living on that line and I'd sat in its associated quarries (Cliffe Hill, Stud Farm and Bardon Hill) so long with one of the regular drivers that we'd both gone through his happy marriage, acrimonious divorce, new girlfriend and subsequent remarriage in that time. Plus, with only one or two trains a week passing through there now, it would make Alrewas seem like Clapham Junction in comparison. I now had the sedentary lifestyle of the South Staffs to immerse myself in and any location offering fewer trains than that was perhaps stretching my masochistic limits just a little too far. Saying that, I became experienced at Alrewas very quickly during the following month, with numerous engineering possessions spread over a corresponding number of 12-hour night shifts. One of these possessions overran, causing a sudden and unnerving glut of trains all queuing up to be squeezed through the single line bottleneck once the possession had been given up. From a delay mitigation point of view, Sloth would have been ideal here because he would have just sent the trains through regardless, although the subsequent court trial and manslaughter charges may have put a dent in any projected profit.

On another occasion, Lichfield box didn't open on time, and with no response to my bells and ultimately no 'line clear', I was unable to deal with the first Virgin Voyager from Central Rivers. The poor driver had to scrunch along the ballast to change ends and return whence he came with his tail lamps between his legs, in the hope of accessing Birmingham via Burton, instead of Lichfield. During the remainder of the month I had a track circuit failure, a train pass without a tail lamp, several trains that could not be relied upon to operate track circuits and some obscure shunt moves that hadn't even been mentioned during my erratic training sessions by some of my equally erratic colleagues. Sometimes it felt like I was working a different box from the one I'd signed for and I occasionally had to stick my head out of the window and check the name board, just to make sure that it was actually Alrewas.

September was the first time I got to invoke the 'stop and examine' regulation. A ballast train had just cleared Wichnor Junction and was heading my way when I noticed on the TD screen that all the express trains on the Derby/Birmingham Line had come to a stand. From a signaller's point of view this is never a desirable look for a TD screen. Apparently, some ballast had fallen from the train and fouled the junction points, causing them to remain set in my direction. I sent the requisite 7 bells to Lichfield and we dealt with the train between us, after which we had some unscheduled diversions until the points were cleared. Having diverted trains provided a welcome respite from the boredom and could make for an extremely satisfying day's signalling. It was natural to feel out on a limb at Alrewas, set apart from the network, but diversions made you feel important and connected again, and it was always nice to be wanted – even if only occasionally.

It was surprising how the more basic or innocuous a box appeared, the more it could test you. Both Tutbury and Alrewas provided me with some of the best signalling experiences during this early stage of my career, but Alrewas could test signallers and sometimes find them severely wanting. I always considered it to be the most dangerous box I worked, simply because of the crossings, their method of operation and the infrequent trains. It can be difficult to maintain concentration over long periods, particularly when very little is happening. It was a strange phenomenon to behold because a signaller could spend hours (or sometimes days) waiting around for a train, finally get offered one, then after all that waiting around, accept it and clear signals without first confirming the status of the crossings. It was that simple. Similarly, having diversions and being busy could be equally bad and a signaller really had to keep their wits about them with crossing use between trains. I was just glad Sloth never made it out here; the thought of that possibility makes me shudder even now.

By the end of 2008 it felt as though I'd been seconded to Alrewas without being informed. Apart from the odd snatched shift on the North Staffs, it became more usual to find me languishing on the South Staffs. I certainly seemed to be doing more than my fair share of 12 hours and nights, up to and including Christmas Eve, when I finished a 12-hour shift at 06:00 at Alrewas, then doubled back to Fine Lane for 18:00. Apparently, Santa Claus wasn't the only one in demand that night and I was beginning to wish I'd never reserved that sun lounger after all.

Just checking the name board in April 2009. A box of extremes, extremely boring mostly, extremely busy sometimes. *Philip Helme.*

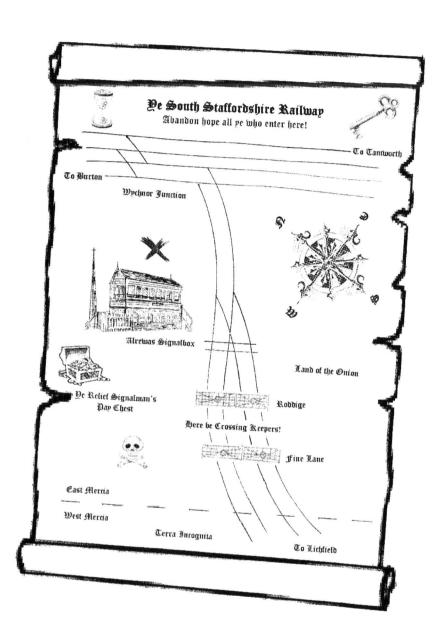

Ye South Staffordshire Railway
Abandon hope all ye who enter here!

To Tamworth

To Burton

Wychnor Junction

Alrewas Signalbox

Ye Relief Signalman's Pay Chest

Land of the Onion

Roddige

Here be Crossing Keepers!

Fine Lane

East Mercia

West Mercia

Terra Incognita

To Lichfield

11. THE ONLY MAN AWAKE IN THE WHOLE WORLD

My first experience of a night shift was rather an extreme one. I was seventeen years old and on my first posting in the Forces, having just passed out from basic training. It was also barely a week since I'd passed my driving test in one of the ubiquitous camouflaged Land Rover 110s, and now here I was driving one on a mobile night patrol. Looking back, it appears I had been sized up for a driver well before I joined BR or decided to obtain my HGV licence, but one of the advantages of being a military driver on tasks such as these was that I was armed. I would have relished being an armed driver in my post military career. It certainly would have made things a lot easier when dealing with an arrogant traction inspector in the loco cab, or a cocky warehouseman closing Goods Inwards just as I arrived on a timed drop, not to mention the satisfaction of being able to double tap all the morons who cut me up on the road during the day. But I digress...

Because of continuing terrorist attacks on the mainland, all MoD establishments were on Bikini State Black Alpha alert, which meant that specific intelligence showed a terrorist attack was likely. No one was sure what 'Bikini' had to do with it though. Some people speculated that it was because of Bikini Atoll, but the Cold War was just about to thaw, and the Bikini State was more of a terrorist threat indicator anyway. I tended to think there was more psychological reasoning behind it and that it was so named in a 'subtle' attempt to keep servicemen keen and alert. Whenever anyone asked, "What's the Bikini State today?" it always had the desired effect, with most men taking an immediate, albeit fleeting interest. Perhaps if society hadn't become so sensitive and politically correct, railway management could have expanded this idea and applied revealing female garment names to certain aspects of signalling to help improve concentration levels amongst signalmen. Imagine how safe an on-track team would be with a lace teddy line blockage or a sheer negligee obstruction of the line. I'm sure it would remain at the forefront of most male minds and doubtless the Tutbury signalmen would approve of the nomenclature. I still remember TITS RA RA even after all these years, so there must be something in it. But I digress again...

Because of the heightened state of alert and the full utilisation of all available bodies, I had been paired with one of the cooks. He was nicknamed Little Chef, because of his resemblance to the roadside eating chain's logo. But aside from being plump, he didn't seem to share many other characteristics that night. Instead of carrying a tray he was carrying a 7.62 Self-Loading Rifle (SLR), and unlike his alleged doppelganger, there was no cheerful smile or perceived jovial manner. In fact, he was rather disgruntled about being dragged from the cookhouse and having extra duties forced upon him. He was also a corporal, which made him my immediate superior. I was just a teenage nobody (as opposed to being a middle-aged nobody now), but one who just happened to be armed with a 9mm Browning pistol, which I thought was cool, as may have been previously gathered. We looked an unlikely pair as we stepped up to the guardhouse for our orders at 22:30. Little Chef waddled in first, with me trailing behind.

"What's all this then?" the provost sergeant boomed. "Trying to kill people with a rifle instead of your cooking is it?"

I knew little about the world back then (and time has not really improved this state of affairs), but I never thought it wise to insult someone who regularly prepares and serves your meals – and certainly never insult a chef who is armed. They are temperamental people at the best of times. Matched against the formidable provost sergeant, the culinary corporal had all the power. The ladle was mightier than the sword.

"We're here for the mobile patrol," said Little Chef hotly.

"You'd better go and see the boss then," replied the sergeant. "Before Wyatt Earp here falls asleep," he added, nodding towards me. It must have been my low-slung holster.

Like most people, I had been doing a shift system of four hours on, four hours off for an extended period and I was shattered. It was impossible to get any sleep during the four hours off because I was sharing a room with several other blokes who were constantly changing shifts or doing various housekeeping tasks. I had been messed about at all hours during recruit training, but this was different, it seemed relentless. I didn't even know what day it was and had reverted to the recruit's default answer, which was a resounding "Yes corporal" to everything that was said to me, regardless of the rank of the person who'd said it. I'd just said it to the warrant officer who'd briefed us on our duties. He was a little shocked, particularly since I was armed, but he looked more hurt than anything else that his rank hadn't been recognised. I expected an ear bashing but he perhaps thought that going on patrol with Little Chef was punishment enough.

Apart from sharing the cab of the Land Rover, Little Chef and I had nothing else in common, so our conversation was rather muted as we trundled around the base. He directed me to do several circuits of the Married Quarters; no doubt hoping to glimpse some late-night bedroom action as he feverishly eyed all the windows but was quickly disappointed and the novelty soon wore off. Thinking back, he was perhaps about to give up the culinary life and had secretly embarked on a rudimentary training course to work Tutbury box. In any event, it must have been about 02:00 when he told me to pull over adjacent to a children's playground near the Married Quarters. I assumed he'd spotted something but just told me to keep a look out whilst he grabbed forty winks. That settled it; he was definitely re-training to become a railwayman!

I sat looking at the empty playground. It felt like I was wearing an extremely tight swimming cap, the pressure of which was threatening to force my eyelids shut and squeeze my tired brain into submission. All I could hear was a constant low buzzing sound. Foreground began to blur into background and time seemed to stand still. I was at the threshold between forced wakefulness and the irresistible pull towards glorious sleep. Suddenly a figure squeezed under the perimeter hedge of the playground and ran towards the swings, and then another one popped out and ran towards the slide. I watched incredulous as two young children laughed and played not more than 30 metres away. I turned to Little Chef. "Hey, look at those two cheeky beggars."

"What?" He grunted, shaking himself awake.

"Over there." I nodded, turning back towards the playground.

"What are you on about?"

I was dumbstruck: the playground was deserted and there was no sign of life at all. I hadn't fallen asleep and dreamt it; it had been a hallucination, yet the children had seemed totally real. Little Chef gave me a pitying look.

"It's time we were getting back anyway," he muttered, shaking his head.

Nearly twenty years had passed since then, but the same wretched condition still plagued me as I sat at Alrewas on yet another 12-hour night shift. Owing to staff shortages and what I perceived to be other relief signallers cherry-picking jobs, I ended up with more than my fair share of nights on the South Staffs, most of which were back-to-back 12 hour shifts that brought me perilously close to exceeding working time limits on many occasions. I'd done some brutally irregular shifts with BR but without exception, I found nights to be the worst. They felt completely unnatural to me and the fast turnaround at the time didn't help. There were only two shifts with BR – PM shift was obviously any time between midday and midnight and AM shift any time between midnight and midday, with this pattern alternating each week. Therefore, you could have a week of 22:00 starts (nights) followed by a week of 02:00 starts (days) – and not much of a social life! I suppose if there had been more to do to occupy the time I would have perhaps felt different, but nights with BR meant hour after hour languishing in the mess room, or worse, in the cab of a loco on some nondescript ballast job, never quite knowing when the torture would end. Nights in a signal box weren't much different, except the shifts were regular instead of irregular, and now thankfully subject to a maximum 12-hour limit.

I didn't dislike nights, just the way I felt whilst doing them. To me they had the same effect mentally and physically as flying to New York each night, and I found it virtually impossible to sleep during the day. Also, no matter how hard I tried I was never able to convince my stomach that having breakfast at 18:00, lunch at midnight and a main meal at 06:00 was the accepted norm. I could never seem to get rid of that constant cardboard taste in my mouth, or the grit from under my eyelids either.

On this current routine of 12-hour nights (18:00-06:00) I was perhaps achieving 4-5 hours' sleep in every 24-hour period – little wonder I (and my stomach) was growing to hate them. I would also try to avoid my family and friends (or rather they avoided me) because of the severe irritability this lack of sleep caused. It could be so bad that I would even fall out with myself.

I always felt like the only man awake in the whole world on nights at Alrewas. The place didn't just feel out on a limb from the railway, it also felt detached from the rest of life too. The few businesses adjacent to the box all closed at night, and because the road was a dead-end, any other traffic was minimal. The A38 passed directly behind the box, but its constant flow only added to this feeling of detachment and isolation – everyone was going places and passing me by. The entrance to the National Arboretum was a quarter of a mile up the road and I could just see the top of the Armed Forces Memorial from the box, which was inaugurated by the Queen in October 2007. It was a true case of 'At the going down of the sun and in the morning. We will remember them.' and I would watch every evening as it slowly dipped behind the obelisk.

I tried to get some sleep during the lull but could never really switch off. Quite often there would be a refrigerated trailer parked opposite the box and every time its internal temperature rose, which seemed to be about every twenty minutes, its generator would spark up and roar away until the pre-set temperature had been achieved again. I didn't know how fridge drivers stood it when they had to spend the night in their cab, but I suppose it was no worse than being stuck on a stationary Class 47 and having to suffer the high-pitched scream of its air compressor at similar intervals.

Nights at Roddige and Fine Lane could be equally excruciating, but aside from listening out for the odd car pulling up at the gates, other responsibilities were negligible. Unless of course you happened to include acting as ringmaster for the flea circus that seemingly resided in the chair at Roddige. There were two block indicators at Fine Lane (Up & Down respectively), so if you were still awake, you might receive some warning of approaching trains. There was no such luxury at Roddige as both block indicators were situated outside in a metal box. As the cabin and the blue box toilet were positioned very close to the Up line, with their doors opening to face the direction of travel, it was always best not to rush outside lest you find yourself inadvertently swept into the path of a train. It was certainly worth making the effort to check the block indicators before venturing to the toilet. More than once I pushed the cubicle door open to come practically nose-to-nose with a train, not to mention a very startled driver. It didn't do much for me either, but I suppose I was in the right place should the four-letter epithet for faecal matter suddenly become an actual function rather than just an exclamation.

Even though it felt like I was doing more than my fair share of Alrewas shifts I didn't mind being there, mainly because I could take Ben with impunity. If someone did turn up unexpectedly it was always a mad scramble to get him back into the van before they reached the box steps, but that was all part of the fun. During daylight hours I would park on the grass verge opposite the box, and with one end of a rope attached to the van and the other to him, it was long enough to allow him to sit on the grass, or remain in the van, whichever took his fancy. Being a typical German shepherd, he would usually remain sulking in the van after I'd gone to all this trouble. On the rare occasions I had to deal with a train, I would nip across, close the van doors and keep him contained until it had passed. I often wondered what the drivers made of this white van rocking violently from side to side as they trundled through the bottleneck at 15mph.

During the dark hours I would bring Ben into the box, always ensuring I locked the door in case someone should turn up without me noticing and blunder in. At least at Alrewas there were no levers for him to attack, but he knew from my actions when a train was due and would stand rigidly in the corner where he thought it might approach from. He could hear it long before it ever came into sight and would bristle up in anticipation. As soon as he saw its headlight he would bark indignantly and run madly up and down the box as it rumbled past. With several Voyagers returning to Central Rivers between 22:00 and 00:30 he would become complacent, expecting all the traffic to come from the Lichfield direction, but the 02:00 and 04:00 freightliner trains would sneak up on him from the other direction and he would be most displeased to find he'd been waiting in the wrong corner.

If it hadn't been for the freightliners, some decent quality sleep might have been achieved between 00:30 and the 06:00 shift changeover, although one of the Lichfield signalmen didn't let their timetable stand in the way of his achievement of such. One morning the 02:00 freightliner 'bleeped in' and I duly called the attention of Lichfield to pass it on. There was no response to my first call, or indeed to my second, third or fourth, which was a little disconcerting, particularly since I could now see the impressively long train of containers snaking inexorably towards me. Usually the operation was seamless. Lichfield would accept and unlock my signals, I would immediately clear them, and the driver could continue at a stately 15mph off the single line without missing a beat. Now he was about to be checked at my distant signal and I still hadn't managed to raise Lichfield. I kept 'calling attention' whilst simultaneously using the landline and phone concentrator to call the box direct. I knew that the signalman had nodded off, which was understandable, but how he could continue to slumber in what must be a dreadful cacophony of bells, alarms and phones was beyond me. There was still no response and I would now have to phone Control to ascertain his whereabouts, particularly as the train was about to come to a stand at my signal.

This was another aspect that added to the feeling of isolation and detachment; a regional route control boundary separated Alrewas and Lichfield. We were under East Midlands and they were under West Midlands, and I always felt neither Control really wanted us and only acknowledged us under sufferance. I was just about to phone the West Midlands Control when I decided to give Lichfield one more 'ding', and I suddenly received an acknowledgement. I offered the train, got a 'line clear' and gave the driver a green aspect – at the exact moment he came to a full stop! He probably turned the air blue cursing me, but fortunately I couldn't hear him, although I did feel a slight warm tingly sensation on my ear lobes. It wasn't my fault of course, just another case of someone else's bad workmanship reflecting on me, but from the driver's perspective, it would seem as though it was me who had fallen asleep, suddenly awoken to find a train at my signal, then immediately cleared it. I didn't expect the driver to understand (not at 02:00 in the morning anyway) that it is always the box in advance that unlocks the signals, i.e., Lichfield in this case, and that he was the one at fault. Consequently, there was no friendly wave from the driver as he trundled past that time. For my part, I only *felt* like the only man awake in the whole world, I didn't expect to be him!

A similar thing happened to me on the North Staffs some time later. I took duty at Scropton at 05:30 to get the RHTT through. I opened the box to Tutbury but received no response from Sudbury – the booked signalman had apparently forgotten to set his alarm clock. (Instead of a lineside equipment failure, which was always the old excuse for a train delay, this was a bedside equipment failure.) The RHTT was on schedule but it had to stand at Tutbury because of Scropton's special instructions relating to train acceptance. The Tutbury signalman would have informed the driver that one of the boxes was late opening and the driver would have automatically assumed it was Scropton, as he was currently standing at Tutbury. Therefore, it was another occasion where I was cast as the villain because of someone else's failure – and I didn't get a friendly wave from that driver either.

Like Scropton with its nearby water courses and resultant fogs and flooding, Alrewas suffered the same with the Trent and Tame rivers close by. Thick night time fogs would often roll in, and in this zero-visibility nether world, you'd be working solely on instruments. Two steady green lights on the panel, the silent passage of the train headcode on the TD monitor, the barely perceptible click of the track circuits, then suddenly the train would materialize from the fog and then dematerialise just as quickly. The passage of the freightliner trains could be quite mesmerizing, with container after container sweeping past, then abruptly nothing. (Not all the flat wagons had containers on them.) Thinking it must be the end of the train, I'd start reaching across to raise the barriers, and then suddenly the conveyor belt of containers would start again. I often felt the freightliner trains were a good indicator as to the state of the economy. If all the wagons had containers on them, the economy must be good. If there were gaps on the train, or worse, the service didn't run at all, then it must be belt-tightening time again. But I tended to find a tightening of the belt occurred naturally to a largely sedentary signalman, especially one who ate questionable foodstuffs at even more questionable times of the night.

There was something about the freightliners though. Perhaps it was because they provided the only discernible link to a wider world during those long dark hours at Alrewas. The containers sitting atop those wagons were constantly threading their way through places like Shanghai, Manila, Durban, Port Said, New York, and now they were rolling past Alrewas Signal Box in deepest Staffordshire. Imagine adding that location to your sightseeing itinerary. Aside from keeping containers moving on the railway, I'd also assisted their worldwide passage by hauling the odd one from terminal to port during HGV days. After one such drop at the Port of

Southampton I got talking to a chap who worked on the container ships and he told me that when they were all secured together on deck, the wind and motion of the ship caused them to sing – an eerie, metallic lament to be sure. I often thought I could hear the odd one sing as they passed me at Alrewas, but as it was 02:16 and I'd had very little sleep, I was probably hallucinating again

To help alleviate some of the South Staffs tedium I applied for a couple of MOM jobs (Nottingham and Lichfield), more as an intellectual exercise than anything else. Although I was happy being a signalman, I held several competencies that would be useful in the MOM role and it seemed a shame not to use them. I sent copies of my applications by email and internal post, as well as dispatching them through the normal post to both Birmingham and Manchester, the two main HR hubs. I didn't know why it had to take nearly an acre of forest just to register an interest, but I assumed it was because these offices were cuboids. Bermuda only had a triangle; these places had an extra side where things disappeared much more efficiently. I followed up these applications with phone calls, but there was no sign of any of the Lichfield applications and only one of the Nottingham ones had been found, in their office bin no less! I wasn't too pleased and drafted a complaint. This I did send to Bermuda, as there was more chance of it being received there. Scientists have posited that there is a black hole at the centre of our galaxy, but I would direct them to look no further than Manchester or Birmingham.

A couple of months later I was called to an interview for the Nottingham MOM position. The day before, during a rare stint at Sudbury, all four crossing barriers had failed to rise after the passage of a train, which caused absolute chaos. As there was no MOM available to assist, I continued to run trains, but had to manually pump up the barriers each time to clear the two-mile tailback of traffic that quickly developed on either side. I went for the interview next day and the first question was "How would you deal with a barrier failure?" Much later I found out that I'd been selected to attend an interview for the Lichfield position too, but of course, no one had bothered to inform me. In this modern age of communication, I found it difficult to comprehend why these applications could not be acknowledged upon receipt and updates sent as they progressed through the system. But that was just plain common sense and courtesy, both traits that seemed woefully lacking in the HR department.

I was still rather disgruntled about all this when a smart black Audi saloon swept into the parking area at the front of Alrewas box early one morning. Not being a regular occurrence, and seemingly a cut above the usual clientele of the adjacent garage, this had to be regarded as rather suspect. It had a look of higher railway management about it, and to give credence to my suspicion, a sharp-suited chap emerged from the vehicle and headed directly towards the box. As the Queen had made it as far as the National Arboretum, I suppose it was only fair that one of Network Rail's high command should make it to the box. Ben was pegged out on the grass next to my battered old van and this person must have thought he'd just arrived at a gypsy encampment rather than a signalling location. My trusty companion gave him the evil eye as he ascended the steps, but did not engage, as the stranger had the good sense not to encroach on his outdoor total exclusion zone, which was roughly eight feet in any direction – his indoor total exclusion zone was limited only by the dimensions of whatever room he happened to be in at the time.

The stranger introduced himself and I inferred his position was somewhere just below the board of directors, but why a person of this heady status had decided to grace me with his hitherto unannounced presence was a complete mystery. I wondered if he was in fact lost, but was eventually enlightened when he stated, "I often see this box from the A38 and was curious to see levers and trains."

The poor deluded fool, didn't he know he was at Alrewas? Although I did briefly step outside and check the name board above the door, just in case *I'd* made a mistake.

"Sorry, but I'm afraid I'm going to have to disappoint you on both counts." I replied, trying not to look too smug about it. He returned my thinly disguised look of smugness with one of dejection, so I explained to him the nature of life at Alrewas, whereupon I took his glassy-eyed stare to be my cue to inquire as to his function in the grand scheme of things.

"I'm the new head of HR."

What a gift! My expression at this point must surely have resembled that of a James Bond villain who, having just caught the redoubtable agent nosing around his lair, was now about to gloat over the heinous but ingenious method of dispatching him. I sat there rubbing my hands with gleeful delight before proceeding to detail all the ills of his department, for which I'm sure he was profoundly grateful. To his credit, he did listen to me, unlike an old boss of mine, who was one of those rarefied academic types who always used to say, "I don't want to hear problems, just solutions." (In retrospect, what I should have told *him* to do was to go forth and make jerky movements, providing the ultimate solution and thus saving us both a lot of time.) After listening to my valuable insight and nodding politely at all my suggested improvements to his appalling, albeit inherited department, he stood up to take his leave, mentioning something about wanting to visit the crossings on his way out. I quickly dissuaded him from any such recklessness as he would most likely be skinned and eaten before sunset, or at the very least, made to squeal like a pig.

Shortly after this visit I noticed some of my recommendations had been incorporated into the recruitment process, which I thought was a little disingenuous, but as they had all been plain common sense and courtesy anyway, I'm sure I would have been embarrassed to accept any recognition for them – unless that recognition had been in monetary form of course. Oddly enough, my recommendation that all incompetent HR administrators should be dismissed and publicly flogged was not taken up, but I still think he got off lightly during this unofficial audience because I never even got around to mentioning Sloth. This was partly because I didn't have a clue where to start, and partly because my therapist had expressly forbidden me from ever uttering his name again.

Incidentally, I once got chatting with one of the relief signalmen at Lichfield and he was telling me about a dreadful person who'd suddenly appeared on their patch, apparently masquerading as some kind of signalman. I know who it was even before a physical description was reeled off – welcome to my former world pal! Some time later I heard a rumour that, as he'd made such a mess of his West Midlands posting, he'd re-located down south, whereupon he'd eventually been sacked owing to some serious but undisclosed operating incident. All that pain and anguish because HR overstepped their (questionable) authority.

There was one occasion at Alrewas when Control didn't acquit themselves very well either. This involved the 00:30 Voyager, which had been involved in a fatality earlier in the day and was now delayed at Birmingham New Street. It was Saturday night and this train happened to be the last one of my shift, after which I could close the box and go home. I phoned Control to ascertain the length of delay, as I was close to exceeding my working time limit again. Thinking about it now, I probably phoned East Midlands Control rather than West Midlands, but the person at the other end assured me the train was cancelled and I had permission to close the box. This was further confirmed when I refreshed my TRUST screen and the word CANCELLED had been inputted next to the train's headcode. I knew the *service* had been cancelled owing to the fatality, but the *train* terminated at New Street and was scheduled to return empty to Central Rivers. Surely it had to come back to its depot at some point? I shouldn't have fallen for it really because it was another classic railway miscommunication, but I made it all the way back home and was just about to unlock my front door when I got recalled. Of course the train had to return to Central Rivers and West Midlands Control couldn't understand why the Alrewas signalman and both crossing keepers had disappeared. I wasn't too happy about having to go back, but once the crossing keepers had been rounded up, we finally got the last train through. What with being the Lichfield signalman's alarm clock, restructuring HR and trying to second guess both Midland control centres, perhaps I *was* the only man awake in the whole world after all – the railway world anyway.

12. MOM FOR A WEEK

For the first few months of 2009 I was still predominantly at Alrewas doing back-to-back 12s, the only consolation being that I missed most of the refurbishment work at Scropton. The old wooden windows had been replaced with double glazing, which I think was considered a crime by Old 'un, but his romantic notions of the job didn't always correspond with real life. I was happy they had been replaced because they were constantly rattling and extremely draughty in winter. I was forever trying to block them up with paper towels and there was nothing romantic about that. With double glazing installed it was suddenly like St Tropez in the box, and I think even Old 'un was eventually won over by the new porch and a refresh of the traditional London, Midland and Scottish (LMS) colour scheme.

Sadly, I lost Ben in May and what felt like eight years of my life with him. I think I grieved for myself as much as I did for him, but he belonged more to my groundwork period and I don't think he quite knew what to make of our signal box adventures. He certainly wasn't happy about me disappearing to Watford every Sunday evening when I was training, but he eventually had the distinction of visiting every signal box and crossing that I worked. He was a regular at Egginton and Scropton, and always accompanied me to Alrewas where we spent a lot of time together during my unofficial secondment. He was a fine companion, particularly on all those interminable night shifts, and his abject annoyance whenever a train passed always made me smile. That's how I often think of him, all bristled up with his chest puffed out, just waiting for a train to approach *his* box.

Ever vigilant – RIP Ben 2009.

I never received any feedback from the previous year's MOM interview, and as a result, didn't give it another thought. That's why it came as such a shock to be told that I would be returning to school (Leeds this time) on the August MOM course. I doubt it was because I'd complained about the sheer lottery of applying for a job through HR, but more likely that management were short of relief MOMs and were experimenting with raising a couple of us from the signalling ranks. Dave, my old classmate from signalling school turned out to be the other candidate and it was my understanding that I would be covering the Derby patch whilst he covered Nottingham. I dreaded to think which part of the country he would be sent to for his medical this time, especially since I'd secured another slot at the occupational health centre 200 metres from his house, but I think HR finally saw sense and allowed him to urinate in a beaker there too. With careful aim, he could have perhaps met this obligation from the comfort of his front room, providing he opened his window first!

For some unknown reason, I was dispatched to York in June for a two-day Personal Track Safety (PTS) course. This certification would automatically be done during the first week of MOM school, so why I had to lug a load of orange gear up to York was a mystery. The 'all orange' rule had recently come into force, which required anyone going on track to wear HV trousers, as well as a HV top. As these trousers weren't issued to signallers, I had to borrow an oversized waterproof pair from one of our MOMs. I felt like the pathetic kid at junior school who forgets to bring his shorts for PE and is forced to wear the enormous and suspicious-smelling ones from lost property. But even those were a luxury compared to having to do it in Spider-man themed Y-fronts in front of all the girls in your class, which was the humiliating punishment once inflicted upon me.

Not content with all the orange gear, I had to take a hard hat and safety boots, wedge all this stuff in the classroom with fifteen other people and their belongings, and then undergo two days of tediously repetitive waffle. At the end of that, we finally donned our orange gear for a ten-minute practical solely on how to cross from one side of the line to the other: I kid you not! Perhaps I was back at junior school after all? I could understand if it had been a running line, but I quickly concluded this was not the case since it was only fifteen metres in length, there was no ballast around it and it was situated in a warehouse. The course was a total farce and that it had been stretched over two days was scandalous. Keeping a good look out, knowledge of warning signage, safe distances and how to make an emergency call are the basics of PTS. Most children have mastered these fundamentals by the age of eight – even those mentally scarred in PE lessons – so there is really nothing more to add except their application in a railway context. Therefore, I feel a well-rounded adult would only require a few hours of classroom study or a half decent real-life practical session of equivalent length, but I suppose there isn't the same lucrative earning potential from that approach; or indeed enough well-rounded adults.

PTS was implemented during my last year at 4 Shed and I was simply handed an orange card by one of the train crew supervisors at the time.

Back then, the original PTS course lasted about twenty seconds and consisted of the following muttered exchange in a corridor:

"Take this."

"What is it?"

"I don't know, I think you need one to go on the track."

"I already go on the track."

"Just keep it with you."

"Er, OK."

Well it was orange. Perhaps it was a case of me accompanying the card rather than the card accompanying me. I didn't see how, after three relatively safe years on track, carrying this card would make things any safer. Fifteen years later I was a qualified signalman, fully conversant with all the track safety rules. I had been passed competent in such by HMRI, *and* signallers could go on the track without PTS if it was part of their duties, but I still had to do the course. To be honest, I preferred the original muttered exchange. Like York, it added nothing to my existing knowledge, but unlike York, it only took twenty seconds and I didn't have to take a load of orange gear on a 300-mile round trip.

My dear old Dad used to call those types of courses SBOs (Stating the Bleedin' Obvious) and from the mid 1990s onwards there seemed to be a proliferation of them – and all exceedingly expensive to undertake if you were not in the employ of a fair-sized company. My back injury notwithstanding, it's no wonder my groundwork business nearly went bust. Things I'd been doing for years suddenly required training and certification and I needed a bit of paper to operate pretty much everything I came into daily contact with. I realized things had spiralled out of control whilst working as a groundsman for the local council. It was deemed necessary for me to undergo a ladder climbing course, which I thought a trifle odd: firstly, because I already knew how to climb a ladder, and secondly, as my job title tended to suggest, a groundsman generally stayed on the ground. But as the cost of the course wasn't being extracted from my pocket this time, I was curious to see what could possibly be learned that wasn't already common knowledge. Perhaps I'd missed out on some hitherto unknown ladder climbing technique all these years.

The instructor duly arrived on site carrying a briefcase and was immediately shot down in flames when asked how he had managed to fit a ladder in there. He might have redeemed himself had he replied that it was a rope ladder, but I've generally found that, like a HR administrator, a sense of humour is lacking in a SBO course instructor. Obviously (but only to him it seemed) we'd be using one of the on-site ladders, and once a suitable one had been propped up, he proceeded to detail its components:

"These are the stiles, and these are the rungs," he stated gravely, pointing to each part in turn – the *only* two parts I might add.

"Hold on, you're going a little fast for me," I replied, furiously scribbling some notes.

"You climb thusly," he continued "Hands and feet on the rungs, making sure you maintain three points of contact with the ladder at all times."

I confess to feeling a little misled here because I was expecting some great knowledge to be imparted, but is there any other way of successfully climbing a ladder? I ask this because I have never knowingly tried to ascend one without using the soles of my feet. I have been guilty in the past of trying to climb with buckets, tools or building materials in both hands, but always managed to maintain three points of contact by hooking one arm around the ladder whilst shoving my torso ever upwards with my feet. After all, most people climb ladders for a specific purpose and not solely to admire the view from the top, hence the necessity of having to carry equipment. However, for an unencumbered person on a ladder, there are only ever *two* points of contact, as one hand usually moves simultaneously with one foot, which, I believe used to be called climbing. But as time was short and real life played absolutely no part in these proceedings, I went up and down the ladder as instructed and he then ticked a box to confirm that, after all those years of incompetence, I was now officially competent and could rest easy.

As a SBO course I never thought ladder climbing could be beaten, that was until a few years later when I was sent on a hand-washing course. Yes, you read that correctly – a course that taught you how to wash your hands! I may have played it fast and loose with ladders on virtually every occasion I used them, so my received, albeit patronising instruction in their safe but largely impractical use was perhaps justly deserved, but I never encountered any such ambiguities with putting soap on my hands and rubbing them vigorously under a hot tap. The last part of that sentence, which encapsulates the entire course content, probably took about five seconds to read and understand, but on the day, it was somehow expanded to take nearly an hour. Afterwards, one person said they'd learned a lot, but what had they learned that they didn't already know? But this was the type of person I tended to nod in uneasy agreement with whilst simultaneously edging away from. These people were dangerous, doubly so it would seem, particularly if you'd shaken their hand or accepted any foodstuff from them *before* the course.

I was reminded of an old trainman at 4 Shed who went by the unfortunate but fitting appellation of Ready Rubbed because of his constant nose picking and subsequent manipulation of the extracted contents. (I suppose Hand Rolled would have been an equally suitable nickname, if remaining with the tobacco theme.) I didn't class him as dangerous, but I never accepted any foodstuff from him either.

Returning to PTS, I'm not saying there shouldn't be some legislation and awareness training, but it should be fit for purpose. At least on these SBO courses I climbed a ladder and washed my hands – I never went on a live running line at York.

August soon arrived, and it was time to head to Leeds for five more weeks in a classroom. The MOM course was scheduled to last seven weeks, but weeks four and five, in my case, were to be spent with the Derby MOMs, hopefully gaining some practical experience. My original LOM had retired and there had been several others in the interim, but all had long memories. Therefore, I was gently reminded to go by train this time, but I didn't mind. Leeds was far easier for me to access than Watford and I had the hitherto unknown luxury of departing on Monday mornings instead of Sunday nights.

The training facility was conveniently located a short walk from the station in the City Exchange, which was where I met with Dave and the other nine members of the class. I turned out to be the oldest of the group, so it wasn't long before I was fending off the Stephenson's *Rocket* jokes again. The only minor inconvenience was that our hotel was situated near Wakefield, so each day we would be bussed in and out during the rush hour traffic, but apart from that, I was looking forward to getting stuck into the course. It was probably the best and most comprehensive operational railway training you could get, and I felt fortunate to be there.

Unfortunately, I was only there for the first three days of the first week, as those who already held PTS were sent home on Wednesday afternoon. Quite why I'd suffered two 12-hour days in York when I could have comfortably completed it here was beyond me, but perhaps it was HR's revenge. After just getting settled at the hotel and orientated around the training facility, it was a sudden and unexpected decamp back to Derby. Fortunately, I was able to secure a couple of shifts with one of the Derby MOMs, both of which primarily involved chasing sheep. Not for any nefarious purposes you understand (although I can't speak for the MOM), just to clear them off running lines around Derbyshire and Staffordshire where they'd strayed. Well, that was how it was explained to me anyway.

The next two weeks at Leeds were intensive but interesting, and with PTS out of the way, we eventually became acquainted with the other elements of the course:

COSS – Controller of Site Safety.
LXA – Level Crossing Attendant (I liked how an X had been inserted into this abbreviation instead of a C.)
Pilot(man?)
PO – Points Operator.
RSA – Route Setting Agent (A rather grandiose title for someone who instructs POs during a complex points failure.)
BSN – Bridge Strike Nominee.
RDN – Rail Defect Nominee.
Lookout/Site Warden.
Handsignaller.
RIO – Rail Incident Officer.

PTS only allowed you to go on the track under the supervision of a COSS, and it was a COSS who arranged a line blockage with a signaller, so getting this competency was really the key to the whole course, and why the entire second week was devoted to obtaining it. Handsignaller, LXA and PO were classed as auxiliary operating duties and were completed during the third week, along with the RSA, Lookout and Site Warden competencies. Friday of that week was spent at Doncaster for the practical. It was an easy day for me, having already pumped my guts out on Sudbury's barriers, as well as clipping and scotching Scropton's and Egginton's crossovers on numerous occasions. (A metal G clamp to clip facing points and a wooden wedge to scotch trailing points.) I was also surprised but pleased to find that, not only did the MOM course provide some solid, albeit theoretical railway training, there had been the bonus of visiting five out of the seven Yorkshire cities. (I have cheekily slipped Bradford into the Leeds conurbation, and once spent an hour in Sheffield changing trains, thus making up my five – only Ripon and Kingston-upon-Hull are absent.)

It didn't seem long before I was back in Derby for my two-week practical experience with the duty MOM. Apart from learning where all the best eating establishments, lay-bys and hidey-holes that MOMs were reputed to loiter in were, we did deal with a points failure, a flood, a bridge bash and of course the inevitable animals on the line. I also had to call in at 4 Shed one day (or rather the prefabricated building that stands on 4 Shed's old car park), which was a surreal experience and rather like stepping through a time tunnel – nothing had really changed and some people were even still in the exact position I'd left them fifteen years ago, but all had aged, including and most especially me. All my weekends were spent back in the signal boxes, to help cover the chronic staff shortage. There was talk of withdrawing me from the MOM course at one stage, which didn't do much for my morale, but even if I could complete it, I couldn't see how I'd ever be released from signalling duties to carry out the role anyway.

I returned to Leeds for the final two weeks, where Pilot(man?), RDN and BSN duties were tackled with great alacrity (well I thought so at the time). RDN and BSN involved how trains may still be run if parts of the rail were missing or broken, or if someone had been careless enough to wedge a high sided vehicle under a low railway bridge – as you do. Last, but by no means least, came the RIO part of the course, which was treated with the proper solemnity and black humour in equal measure: just as it should be.

"This job will change your life. The first time you respond to a fatality, it will change your life." That was the opening statement from our instructor as we began the RIO course. I thought back to the first time I'd responded to a fatality. I was seventeen and still undergoing recruit training in the Forces, but somehow, I'd managed to pass weapons training on the SLR, which unfortunately rendered me instantly useable for guard duty. Instead of the weekend pass I'd been expecting, I would now be spending Saturday and Sunday on alternating shifts between the guardhouse and main gate. My first fatality very nearly arrived on the Saturday night, and it was one I would have been directly responsible for, had things not gone differently.

I was in the sangar (a fortified sentry post located on the perimeter of a base) covering another recruit who was about twenty metres away checking vehicles entering the main gate. The muzzle of my SLR was poking through the slit and I was looking along it, trying to remain alert and interested. It was around 23:30 and it had been quiet for a while, but it wouldn't last because all the pubs had closed, and most people would be making their way home. The main road past the camp was always a source of tension and the gate personnel were prime targets for drunken youths.

A few cars drifted past tooting their horns, then a silver hatchback pulled up and my partner approached it, but I suddenly felt very uneasy about it. There was something about the way it had pulled up and the angle it was facing – it all seemed wrong somehow. I already had my partner covered, as a blonde-haired, baby-faced youth rolled down the passenger side window. There was a brief muttered exchange then the youth suddenly produced a pistol from his lap and pointed it directly at my partner's head. The Rules of Engagement at the time dictated that, in this situation, I could now open fire without first shouting a warning. I had Baby Face clearly in my sights, and at this range, even with my questionable marksmanship skills, there was no way I could miss, and there was no way he could survive it.

The whole thing probably took less than two seconds, but it seemed much longer. Time seemed to slow down and there was an eerie silence. My mind became fully focussed and my responses automatic. There was only him and me in the universe now. I felt my trigger finger tightening, and almost certainly in the next instant, his head would explode into a bloody mass. Even though time had slowed down I remember being surprised at the amount of jumbled thoughts being processed in my mind. There was a feeling of not wanting to be in this situation, but now that I was, there was little I could do about it. What would I be doing if I were at home right now? What would my family and friends think? Would the lads and I still be going out for a drink next week? Perhaps the most surprising feeling was a brief flash of exhilaration, followed by an even briefer flash of what I suppose was hesitation. But there had been weeks of indoctrination on the weapon, and now everything had clicked into place beautifully for the final and ultimate test; one pure moment...

Then it was all over. My partner had involuntarily staggered backwards into my line of fire and I suddenly had no shot. I heard someone laugh, and then the car screeched off, leaving my partner staring blankly after it. There was a brief element of comedy when one of the NCOs (non-commissioned officer) suddenly burst out of the guardhouse with a Sterling submachine gun at the hip (amazingly, people were still being trained on this vintage weapon). He looked like something off the cover of *Warlord* or *Victor* comic and only needed a couple of pineapple grenades to complete the ensemble. I had to admire his enthusiasm though because he desperately wanted to empty its entire 34 round magazine into the now distant car – until he was subtly reminded of the Rules of Engagement.

It had all been a prank anyway. We found out later that the inevitable car full of drunks, who, after kicking out time, had decided to bait the local military. Baby Face's weapon had been a water pistol, which was a rather dangerous escalation of the insults usually hurled at us. I doubt Baby Face ever knew how close he came to losing his life that night, because if that was the start of his career in stupidity, he must be long dead by now.

In the event, my first dead body came the next day, barely as we had recovered from the previous night's escapades. On the Sunday afternoon, several of us were called to attend an accident on the main camp and arrived to find that a HGV had reversed over a young serviceman, who'd slipped under its wheels whilst calling it back. I knew he was dead, but initially he didn't look too bad, until he was turned over...well, the less said the better. It was the manner of his death that remained with me though and I became more attuned to the risks when operating in similar circumstances, particularly later as a trainman. All the times I was on the ground, dodging trip hazards and trying to hand signal trains into dark and dangerous blind sidings, I was determined that a similar fate would never befall me. Perhaps this first fatality did change my life after all, for the better I like to think.

There were several dangerous sidings in the immediate vicinity of 4 Shed, including Etches Park itself. The RTC sidings and St Andrew's oil terminal both required trains to propel in blind and were only partially lit during the hours of darkness. Chaddesden Sidings had no illumination at all and the trainman had only a hand lamp to rely on whilst stumbling around, trying to check his train *and* where his feet were going at the same time. The fate I dreaded most ended up happening to a colleague of mine whilst he was calling a train back into the RTC sidings. He was standing on an embankment, well out of the way, but unfortunately lost his footing, slipped down the bank and went under the wheels of the slowly propelling train. One of his legs was severed, and even though an ambulance arrived quickly, he was dead within two minutes from shock and blood loss.

My next fatality happened even more quickly than that. I was secondman on a High Speed Train (HST) and we were passing through Kettering station at 90mph. Suddenly there was a brief flash of a face in the corner of the windscreen on my side, then a bump, and it was all over. It took us three quarters of mile to stop. Unless the body ends up sitting in the cab with them, most drivers tend to phone the signaller and say, "I think I've just hit someone." To which the signaller usually replies, "You *think* you've just hit someone?" Deep down you know you have, it just takes a little time to process. This incident was especially tragic because the victim turned out to be a chap in a wheelchair who was being pushed across the barrow crossing at the end of the platform. To this day, I don't know whether it was an accident or a suicide. There was talk at the time that he was terminally ill and had told the person pushing his wheelchair to give him one last shove, but I tended to think it was just a terrible accident.

There was no trauma counselling after any of these events, simply because the process did not exist in the form that it does today. Years later, and for no apparent reason, images of these incidents still occasionally pop into my head and replay as if on a continuous loop, until they are replaced by other random daily thoughts. This may go some way to explaining my many eccentricities, and if after reading this book, there are any budding psychologists out there, who wish to tackle my case, please feel free to drop me a line – providing the men in white coats have not already been summoned that is! Also, my years of solitary confinement in a signal box may have to be considered too. However, I have found that it is often the psychologist who is more mentally damaged than the client, so it may be a case of me confronting their problems first. At the time of writing, I know of two chaise longues (Egginton and Tutbury) upon which they may recline and detail their case to me.

With the MOM course successfully completed I was supposed to have a further two weeks riding out and gaining some more practical experience, but there was little chance of that. For the most part, I was returned to the signal boxes and life on the relief circuit again. To be fair, the LOM (another new one) tried his best to get me released from the box whenever possible, but having one day riding out, then one day signalling just wasn't practical, or safe – I decided that I was either learning the MOM role or I was signalling, not both. Plus, not being fully conversant with all the eating establishments, lay-bys and hidey-holes yet, it wasn't always easy to track down the duty MOM on these ad hoc training days. At the time, I was immersed in some house renovations, so I didn't try too hard to track one down anyway.

In November I passed the ruling with the LOM and the approval with HMRI. I even managed to get the necessary on-track visits done and gain the full COSS qualification, but I was soon back to the 70-hour weeks and 12-hour nights on the relief circuit again. It was disappointing because I'd worked hard and had learnt a lot but was never given the chance to put that knowledge to use.

When it became apparent that I wasn't going anywhere fast as a relief MOM, I got another German shepherd dog from the shelter in January 2010. Skye was about four years old and, her previous owner's neglect notwithstanding, a fun madcap canine that loved life and people but having not been socialized properly, she hated other animals and had to be kept separate from them. Around the same time, I decided to apply for a resident position at Scropton. Young 'un had been gone for a while, and Old 'un had been forced to retire just before the age discrimination law was brought in, so I decided to give up the life of a journeyman. I loved the relief life at first because of the variety – once working four different locations on three different shifts all in one week. I don't remember working my way up and down the line consecutively in one week, but it would have been an achievement. Nevertheless, I began to cool towards the relief lifestyle when I felt I was being taken for granted and that some of the relief were still being favoured above others. I reasoned it was better to remove myself from the equation rather than to fall out with anyone. It was probably the nights and excessive hours at Alrewas that soured me the most, but I liked the idea of a permanent base and my own locker, not having to carry my rule books everywhere, and best of all, a regular shift pattern with no nights. Also, I could have permanent place for Skye without upsetting anyone.

I felt my decision to become a resident was vindicated when I ended up with two weeks of nights at Scropton for engineering work in February. I was beginning to think I was the only relief that could work nights, but the shifts passed steadily, and I felt very comfortable there. If the Scropton residency hadn't come up, I probably would have held out for Egginton, as it was a nice roomy box with a bird's-eye view and was also the closest one to home. Unfortunately, because Skye had never encountered steps before, I always looked and felt completely ridiculous (not to mention knackered!) trying to carry a full-grown, and somewhat reluctant, GSD up and down the mountainous ones there. I liked Sudbury but could never really relax there because of the constant rumble of traffic and the nagging fear that all four barriers would fail at any moment. I didn't dislike Alrewas, just the night shifts, although the boredom could be a killer if you weren't prepared for it. I suppose my heart really belonged to Scropton. Its low-tech way of working suited me just fine, and ever since my first visit, I felt like I belonged there. There was nothing wrong with Tutbury, except for being too much in the public gaze; therefore, it remained at the bottom of my preferred residency list.

In May I ended my time on the relief with one last week of 12-hour nights at Alrewas, which I suppose was fitting really – rosters certainly got their pound of flesh from me. I did manage to obtain a couple of weekends at Uttoxeter before my residency became official, acting as points operator for a blockade that was taking place between there and North Staffs Junction. Trains were still running to and from Crewe and I helped cross them over at Uttoxeter. I held the MOM competencies for a further year after that, but in all that time, I was only an active MOM for about seven days – or in other words, MOM for a week. It was a dreadful waste of time, money and effort, but I valued the experience.

13. A RESIDENT OF SCROPTON

Initially I was unsure whether I'd got Young 'un's or Old 'un's job, but it seemed fitting that a middle-aged 'un had been drafted in to cover all possibilities. As it happened, both situations were vacant when I arrived to take residency on 17 May 2010 and I could have had either berth but elected to stay on Old 'un's shift because it was the non-talkative one and suited my temperament much better. Skye didn't mind and was enthusiastic about any situations that came along, vacant or otherwise.

And this was the thing I'd noticed most about her. Whereas Ben was often dour and resigned (very much like me really), Skye loved it all. She would join me in the box during the dark hours and I eventually made her a secure place in the locking room below for all other times. Typically, whenever I'd just got her ensconced downstairs, a procession of people would turn up wanting access; the MOM, S&T, PWay and innumerable representatives from various utility companies – sometimes one after the other. Skye wouldn't hurt anyone, she was just inquisitive and tended to wrap herself around the legs of unsuspecting visitors and trip them over. With space at a premium down there, particularly headroom, I would temporarily transfer her to the van until the maddening crowd had dispersed.

Enjoying work and play in equal measure – Skye on duty, July 2011. *Philip Helme.*

These constant interruptions, primarily by people in company vehicles that had the words 'Response Unit' written on the sides, were perhaps in retaliation for when I once sneaked across to the yard and covered up the first three letters with a bit of paper. Childish no doubt, but immensely funny to a signalman with too much time on his hands, especially when the driver of the newly titled 'ponse unit' departed without realizing. (Not quite ponce, but close enough.)

The thing I'd discovered about Scropton early on was that it was an 'all or nothing' box. Whenever I was dealing with trains, typically between five to and five past each hour, everything else seemed to happen as well; the box telephone would ring, Mill Lane Crossing phone would bleep, PWay or S&T would want a line blockage, someone would pop up wanting directions, and of course there would be a queue of traffic waiting at the gates. It was frustrating really because after the trains had gone there would be about 40 odd minutes when nothing much happened, and I would wonder what all the fuss had been about. I know it's only natural for people to begin or end journeys on the hour, but if the locals especially, just tweaked their journey start and finish times to before ten to or after ten past each hour, then they would rarely get held up, thus saving everyone a lot of heartache. But this was something that never altered throughout my tenure at Scropton – in fact it got worse. I think some motorists had no destination in mind and just enjoyed the novelty of driving back and forth over a level crossing.

With the farm traffic and the signallers' constant traipsing in and out for the gates, Scropton was a difficult box to keep clean. As British weather can only really be described as wet with dry periods, or dry with wet periods, this usually equated to an inch of liquid mud on all walking routes during the former, and an inch of dust on all surfaces during the latter. Well, I say dust; it was more like topsoil. Old 'un had always kept the place to a reasonable standard (he being an ex-Guardsman I expected no less), but this had lapsed by the time I arrived and my first week was spent knocking it back into shape. There was only me to do it initially because the relief were covering the opposite shift and it was three months before one of them decided to take the plunge and fill the other resident vacancy.

No matter how hard I tried I could never get used to pulling levers with a cloth and it was one of those box traditions I immediately dispensed with. I also never bothered polishing the levers and brasses like Old 'un had either but decided I would give the frame a fresh coat of paint when I had the chance. That was until I heard a rumour that all the North Staffs boxes were to be closed within a few years, which dulled my enthusiasm somewhat, so I never bothered in the end. I may have dispensed with the lever cloth, but I did manage to keep other notable old signal box traditions alive, such as cutting hair and cobbling boots; mainly my own, although I found the quality of these enterprises to be directly proportional to the amount of female attention I got thereafter. Hattie at Tutbury notwithstanding of course!

Mentioning old traditions (Hattie's perhaps being the oldest one of all), it is hard to believe that Tutbury still retained oil signal lamps into the twenty-first century. When I used to work there on the relief, the lamp man would appear every Thursday afternoon and, like a circus acrobat, climb the rusty signal post ladders of TY6 and TY2 and wobble precariously whilst replenishing their paraffin reservoirs. He only ever made two points of contact with the ladder as well, usually just his feet, as both hands were employed steadying his oil can whilst he transferred its contents into the reservoirs. He always seemed to want to carry out this balancing act just as I was dealing with trains and I found it unnerving to see his head level with a signal arm that was about to fly up or crash down like a guillotine blade. I would occasionally shout a warning, which made things worse because he would try to see who was shouting, but I had visions of chin-chopping him or clunking him on the back of the head, much like the fate that befell Alec Guinness in *The Ladykillers*.

Scropton's only dealings with the lamp man were when he wanted to cross at Mill Lane, usually just in front of a train, to access Tutbury's Up Distant. The oil lamps were replaced with LEDs in 2010 and the acrobatic lamp man was no more (perhaps he'd failed the ladder course?), although his spirit probably lived on in the form of a bird. Most afternoons at Scropton, an especially plump pigeon would perch on the Up Home signal arm, no doubt to obtain a literal bird's-eye view of the adjacent bird feeder. Whilst dealing with gates and bells, I would forget it was there, until I pulled the lever and launched it into startled but assisted flight. It must have enjoyed the thrill because it was a regular occurrence.

As well as the remaining oil lamps, all signal lamp bulbs were replaced with LEDs too. I was told these were more efficient and lasted longer, but I found this not to be the case at Scropton, going from zero lamp failures with the old bulbs to averaging three a year with their LED replacements.

As a resident, my roster became much simpler and I just alternated between a week of earlies and a week of lates. With the railway week starting on a Sunday, the one before a week of lates became my working Sunday, and as there still seemed to be a staff shortage, 2010 marked the beginning of nearly three years of me doing thirteen days in a row, Sunday off, then another thirteen days in row. Of course, there was the appropriate annual leave each year and obviously many other days off too, but all I seem to remember was this relentless thirteen-day cycle – not that I was complaining financially of course. It was also my choice to do it, and if work was offered, I never turned it down. I remembered too many times in the past when I wondered where the next wage was coming from, particularly during periods of self-employment. Also, if the boxes were scheduled to close, I wanted the work while I could get it. Weekends and Bank Holidays have always been largely irrelevant to front line railway staff, and throughout my working life, I have never had a Monday-Friday 9-5 routine – I doubt it would have suited me anyway. Besides, who wants their holidays at the same time as the rest of the population? However, I realized I may have spent a little too long at work when I started answering my home and mobile phone with the words "Scropton Signalman." Let's be honest, seven days in a row was enough, never mind thirteen.

In July a shanty town was set up in the old station yard opposite the box by a company contracted to carry out work on the railway bridge over Scropton Brook. This work didn't affect the running of trains, but the signalman's idyll was shattered for six months whilst it was carried out – with yet *more* people converging on the box. That same month also became the first time I had to send 6 bells for an obstruction of the line, (apart from all the occasions I'd had to rattle it out when the resident signalman at Tutbury forgot to send me 'train entering section' that is – a criterion of TITS RA RA, if, like him, you'd forgotten). This time it was a bona fide obstruction in the form of a tree that had fallen between the rails of the Up line near Archers Crossing, which I wasn't aware of until it suddenly reared up and smacked the cab of the first Up train – a Class 153 – which was about the same time as the driver became aware of it too. He put the brake into emergency as he passed the box, coming to a stand just beyond Mill Lane Crossing, from where he contacted me. Fortunately, there was no damage and he was able to continue, but it provided a good illustration of the stopping distance required for a train at 70mph, even a single carriage Class 153.

The following month I received a rare 'loco running round its train' practical lesson, when a Class 66 left its ballast wagons on the Down and proceeded to Uttoxeter to be crossed over, before returning to me on the Up. Unfortunately, the entire manoeuvre was carried out within an engineering possession, so no bells or signals were required, but it was interesting to observe, even though I didn't do anything except pull Scropton's recently refurbished crossover and put the loco back onto its train. I secretly wanted to couple up and do a brake test and was a little disappointed when the travelling shunter did it – I guess old trainman habits die hard.

In September a Class 153 failed in Tutbury's Down platform and another one was sent from Derby to assist it. They both eventually arrived at Scropton, whereupon I crossed them to the Up and sent them back, no doubt for attention at Etches Park. When I was on shed duties as a trainman, I would sometimes flip through the repair books of the locos I was in, often marvelling at the descriptive missives written by drivers of any faults they'd encountered during their shift. Underneath almost all of these would be scrawled the same three words by the fitter, 'No Fault Found.' I wondered if that would be the case with this unhappy Class 153.

September was also the first anniversary of me gaining my MOM competencies and I had to undergo the annual Assessment In The Line computer tests if I wanted to keep them. I spent a whole day in the MOMs' office at Derby and it was torture – eight hours of wading through pointless, idiotic questions. It was hard to believe there were pass or fail questions about what combination of equipment a level crossing attendant required; whether it was pen, paper, keys or spanner, keys, hand lamp or flags, hand lamp, keys – what did it matter? Just take everything you need to get the job done. The exact combination of items, as dictated by the computer, was the last thing on my mind when the barriers failed at Sudbury and there was two miles of waiting traffic in both directions. The whole assessment experience was extremely painful and I've had prolapsed vertebral discs that have been less so. But I'm not going to elaborate further on those computer tests, except to say, as just about every signaller will tell you, their quarterly assessments were a complete and utter waste of time. In 2016, this excruciating exercise was reduced to just once a year and re-branded as an Occupational Development Day. Subsequently, whenever your turn came up, you were listed as ODD on the roster. Still, I suppose it was marginally better than BO – Booked Off.

At this point I was still doing my quarterly assessments, as well as the annual MOM assessment. The signallers' assessments I could (just about) understand, but as I was rarely let out of my box for any MOM duties, I felt I was suffering that one for no good reason. Before the end of the month I managed to get two days acting as COSS for a vegetation team and ended up clearing some lineside vegetation between Tutbury and Scropton – the Scropton Signalman having to clear his own vegetation, the indignity of it all! But apart from another stint as a points operator at Uttoxeter in November and a couple of hours acting as pilot(man?) during another blockade there, that was it for the year – or for any other year as it turned out. But I wasn't bothered because I'd set my stall out at Scropton and was satisfied with that.

2010 ended with five inches of snow and a three-week deep freeze, where temperatures regularly dropped as low as minus 12. All the pipes froze up and we had to bring our own water to the box, not just for drinking and washing, but toilet flushing as well. It certainly made you aware of how much water you used, especially when you had to hump it about yourself. But I suppose it was no different from working at the South Staffs crossings, or even a shift on an old BR ballast job come to that. Then there was only a hotplate in the cab of a loco or a stove in the brakevan – no other facilities were available. There was no toilet or washbasin (and strangely no hand-washing course either), everything for a shift had to be carried with you. Some trainmen resembled machine gunners as they trudged out to their locos. But instead of ammunition belts across each shoulder and a tripod and general-purpose machine gun in either hand, they had their guard's bag over one shoulder, their food bag over the other and a two-litre bottle of water and a teapot in either hand.

As a small aside, I was always amazed at the ingenuity of train crews when it came to the carriage of milk on these jobs. Everyone took a turn at making tea in the communal pot and each would bring just enough milk for this purpose. In fact, it always seemed to be the *exact* amount of milk (obviously because there was no fridge), but the variety of containers used to transport it was mind boggling: flasks, jam jars, swing-top beer bottles, sauce bottles, even medicine bottles, everything except a milk bottle, although the only proviso was that these containers could be re-sealed again. Admittedly, every container had formerly held contents for human consumption, and (possibly) had all been washed out before re-use, but as previously mentioned about foodstuffs, not all cups of tea were willingly or gratefully accepted, and some were treated with downright suspicion and very often ill-disguised disdain.

As no MOM duties had been forthcoming, or even mentioned by the time the 2011 assessment came around, I decided to cut my losses and just keep the PTS and COSS qualifications, thus reducing my computer torture to a minimum. Certain elements of management were unhappy about my decision and it was always used as a stick to beat me with thereafter, but there was no way these competencies could be sustained without some solid practical experience, and I just wasn't getting any. The other relief MOMs resented being on signalling duties, or thought they were missing out on overtime whenever it was mentioned I might be let out of my box to gain some experience, so it got to the point where it was simply easier to keep me in the box and out of the loop. I suppose I unwittingly helped in this regard, because although I was officially a resident signalman, I covered other signal boxes during the on-going staff shortage. During 2011 I worked the occasional shift at Sudbury, Egginton, Alrewas and even Hilton at one stage. That was the same year we received notice of the North Staffs re-signalling project and the proposal to close all the boxes by the end of 2015 (later extended to 2016). Typical: particularly as I'd just got settled in one.

Back at Scropton I had occasion to operate the increasingly reluctant crossover again for a wrong direction move from Tutbury. After that, I had to book it out of use because the point ends were not going fully across and leaving a two-inch gap. It also looked slightly out of gauge, therefore ideal conditions for a wheel to ballast interface (if you happen to sit behind a desk and never get your hands dirty), or a simple 'dropped in the dirt' derailment to everyone else. In March I covered an unusually 'busy' shift at Alrewas – signalling three trains in 12 hours – but it was to be my last. That decision was made when the LOM (another new one) popped up at Scropton shortly after and told me that management weren't renewing my PTS and COSS qualifications because it wasn't in their interests. I found their ingratitude a little hard to take, particularly since I had worked so hard. I told him that was fine, and while they were at it, to cross off all my signal boxes and crossings, except this one, because it wasn't in *my* interests to keep them on anymore. I hadn't come here just to start working as a relief again. After that rather blunt exchange, I really became a resident of Scropton, solely and exclusively – and thus ended the great relief MOM experiment.

One day, a couple of rail enthusiasts arrived at the crossing, both fully laden with camera equipment. This was nothing special as a lot of enthusiasts gravitated here, particularly if something unusual was booked to pass through. I always had a chat with them, firstly because they knew more about what was happening than I did, secondly because life as a signalman can get a little lonely (although not *that* lonely) and thirdly because I had a pop star complex, and these were the natural groupies. I wasn't aware of any special happenings and was intrigued as to their presence. There was only the weed killing train due to pass on the Up, but surely, they hadn't come to see that? Apparently, they had because it was booked to cross over at Scropton and return to Uttoxeter and they wanted photos of it doing so. I hated to dent their enthusiasm but assured them that wouldn't be happening, primarily because the crossover was booked out of use and had officially been so for several months. Even if this information hadn't yet filtered through to Train Planning (an oxymoron, surely?), I would have had advance paperwork detailing this proposed move, allowing time for me to query it. Of course, that last sentence must be read with a massive tongue in cheek and the truth slowly began to dawn on me as I returned to the box to accept the train.

I cleared all my signals and the train duly approached, a little hesitantly it must be said, as the driver seemed rather confused about receiving a clear path through Scropton. After several uncertain power and brake applications, he finally came to a juddering halt at the Up Section, well beyond the crossover. One of the enthusiasts gave me an 'I told you so' nod and we all waited to see what would happen next. As the next Crewe-Derby service wasn't far behind, and its driver would no doubt be most perturbed to find a weed killing train blocking the path, I took the initiative and phoned Control. Of course, they knew nothing about it either, but I told them I was willing to assist, providing the LOM gave me permission to operate the crossover. I didn't fancy trying to explain why an expensive piece of equipment had dropped off the track if I were to act independently. After receiving permission, I pulled the crossover and clipped and scotched its point ends, thus closing the two-inch gap. Although the train appeared to lean alarmingly as it came through, it stayed on the rails and the enthusiasts got their photos. One of those enthusiasts turned out to be Bryn Davies – and I've not been able to get rid of him since!

Scropton suffered heavy flooding in June, causing the village to be temporarily cut off. I was on a late shift at the time and the water levels rose extremely quickly. I had to leave my van at the box and was just contemplating a walk along the track to Tutbury with Skye, when one of the locals, who'd had the good sense to park his vehicle just outside the village, very kindly offered us a lift home.

A couple of days later there was a flash of lightning directly above the box, which temporarily knocked out the power and, unbeknown to me, caused the metal fascia of the phone concentrator to retain a residual charge. I became aware of it when my fingertips brushed the fascia and the resultant discharge sent me flying halfway across the box. In all my years of working mechanical signal boxes, I had never had a signal cable break on me, but this shock threw me across the box in what I assumed to be a similar fashion. Flood and lightning; two worthy insurance claims in one week. Three, if you include pestilence, i.e., the constant stream of visitors on the early shift.

Looking in the Down direction, Bryn Davies provides a nice shot of the layout around the box in November 2012, with yours truly on duty.

Perhaps the most hair-raising experience I've suffered at the box (apart from being tased by the phone concentrator as described above) was during a 05:30 start for the RHTT one November. After it had whooshed past (literally) on the Down, I sent 'train out of section' to Tutbury and went to open my gates. Once done, I turned to go back to the box but saw two headlights snaking their way towards me on the Up. The logical part of my brain told me that no train had been signalled, or even accepted, but my eyes temporarily delayed this message, deceiving my brain into believing that one was currently bearing down on me. This frightening revelation instantly manifested itself by a furious pounding of the heart, the raising of hairs on the back of my neck and, curiously, a millisecond in which to regret all the times I could have made peace with my maker but hadn't. The logical part of my brain kicked in when I realized the headlights belonged to a tractor, following the perimeter of an adjacent field that perfectly mirrored the curvature of the railway line. And so, somewhat relieved but drained, I returned to the box.

Rather like the ebb and flow of various LOMs on the North Staffs, so too with my opposite number on the other shift. The position had originally become vacant again in 2012 and was covered by the relief until a signalman from another area arrived in 2013. He was only supposed to be helping for a couple of weeks but was still in situ almost three years later. I personally thought they should have given the job to Bryn, being as he seemed to spend the most time there. 2013 was a bad year for signallers and crossing keepers on the North and South Staffs, as five were suspended because of forgetting about the crossing gates at Alrewas and trying to run trains through them, giving me visions of the Denby Branch all over again, (see *Derby Trainman*). Three out of the five were sacked, although one was dismissed for an unrelated incident at Egginton. After such controversy, the system was altered at Alrewas, as it should have been some years before, but that was no longer my concern. To cap it all, a crossing keeper at Hilton was seriously injured when a car collided with one of the gates. Fortunately, he survived the experience, but as a result, any personnel operating manual crossing gates, Scropton included, now had to wear full orange gear – not that it offered much protection from ground impact after being catapulted twenty feet through the air. With all this staff shuffling, there were many 12-hour shifts throughout the year.

One lazy August afternoon I was sitting in the box when the Down Distant lever suddenly began to rattle in the frame. There were only two possible explanations for this (well, three if you count a supernatural one). The first was that somebody was physically pulling the cable and the second was that a large animal was trampling on it. Just as I was turning these thoughts over in my mind, Tutbury phoned to say that a cow had been reported on the line at Weer Lane Crossing. Feeling quite pleased with my evaluation of the situation, I acknowledged the message, replaced the receiver and glanced out of the window, immediately spotting what I presumed to be the said cow ambling towards me on the Down line. Most ROC signallers never see trains, let alone animals on the line. They only ever receive reports by phone and thus respond at a convenient remove. For a manual box signaller, no matter how many times it happens (and it was quite a few at Scropton), it always comes as a shock to see a sizeable animal blocking your previously clear tracks. There wasn't much time before the next train, so I tried to grab hold of the hapless beast, but it ran in the direction it had originally come from. As it happened, the cow wasn't necessarily the main problem because several farmers were on the track too. I only found that out when the Down train came through at caution and its driver reported such, although he hadn't seen the cow anywhere. Of course, the Up train arrived at the box at the same time and I instructed him to proceed through the section accordingly, only for both drivers to stop level with each other and have a chat. Then a police helicopter appeared, followed by the errant farmers and eventually a breathless MOM. Apparently, the cow had made its own way back into the field and was now suitably contained, whereupon everyone dispersed, and life returned to normal again.

Management speak had translated 'cow on the line' into 'bovine incursion' and as I sat idling in the box after this latest incident I wondered what other 'ine' incursions there could be:

Canine – dog – hopefully never.
Feline – cat – all the time, but they are clever enough to get off the track themselves.

Ovine – sheep – regularly.

Elapine – snake – only if higher management were out and about.

Leporine – hare/rabbit – didn't see many so I assume the farmers had shot them all.

Murine – rodent – occasionally, though relief signallers rarely left the comfort of the box.

Ranine – frog/toad – quite a few on the crossing during wet weather.

Piscine – fish – only when it flooded.

Vulpine – fox – (see Leporine).

Rupicoline – rock dwelling creature – not as rule, but I knew a few people that lived under them.

Asinine – extremely stupid – all the time, but as HR never left their office, it was usually the two-legged pedestrian or four-wheeled motorist variety. (Unfortunately, Asinine isn't a legitimate category, but I always wanted to use it for 'donkey on the line' just to see if anyone fell for it.)

Possibly a little late in the day, the Environment Agency began flood defence work at Scropton in August 2013, which continued for a year. Their shanty town was far too big to be accommodated in the old station yard and was set up in a nearby field instead, with the signalman's peace disrupted once more. As the work progressed, about 50 line blockages were taken each week for a period of two months, and after normally averaging only three line blocks a week, this was rather a shock to the system. As a result, the other resident signalman, who had been told it was a steady box and that he would only be there for a few weeks, began to feel somewhat misled. I am not sure what difference the flood defence work made either, and in some cases things became worse, with heavy flooding occurring five times in as many weeks during autumn 2019.

14. LOST IN TRANSLATION

The 'mis' prefix can precede many words, but perhaps 'management' and 'communication' should carry it permanently. It can also apply to 'interpretation', but one person's interpretation can differ wildly from another person's; therefore, it is sometimes difficult to distinguish a misinterpretation.

I always thought it was a mistake for any company to proclaim itself 'world-class' as Network Rail once did. Much like one of those 'Winter Wonderland' grottos that always pop up around Christmas time, you know it is going to be an immensely disappointing experience. So it is with companies that proclaim themselves world-class, especially if you happen to work for them. In my humble opinion, they certainly weren't world-class regarding their interpretation of good communication.

I was told on many occasions that our radio and telephone communication procedures were based on the military model. Which military, I didn't know, but it was nothing like I ever used in HM Forces in the late 1980s. The radio procedure I learnt was simplicity itself compared to the Railway Safety Critical Communications Protocols that were now being forced upon us – the title itself was enough to put you off. These protocols demanded that every time a message was stated, the hapless person at the other end had to repeat it back exactly. This differed considerably from a standard military exchange. To my mind, a repeat back is completely unnecessary and only serves to cloud the issue. It is the *message* that is important, not the repeat back. The objective is to reach a clear understanding and that can be achieved simply by asking the recipient at the end of the message, "Do you understand?" If the answer is no, the message should be relayed again until a clear understanding is achieved. The ABC of good communication is Accuracy, Brevity and Clarity, but a repeat back does nothing to aid these noble principles, quite the opposite in respect of brevity! I much preferred the no-nonsense military procedure, an example of which is detailed below:

"Hello 6, this is 66 Alpha, message, over."
"6 send, over."
(The message is relayed.)
"6 Roger, out."
(If any part of the message wasn't received or understood, a simple 'Say again', or 'Say again from' by the recipient was enough.)

Most corporal clones usually kept their communications short and to the point and few asked if there were any questions at the end. These communications were very often delivered in situations equally dangerous as a railway environment (a contact report for instance), but you were told everything you needed to know at the time and woe betide anyone who hadn't understood.

Network Rail then introduced the 'handshake'. If the repeat back was over-egging the pudding, the handshake was the equivalent of cremating it in the oven. The handshake was where any railway personnel phoning a signaller would have to reel off their name, designation, company and place from which they were speaking – although some lineside callers weren't always entirely sure of this information themselves! The signaller would then have to repeat this information back to them every single time it was given, which could be as frequent as every few minutes if the caller happened to be conducting S&T maintenance. The concept may have had slight value in a busy power box where there were multiple phone calls and distractions, but at most of the quieter manual boxes it was excruciatingly pointless and irrelevant. Like the repeat back, what was the objective of the handshake? Once someone had identified themselves on their first call, I didn't see the need to keep repeating their Curriculum Vitae back to them on subsequent calls, particularly someone I knew personally, dealt with regularly and could invariably see from the box. It wasn't as though I'd suffered a sudden bout of amnesia or the caller kept affecting a comical accent each time. Speaking for myself, I wasn't bothered who they were, what they were or where they were, only what they wanted and how long they were likely to inconvenience me. Additional information could be added as required – or better yet, when I asked for it.

These ideas (most not fit for purpose) were usually a direct result of the ever-changing chief executives, who seemed to stay for a couple of years and inflict as much damage as possible before moving on. Most came from outside the rail industry and tried to implement ideas that possibly worked well in their previous business model but were largely nonsensical or unworkable on the railway. The railway isn't a supermarket, a financial institution, an oil refinery or a car factory, it has a fickle nature and a life all its own.

The in-cab phones of the early 1990s may have morphed into GSM-R but Scropton didn't get a fixed terminal until 2013. To be honest there was absolutely no point in this location having one; its value was negligible and it merely occupied valuable space. The system was undoubtedly of great benefit to the driver in the cab, but once the North Staffs signallers had had a play, the novelty soon wore off and most just sat in the corner bleeping intermittently and gathering dust (the terminals that is, not the signallers – although thinking about it, that statement could apply in either case). In true railway style we were trained in the use of GSM-R nearly a full year before any terminals appeared in the boxes; subsequently no one could remember how to operate them when they did arrive. Most of us had to learn the same way a child learns: by pressing all the buttons until something interesting happened. I'd always considered the telephone to be a poor means of communication anyway; there was no room for body language. Funnily enough, block bells fitted the ABC criteria perfectly and were the best means of communication by far – those Victorians knew what they were doing all right.

Scropton is really a communications museum and the signalman is the curator – as well as one of the exhibits. The above photo, taken by one of Scropton's many fleeting visitors in 2015, shows the evolution of communication, starting with body language, hand signals, speech, writing slope, mail pouch, semaphore signals, telegraphic block bell, telephone, fax, email and GSM-R. The rear-view mirror could double as a heliograph, the Bardic as an Aldis lamp and smoke signals could have been employed had not the stove been removed to make room for all this electronic paraphernalia. Even one of the local pigeons could have been trained to deliver messages, so apart from jungle drums, all methods of communication were available – and still no one knows nowt!

As an aside, mentioning stoves, it sounds comical now but in BR days there was a stove in every brakevan, and a more unsafe environment for one I could not conceive. The stove (including stovepipe) would invariably be glowing red and, as riding in a brakevan was akin to being on a fairground cakewalk, every bump and lurch had the potential to send you careering into it. However, when you consider that you were essentially travelling in a wooden shed at speeds of up to 60mph, often attached to wagons containing hundreds of tonnes of flammable, explosive, toxic or radioactive material, I suppose first degree burns from the stove were of little consequence. I dread to think of the risk assessment and endless paperwork that would be required to ride in one nowadays. Not forgetting that you were also carrying ten detonators (fog signals) around with you too. The legislation for the simple act of turning on the taps in the box for so called 'flushing' purposes was extensive enough, never mind rattling around in a brakevan with a red-hot stove and ten little explosives. (This tap flushing seemed particularly self-defeating at Tutbury, being as there was still the suspiciously encrusted mug of stagnant water sitting atop the gas fire.) As previously mentioned, Scropton used to have a stove too, but it was removed in the 1990s. The main danger being that if a cable snapped mid-pull, the signaller could end up with branded buttocks, or worse.

Before GSM-R, drivers would use their cab phones to ring the box telephone, whereupon all the necessary safety critical communications would be completed, and the signaller would issue the relevant message. One of the reasons I liked Scropton so much was that I could sidestep most of this tedious waffle and speak to the drivers directly, but unfortunately, this wasn't a view shared by all. On the occasions I had to caution trains into the advance section, I would let them approach my home signal until they were almost at a stand, then clear the signal slowly. Most drivers would immediately be aware that something out of the ordinary was happening, by which time I would be standing on the box steps or crossing waiting to talk to them. In effect, I was continuing to caution trains by the original flag method – only without the flags. I admit this was no longer an accepted procedure, but it was common sense at Scropton. However, some drivers began to ignore me and, rather than engage in face-to-face communication, just trundle past towards the section signal (241 metres away on the Down and 362 metres on the Up) and phone me from there. Strange as that procedure was, I eventually learned not to feel too slighted and continued to give them the opportunity to stop and talk if they wished. For some who were wholly reliant on phones, perhaps they hadn't had the training for an 'old-fashioned' face-to-face conversation (still the number one preferred method of communication at the time, according to the Rule Book) and just wanted everything to be stated on a recorded line. It's a good job the message I had to impart was never 'The GSM-R and phones are out of action', because then they would have had to walk from the section signal back to the box. no doubt with much egg on their face.

Dealing with drivers face-to-face was my common sense interpretation of the rules. Admittedly it was easy to do at Scropton, but the example helps to reiterate the earlier points I made about the Rule Book in Chapter 2. Another example concerns sheep on the line. It was usually cows on the line at Scropton, but I had my fair share of sheep when I was a relief signalman. (I'd rephrase that last sentence if I could!) During those first few years, whenever sheep were reported on the line, trains would be cautioned through the affected section. Then a rule was introduced that stated trains should only be cautioned if there were six or more sheep; a rule which never actually appeared in the Rule Book, but in the Periodical Operating Notice. This rule made no sense to me whatsoever. I knew it was done from a delay mitigation point of view, but why six, and who's counting? Do six sheep equate to one cow? There may have been three sheep on the line when the initial report was received, but two minutes later there might be 30, plus pursuing farmhands, particularly since sheep tend to follow each other, well, like sheep really. In the absence of accurate on-site information, it would be safer to just caution trains. I always did and doggedly stood by that decision. To my mind, continuing to run trains normally when you know there are animals on the line is negligent. It's morally negligent at the very least and extremely unpleasant for everyone involved. Also, most of the Class 15x units that plied our route had part fibreglass cabs and anything that impacted at speed, even a single sheep, had the potential to end up sitting alongside the driver. If it was known there was a *single* swan on the track (between the rails), the Rule Book stated that trains had to be cautioned, so I could never really understand the logic, apart from that all swans belong to the monarch.

As it happened, some signallers weren't even interpreting a cow on the line as an obstruction anymore, but the Rule Book clearly stated that a 'large animal' should still be classed as one. Other than a bull, Shire horse or escaped circus elephant, I was hard-pressed to think of anything larger than a cow roaming our shores, unless 'Nessie' was holidaying in Scropton Brook, but evidently some of my colleagues interpreted things differently. In the end, this is why the Rule Book can only ever be a code of practice – guidance for the wise. Just as the Highway Code cannot dictate how you should drive in every situation, the Rule Book does not adequately cover every occurrence or location. Interpretation of the rules should be acceptable if done safely using common sense, experience and local knowledge.

I realized that the counting of sheep could cause drowsiness in some people, so whenever I received a report of an 'ovine incursion', I automatically rounded up (or should that be shepherded?) their alleged number to six and just cautioned trains. It wasn't long however, before this ridiculous sheep counting exercise was played out for real between Scropton and Sudbury. I had arrived to take duty just after one of my colleagues had signalled a train into the section normally (as per instructions) following a report of only five sheep on the line. (Incidentally, the initial GSM-R call for this had gone through to the wrong box, with Tutbury having to relay it to Scropton!) The train inevitably struck some of these unfortunate animals and the driver had to stop, report the incident and request a line blockage to examine his train, all obviously taking far longer and causing more paperwork and phone calls than if my colleague had just cautioned the train. Not forgetting of course, that this avoidable collision could have easily damaged an air pipe on the train, which then would have resulted in a failure: the average amount of time to deal with such an event on our line being about 90 minutes. Fortunately, this was not a scenario the passengers would have to endure, and the train resumed its journey. When the MOM finally responded, after being summoned from another incident over 30 miles away, he had the wonderful job of removing the carcasses, after first taking line blockages with the relevant signalmen of course. After he had cleared the line, I then had to caution the next train through (yes, you read that correctly) because he reported that several farmhands were now on or near the line.

As far as I could determine, *not* cautioning for sheep (of *any* number) was, at best, counterproductive and, at worst, sheer bloody madness! Also, looking at the 'big picture' (as Control were often urging me to do), what about the Etches Park/Eastcroft depot staff who had the unenviable task of cleaning the unit afterwards, or any of the involved railway personnel who perhaps had post traumatic stress from a previous human fatality and may have suffered flashbacks because of this incident? The whole thing could have been easily avoided with a simple caution and this incident had proven it beyond all doubt. Unfortunately, Control's big picture was to take a region wide average of these delays involving sheep (i.e., fewer than six) and deem the overall result acceptable, but then they didn't have to deal with the incidents or the aftermath first hand.

Purely as a footnote, not only did the above incident deprive a farmer of at least two sheep, it very nearly deprived me of my life too, and helps to highlight what this chapter is really all about. With the caution in place for the wandering farmhands, I, and my neighbour at Sudbury both had a train arrive at the same time, but with my more expedient method of face-to-face communication, I sent my train into the affected section well before he sent his. I knew this because I'd not yet received 'train entering section' from him, plus, as I looked towards Sudbury, over two miles distant, I saw what I thought to be the train's headlights still at the box. As I had the inevitable queue of traffic at my gates, I decided that now would be an opportune moment to nip across the tracks and inform the waiting motorists that they wouldn't be delayed much longer. I was halfway across when the Up train rounded the curve from Sudbury at line speed! In the five seconds of life that were suddenly left to me, I managed to dive clear whilst simultaneously giving a hasty acknowledgement to the driver's horn warning as he zipped past. I had misinterpreted the headlights on the horizon, the signalman at Sudbury had neglected to send me 'train entering section' and the driver had evidently misunderstood (another apt 'mis' prefix) the instructions about proceeding through the section at caution – unless of course 70mph was his interpretation of a suitable cautionary speed. Also, and entirely relevant for this chapter, assuming the safety critical communication protocols had been observed correctly at Sudbury, the repeat back had been a waste of time too – but I may have mentioned that before.

The odd bovine and ovine incursions continued to crop up between Scropton and Sudbury and we had to caution trains between us four times in as many weeks during one month. Of course, the GSM-R calls for all these incursions got routed directly to Tutbury, who then had to relay them to us. (Was NR still actively pursuing world-class status I wondered?) I had been told that GSM-R was better because a signaller could respond quicker in an emergency, but only – and this would seem to be the most important bit – if the call had gone through to the correct box in the first place. As already stated, the value of GSM-R was negligible at Scropton because there was little chance of being able to stop a train quickly in an emergency there. The signaller would probably find out at the same time as the driver, or more likely after. But there was no chance at all if we were fated to only ever receive second hand information from Tutbury – too many repeat backs for a start.

Bringing trains up to the box and having them stood on the crossing as you gave drivers the spiel was not without its hazards. Whilst cautioning for one of the ovine incursions, I had a light loco slotted in between the normal passenger trains. After I'd sent it on its way, I found that it had generously deposited about 50 gallons of diesel on the crossing; I was paddling in it! I wish I'd known beforehand. I could have got a few buckets underneath and re-fuelled my van for free. In the event, all I did get was a sweet, sickly stench and a rather slippery rainbow-coloured walking route for the next two weeks. I knew the loco had a large capacity fuel tank, and even if that rate of loss were to continue, there would still be enough to reach Crewe. I did ask my neighbour at Sudbury to query it with the driver though – and no, I didn't feel the need to do any handshaking or have him repeat anything back.

122

15. LIVING IN A BOX

(The last of the lone workers)

It used to be called 'Waiting Time' with BR, but I was never sure which word the emphasis was supposed to be on. *Waiting* Time seemed appropriate in a loco cab and was accrued in quarries, collieries, power stations, engineering possessions and sidings. Waiting *Time* tended to happen in a signal box and seemed to sum up the experience quite well. However it was emphasised, the method of recording this time was identical, in so far as the BR Driver's Ticket and the Train Register Book were both a grid format where the travails and triumphs of each shift would be reduced to lots of little times in lots of little boxes. Both documents detailed a shift, but very little of the human story behind it. In a truck cab it was officially called 'Passive Work', i.e., activity other than driving and statutory breaks, but at least a tachograph chart showed the peaks and troughs of a shift and was not as easy to manipulate as the previously mentioned railway documents (Sloth suddenly springs to mind here!) Incidentally, Passive Work was rarely anything of the sort. It was generally the period where you loaded or unloaded your truck, usually by yourself, and often quite aggressively.

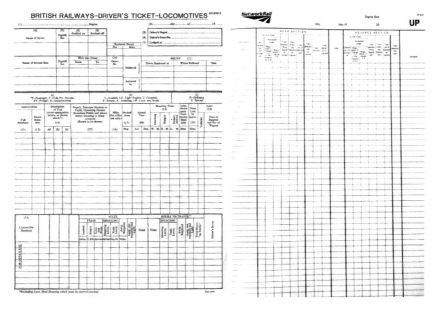

A BR Driver's Ticket circa 1990s and an Up page from a Train Register Book (not the one Sloth removed, I hasten to add).

With an average of two trains an hour on the North Staffs, and even fewer on the South Staffs, that could amount to a lot of Waiting Time, but that was one of the essential skills required for the job. The first and perhaps most obvious question asked of any prospective signaller was; how do you maintain concentration when there is a lot happening? But equally important, more so for the boxes in question was; how do you maintain concentration when there is nothing happening? And taking it a stage further, how do you manage it when you are alone and there is no one else to encourage or motivate you? I had been a lone worker for about two thirds of my working life and it suited me. In fact, I thrived on it, but whether that's a good thing I don't know. I believe that someone who works alone can always adapt to working in a team, but a team worker cannot always adapt to working alone.

I recall reading about Joshua Slocum, who, between 1895 and 1898, sailed alone around the world. He wrote that he had found it was not good to be alone, and so made his companionship with what there was around him,

'...sometimes the universe, sometimes my own insignificant self...pages of my history were recalled which had long been forgotten and that seemed to belong to a previous existence. I heard all the voices of my past, laughing, crying and telling what I had heard them tell me in many corners of the earth'.

Not only did Slocum so eloquently describe himself on his boat, he also described me in a signal box, and perhaps much of what this book is all about. On certain shifts, during the lull between trains, my mind would sometimes escape the confines of the box to revisit faraway places and recall voices of people long gone. On a Friday or Saturday late shift I would often think about all the pubs and clubs I used to frequent or what I was doing on a particular night ten years ago. The downside of this was that trivial problems (current or historical) or perceived slights (real or imagined) could be brooded upon and often get magnified out of all proportion when alone in the box. I always tried to adopt the philosophical maxim of 'If you must look back, let it be to smile at perils past.' Besides which, I had Skye, who accompanied me on every shift. She was my world and I was hers.

When not revisiting faraway people or places (or hearing voices), having such appreciable amounts of time on my hands allowed me to ponder some of the great mysteries of life, like why Spanish men wore flamboyant costumes and goaded bulls into fighting them. Surely being Spanish was enough and the costumes and goading were unnecessary? And why a successful person is often said to have a meteoric rise, but an unsuccessful person is never said to have a meteoric descent or impact, when the last two are descriptively accurate and undoubtedly appropriate in the more spectacular cases of failure? Also, why does an interview panel bother asking candidates where they see themselves five years hence? Surely the obvious and only answers are as managing director or chief executive, anything less is clearly showing a lack of drive and commitment. And when you read about pop stars earning more money dead than alive, are they still being taxed? It must be terrible being dead and still getting taxed on your earnings. Benjamin Franklin was absolutely correct when he said 'In this world nothing can be said to be certain, except death and taxes' but I'm sure he didn't expect the latter to continue after the former.

Scropton was the most accessible box on the North Staffs, and along with the regular crossing users, there were intermittent visits by rail enthusiasts and photographers. At one stage I did begin to think Bryn's regular appearances were a figment of my imagination, a bit like the film *Fight Club*, although in a further plot twist, I was playing the part of Tyler Durden and him Jack. I'd also mentored an assortment of trainees by this time, including two women, and it was around this point I gathered that the TITS RA RA mnemonic was only ever used on all-male courses. During a casual discussion on signalling regulations with a young lady trainee I asked, "What about TITS RA RA then?" and nearly got my face slapped! Another visitor who popped up periodically was the Railway Chaplain, but I always welcomed a man of God simply because on some days, I needed all the help on offer. Crossing Scropton's threshold was about as close to time travel as you could get and whenever a visitor turned up, I often said, "Welcome to Scropton, you've just stepped back to 1884." Most of these visitors were shocked to find some parts of the railway still operating like this.

No matter how much I often craved it, I wasn't always left alone. There were statutory visits from the LOM and MOMs, regular line blockages and maintenance requests from S&T, PWay, periodic lighting, fire extinguisher and water inspections, not to mention all the utility company visits – the list was endless really. Sometimes they'd roll up one after the other to make demands, usually on the early shift, and my heart would sink every time a van pulled into the adjacent yard. Some early shifts were so frenetic I often thought that if Scropton and Birmingham New Street were on the same scale, Scropton would be busier, certainly in respect of footfall.

The LOM visits were routine, and to be fair, if you didn't cause them any problems, they didn't bother you unnecessarily. I kept a shaving kit at the box and, one morning, I was all lathered up during this mundane activity when I noticed the LOM's van pull up. I couldn't really wash all the foam off and receive him with half a beard; I'd look even more unprofessional than I already did – and certainly more deranged. So, I decided to continue, instantly placing myself in a far weaker position to defend against the banter that would ensue once he crossed the threshold. He came in, shaking his head.

"You lot are always up to something in these boxes. I've just visited that mad Scotsman down the line and he's walking around the box with no top on!"

I didn't bother enquiring as to why the 'mad Scotsman' was in this partial state of undress. That he was a manual box signalman of many years' standing was a perfectly satisfactory explanation as far as I was concerned. I ventured that being a Scot, he perhaps didn't feel the cold as much as the rest of us, but the LOM just sneered.

"It's a good job you weren't here when Old 'un was," I continued, finally completing my ablutions. "You might have found him wearing a cape, clutching a plastic skull and lamenting the loss of poor Yorick to someone called Horatio."

This went somewhat over the LOM's head, so I explained that Old 'un had been an actor who occasionally rehearsed his lines in the box. I gathered by the look on the LOM's face that this offered little in the way of an explanation for the eccentric behaviour of manual box signallers, although we both knew of several people that had been tipped over the edge by signal box life. (There had been six 'mental health' casualties in four years and all but one had been an Alrewas resident or relief.) I reminded him about how problems sometimes got magnified out of all proportion when alone in the box.

"I'll start worrying when I see you licking the windows," said the LOM.

"That's been done," I replied. "Start worrying when you see me licking the windows from the outside."

We both laughed, although perhaps a little too maniacally in my case.

"It'll never happen to me," I assured him. "I learned to embrace the madness years ago. After all, a man is only as crazy as the world he tries to live in."

The LOM was now looking for a place to sit and shuffle his paperwork, but as the world I currently inhabited measured 10 x 15 feet, with only about half that as actual usable space to set my stall out (similar dimensions to a cell at Alcatraz, I might add), finding a vacant perch for visitors wasn't always easy.

"Look at this place. Your stuff is spread everywhere. Anyone would think you lived here."

Therein, illustrating the point *and* the problem quite well I thought.

Sometimes the yard was just used as a place to loiter, and happily, no orange clad people would emerge from the assorted white vans that constantly rolled up. There the occupants would remain, snacking, snoozing and playing with their phones. After several hours, some might venture across to make use of the box facilities, and encountering me in apparent unfettered and leisurely residence, offer the usual sarcastic "You've got hard job haven't you." To which my obvious rejoinder was always "Look who's talking". I have read that solitude, particularly with a good book, is a blessed state, but physical labour in isolation can be lonely. I agree with both sentiments, but as physical labour at Scropton generally only occurred in short bursts, I can't say I ever felt lonely. I have felt the odd twinge in other solitary work, particularly when working as a groundsman at a large comprehensive school – a place ordinarily bustling with life and noise, then dark, silent and eerie during the evenings, weekends and holidays – the loneliness was surprisingly acute. Now, having done my time 'on the shovel' so to speak, I truly appreciated and oft rejoiced in a more sedentary pace. How many of these fleeting visitors could stand the isolation, boredom and potential loneliness of a signal box day after day? When questioned, most admitted that they would find it hard and probably not last a week. For all the sarcastic statements, no one was in a rush to take my place and one person's promised land was another person's desert. To paraphrase Pascal: 'When someone complains of their hard life, try giving them nothing to do'.

I've probably always had mild obsessive-compulsive tendencies, which became more pronounced when working in the box, but for this line of work, I think it was more of a blessing than a curse. Because of this slight 'anxiety' I didn't have too much difficulty maintaining concentration, and working to a set procedure each time helped satisfy the compulsion, although it probably perpetuated it too. During my time as a relief signalman, it had been interesting to note some of the resident signallers' idiosyncrasies, but it wasn't until I'd been a resident for a while that I realized I was displaying similar traits. (Relief signallers don't usually suffer as much, not being tied to the same box every day, year after year.) The resident signalmen at one box were like an old married couple. One would spend most of his shift arranging the box furniture exactly to his liking and then the other one would come on duty and put it all back again. For reasons of private amusement, whenever I had to visit their box, I would try to schedule my appearances to coincide with their shift changeover. Another example was the overzealous cleaning at Tutbury and by Old 'un at Scropton, as well as perhaps all the brass rubbing at Sudbury. Some might label it as mild OCD, but apart from pride, perhaps it was just a way of maintaining concentration and creating a buffer zone against the outside world. It also explained why some signallers were resistant to visits or got unsettled about having their routine disrupted. After all, even Superman had a Fortress of Solitude.

The desire for cleanliness was understandable considering some signallers, including me, spent far more meaningful time at work than they ever did at home. It also explained the wide variety of comfy chairs in almost every box. Management never really grasped that this was a necessity for box life and wasted a small fortune experimenting with several different types of unsuitable chairs, when a battered old armchair from home invariably fitted the bill.

You certainly had to be happy (or if not happy, at least comfortable) in your own company, and have the wherewithal to survive life in a signal box. The wherewithal in this case meant having something to occupy you between trains. Some signallers employed their laptops and mobile phones with gusto, whereas I occasionally made use of a portable CD/DVD player (late shifts only), even though such items were of course forbidden on a safety critical role. I couldn't see any harm using these devices during the lull, provided they were switched off whenever trains were about. After all, limited Internet access eventually became available and was allowed in most boxes through the TRUST computer, and virtually this entire book was written in the box using the available word processor. (So, if there are mistakes in the text, blame the distracting trains!) But having grown up without all this electronic clutter, particularly during all those mind-numbing hours in a loco cab or brakevan, I wasn't dependant on it in the box now. It really all came down to self-management and discipline. Technology was supposed to be the servant not the master, but it was evident that most people had allowed those roles to become reversed. Some of the younger signallers disliked having their electronic pursuits curtailed, but I often wondered how they would survive if the ban were ever rigidly enforced. During the occasional LOM crackdown, I was always reminded of a phrase first coined by Buddy Rich (musician) and later used to good comic effect by Jerry Seinfeld (comedian) 'Let's see how they do, up there, *without* all the assistance'. (For a full explanation, look it up on the Internet, but only if you are not currently engaged in a safety critical role.)

I did laugh when Nokia released their updated 3310 mobile phone though, with one advert asking, 'Do you remember the 3310?' Remember it? I was still using one! I had resisted having a mobile phone until 2001, but as a lone worker, my then employer, for my own safety, had literally forced this model upon me. I was still a lone worker but now forbidden to use it, or even have it about my person whilst in the box, which, of course, was no hardship as far as I was concerned. It was the same with the TRUST computer, GSM-R or any other technological aid. During periods of failure, some manual signallers couldn't seem to function without them, nor understand my apathy when the screens did go black.

Being more of an analogue man in a digital world didn't mean I couldn't appreciate the value of such things though, as some of the company emails were a rare source of entertainment. I particularly liked the one about using meditation to relax and de-stress, which stated: 'Switch off from the digital world. Switch off your laptop. Switch off your mobile'. It concluded: 'If you don't know how to meditate, you can look it up on the Internet or follow an app'.

The signallers also received emails concerning operational matters. A frequent one read '1Kxx: please note this service is full and standing leaving Derby' with 'This train is correctly formed of 1 coach' underneath. Who's kidding who? An uncommon one stated 'This train is delayed owing to a MOP trapped on the crossing.' The MOP, in question wasn't the long-handled cloth-headed type (well...) it merely stood for Member of Public, an abbreviation I always found vaguely amusing. Perhaps it was the perfect but unintentional image it conjured up, or that the term sounded suitably derogatory without being obviously impolite? There was also the brilliantly worded 'There is no lighting at Uttoxeter station. Please advise customers to take extra care when alighting' and a personal favourite: 'There are 40 cows on the line at Barthomley Junction. As a result, trains are unable to moove in either direction.' I never knew if that was genuine or a deliberate typo! One message from our roster clerk read 'I am still sorting out the annual leave for this year, please bare with me.' From the appearance of some of my colleagues, I doubted she meant it literally! The boxes also received a daily email from the LNE Route Performance Analyst, but unfortunately, because its title was so long, it always showed in my inbox with the last three letters missing, adequately summing it all up.

Only occasionally did I look on the company intranet, although I sometimes wished I had studied it more because some of the forums could be comedy gold. One thread discussed which actors would best suit the roles if signal box life were portrayed in film. I make no apology for stealing parts of this thread because I thought it was so good, but I should perhaps apologize for adding my contributions to it. I realize some of my characters are a little dated – and even deceased or not even real in some cases – but I welcome nominations for a modern reboot:

Mel Gibson – early shift (as in *Lethal Weapon* – all hyped up and borderline unstable).
Michael Madsen – late shift (as in *Reservoir Dogs* – never sure what the late shift gets up to).
Robbie Coltrane – night shift (body double).
Bruce Willis – relief signalman (as in *Die Hard* – doesn't play by the rules, disrespects superiors, grubby vest).
Denholm Elliot – signalman next door (as in *The Signalman* – rather odd and far too slow answering his bells).
Charles Bronson – MOM (old stone face grudgingly gets the job done).
Jurgen Prochnow – LOM (captain of *Das Boot* – tense and broody).
Charles Dance – Operations Manager (powerful and unhinged).
James Earl Jones – Route Control Manager (Darth Vader voice).
Keith Harris – Train Delay Attribution Clerks (Orville and Cuddles voices respectively).
Alan Rickman – COSS (keeps ringing up for a line blockage in that annoying Sheriff of Nottingham voice).
Will Hay, with Albert and Harbottle – S&T day shift (keep pulling out fuses and arguing with each other).
Tony Hart, with Chas and Morph – S&T response team (slightly bewildered but resigned older chap partnered with two shaven-headed, hyperactive younger chaps, one pale white, the other with an orange spray tan, both unintelligible and always shouting "Oi!" or "Toneeeey!")
George, Zippy and Bungle – various level crossing user telephone voices.
Arthur Askey, Norman Wisdom and Reg Varney – train drivers (speaks for itself).

Another popular forum thread was signal box cuisine and there seemed to be numerous pages devoted to what signallers were eating in the box. I'm afraid I was very dull in this regard as I only ever bought the same unexciting sandwiches, but if I happened to be doing twelve hours, I would sometimes get adventurous and give something a few revs in the microwave. Unfortunately, I'm one of those people who generally just views food as a means to an end (literally), but I realized my daily menu had become exceptionally boring when I began to look at what Skye was eating and often felt envious.

Some signallers used the time to better themselves through reading, writing and scientific study, and some even completed professional qualifications during their hours in the box. Others just allowed lowbrow newspapers to dictate their view of the world, ate takeaways and complained about the working conditions. These were usually career railway people who didn't know how cruel the world could be on the outside, but each to their own and whatever got you through a shift. Reading material had to be carefully selected though. I was once given a book on historic railway disasters, all of which still had the power to strike terror into the heart of any signaller. A signal box was the worst place to read about such events and there was always that agonizing moment in the text when a railwayman in some lonely place realized that, through his error, disaster was about to overtake him.

You can name just about any hobby and it probably could or had been done in the box. Before anyone asks, I am not classing deviant behavior as a hobby in this instance, although I would include 'pesting' in the list of activities. Incidentally, one of the old shunt drivers at Toton wasn't beyond a little self-gratification in the cab of his Class 08 (how this was discovered I do not know – nor did I wish to!), but the resultant delay in wagon movements around the sidings would exasperate the yardman. With no acknowledgement to his vigorous 'calling on' hand signals (possibly because similar actions were occurring in the cab), he would start trudging towards the loco shouting "Come when you're ready!" which only served to endorse the behaviour in my opinion. I suspect this driver and Ready Rubbed would have made a great pair and had a hand-washing course been available back then, I could think of no two better candidates.

I am also not including clock-watching or talking to oneself as hobbies, even if the latter was sometimes the only way of achieving sensible conversation. What follows is a small sample of some of the box activities I encountered, which are in no specific order: gardening, bird-watching, photography, astronomy, learning lines for a play, model making (well, I was assured that the sticky residue sometimes encountered on the levers was in fact modellers' glue), knitting (only ever done by signalwomen as far as I know, but some signalmen took so long to answer their block bell I often assumed they were counting stitches too), playing an instrument (other than a block instrument), drawing, someone even wrote a book. I know what you're thinking. All that time on his hands and *this* is all he could come up with!

In the early days of my residency I used to have a dumbbell (not my opposite number on the other shift, but an actual metal weight), although I eventually decided that wrestling with Scropton's levers and gates provided enough exercise, not to mention the odd snatched dog walk in between trains. Once, when I was fitting a new kitchen at home I brought in all the flat pack units and assembled them in the box. Unfortunately, I got a little carried away and managed to trap myself in a corner – the corner which just happened to be the furthest one away from the door and the block shelf. It was also wise to be careful about assembling things that were too big to fit back through the door and around the dogleg of the porch. Someone once brought in a box of screws to sort out, but I believe this was a crossing keeper on the South Staffs and so he could be forgiven for scraping the bottom of the hobby barrel (or the screw barrel in this case).

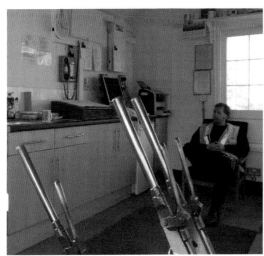

The author is caught clock-watching in 2009 – always a popular box pastime – and writing another TOL chapter in 2014. *Philip Helme/Bryn Davies.*

When you start bringing in a box of assorted screws to sort into different types and sizes, you know things are desperate (or maybe you don't? Perhaps you've already entered that happy, carefree state where you think everyone is deranged but you), but I suppose it was no worse than sitting in the cab of a truck, trying to pass a mandatory 45 minute break and wishing instead that you could be using that valuable time to reduce the distance between the next tip/drop you were so achingly close to and the insalubrious lay-by you currently found yourself in. During those enforced periods of inactivity, I found it difficult to suppress the urge to start fiddling with things in the cab, such as dashboard switches, which oddly enough, only ever got pressed on those occasions and never under normal driving circumstances. I'm showing my age with cab layouts, but I could rarely resist pressing the cigarette lighter, waiting with increasing anticipation for it to pop out so I could check the quality of its glowing element and test its heat output against my hand before it faded. However, I would invariably find it had been clogged with ash and rendered non-functional years ago. I expect most people have peeked in the ashtray and behind sun visors at one time or another, primarily to ascertain if the passenger side has got a little vanity mirror. I once pulled one down to find the mirror had been removed and someone had scrawled 'You ugly bastard' in its place. Similarly, I once noticed the plastic cap in the centre of the steering wheel had been interfered with, so I pulled it off to investigate, knowing full well that only the main securing nut was beneath. However, along with the expected nut I also discovered a neatly folded note, which read 'Put me back you nosy bastard!' I thought both endeavours to be highly imaginative, and remarkably prescient (well, the ugly and nosy bits anyway, not the illegitimacy), but when you get to that stage, surely boredom is an insufficient word to describe the condition.

It's no wonder that it was made an offence for signallers to tamper with box equipment because I can only imagine the chaos if it were otherwise. I did hear about one particular relief signalman, who, thinking he had sufficient time between trains, decided to dismantle the block bell and tapper, only to have an unexpected train appear at the most inconvenient moment – which is when the delicate, but crucial spring connecting the bell hammer to the block instrument flirts off and disappears behind the lever frame, just in case you were wondering.

So, it isn't enough to occupy your mind, you also needed something to occupy your fingers as well (stop sniggering at the back), hence the crossing keeper with the box of screws, and partly why I carried on smoking cigars. I did try to quit several times, switching to sweets – usually herbal tablets or the preferred staple of old-hand shed drivers, liquorice and aniseed, before finally settling on humbugs – but because I was eating so many of the damned things it also became injurious to my health and I had to take up cigars again. (I finally managed to quit both in 2018.)

Incidentally, there are several reliable indicators of advancing middle age, in addition to feeling a physical wreck most of the time and only being able to put your socks on when sitting down. One is having a manager who is frighteningly younger than you and another is having the occasional penchant for old-fashioned boiled sweets, but maybe the latter can be put down to trying to recapture an element of lost youth. Either way, boiled sweets, like the past, should be left well alone. Another indicator is genuinely looking forward to receiving socks as a Christmas present, but that's more advanced middle age.

Scropton had its moments and sometimes there were actual signalling duties to be considered, other than the normal 'train goes down, train goes up routine'. Apart from periodically having to clip and scotch the point ends of the increasingly reluctant crossover, being on the edge of a large dairy farm occasionally meant livestock on the line. I likened these duties to some of the strange old country pursuits I'd read about. Instead of cow tipping, cheese rolling and hole watching, we had cattle chasing, point clipping and clock-watching. Fortunately, there was no morris dancing, unless of course you happened to accidentally walk into the release lever, but a bit of maypole dancing by the farm girls wouldn't have gone amiss, although it was best not to upset the local farmers. Aside from them all being armed with shotguns, the resident signalman could well end up being the next sacrifice in the wicker man. Start worrying if you found a corn dolly on the box steps.

Like any other job, some shifts went hard some went easy. Most went easy. They had to; otherwise the 70-hour weeks at Alrewas or the continuous cycle of thirteen days in a row at Scropton simply could not be sustained. Funnily enough, the shifts could be a lot like writing a book. Some days you would be totally blocked, and on others, the ideas would come tumbling out. I once had a trainee who told me that he didn't think he could cope being on his own for long periods with little to do. He was already fed up and wanted to quit. I felt sorry for him because he was unable to apply a bit of imagination or muster the necessary wherewithal to carry him through. I suppose I was fortunate because I never really felt like that – not to any great or lasting degree anyway – but I told him I once did, in a vain attempt to make him feel better.

"What happened?" he asked.

"The next train came along," I said. Or in my case, the next visitor, project, hobby, voice from the past, dog walk, idea, paragraph – or simply just the absurdity of trying to fit modern life into 120-year-old working practices, or indeed, vice versa. Whatever it was, you certainly needed something to involve yourself in whilst at the box, if only to stop those already close walls from closing in any further.

Some signalmen are cowboys, but not all cowboys are signalmen. The author rounds up another one, June 2014. *Bryn Davies.*

16. CROSSING THE LINE

It was autumn 1989 as the RAF Puma helicopter whipped across the steel-grey Irish Sea. A small group of us had just been picked up from an exercise in North Wales and were supposedly returning to base, but our helicopter was needed urgently, and we were diverted across the water. As we swooped into County Tyrone, barely audible above the noise and vibration, someone shouted, "Action stations, landing zone coming up!" and we prepared for a rapid debus. Our billet for the night was the floor of a Royal Ulster Constabulary (RUC) station, which happened to be in an area where a terrorist sniper was operating with apparent impunity.

Next morning, I found myself doing a brief stint on a vehicle checkpoint (VCP) and the atmosphere was very tense. It felt as though I was in the sniper's crosshairs the whole time (perhaps I was) or that the next vehicle I challenged would decide to crash through the barrier. Thinking back, I suppose it wasn't totally dissimilar to the feeling I got having just made a train cancellation announcement at Tutbury, which probably explained why I always ducked down after making it! But as the threat of an Armalite rifle-toting passenger was minimal (even at Tutbury), the feeling on the VCP was much more palpable and prolonged. Certainly, everyone I stopped that day was angry, mainly because of my presence there in the first place, but also because I was holding people up and impeding their progress.

It was now autumn 1992 and my mind had wandered back to that day as I sat in the secondman seat of a Class 56, rattling down the Denby Branch. Steel-grey ballast and rails had replaced a steel-grey sea, but the low afternoon sun dappling through the lineside trees had created a hypnotic rotor blade effect, which was exacerbated by each sleeper that flashed past. There was little difference in noise and vibration either as both machines seemed to have the same suppressed engine scream, which was invariably accompanied by the smell of hot oil. I was suddenly jolted from my reverie by Big Bill, my driver, who shouted over the din. "Action stations, Kilburn Gates coming up!" I climbed down from the cab and prepared to swing the gates across the road, ready to annoy people, hold them up and generally impede their progress again. It wasn't unknown for vehicles to crash through the gates here too, but at least I wasn't sniper bait, although I suspect some motorists would have happily rubbed me out if they could have done.

Nothing changes...fast forward several years and there I was at Scropton doing it all over again! I may have spent a lot of time in wooden boxes, but it would also seem that I've had more than my fair share of operating barriers and crossing gates too, not to mention upsetting motorists. It didn't seem a terribly long distance from a troubled street in Northern Ireland to the semi-rural idyll of Scropton Crossing, via the gates of the Denby Branch, except for the passage of twenty-five years. Perhaps this snippet should really have gone in Chapter 9 (another full circle), particularly since I'd also received my formal 'education' at the comprehensive school across the road from Denby North Crossing. Never an enthusiastic student, most of my time was spent playing truant in the adjacent sidings and I think it's fair to say that any education I did receive took place there and not in the classroom.

Then and now: the author in a contemplative mood at Denby North, 1992, and in a more modern update at Scropton almost 23 years later – or simply more orange, less hair. *Jim Riley/Bryn Davies.*

I once had a wonderful cabaret staged for me at Scropton by a van driver, who obviously wasn't familiar with this type of crossing. I had just closed the gates and returned to the box when I heard the inevitable sound of an approaching vehicle. The driver showed no indication of slowing down as he approached the gates and I truly believe that he expected they would open automatically as he got nearer. It must have suddenly dawned on him that this wasn't going to happen because he jumped on his brakes at the last minute and came to a stand literally five inches from them. I knew it was close because I found myself poised and ready to bang out an emergency 6 bells to the boxes either side. Some training must have sunk in somewhere! There was a brief pause whilst he considered his next move, but I remained near the block bells just in case he decided to crash through the gates after all. I relaxed a little when his next action was to merely blast his horn. Now the cabaret would begin...

It always went the same way. First there would be a blast on the horn then the driver would get out of their vehicle, slam the door shut, approach the gates and look both ways. After several head turnings they would decide it was safe and reach over to try to open the gates. That the line speed was 70mph and a train could appear at any second never seemed to faze them. Apparently, a quick look left and right was all that was required to ensure safe passage, so why was I here opening and closing gates? They always seemed oblivious of the signal box right in front of them too, or perhaps thought that I'd decided to shut the gates out of spite. Nevertheless, at this point in the proceedings I would usually shout from the box that the gates were closed because there was a train coming.

This driver did all the above actions but also added some new ones, such as throwing his hands up several times, stamping around his vehicle, getting back into the cab and talking animatedly on his mobile phone whilst pointing angrily at the gates. I would have shouted an explanation at this point, but I found myself utterly transfixed by this impromptu performance. Surely, he could see the signal box, with me standing in the window, desperately trying to suppress a smile? It's not as though I was hiding either, dressed as I was neck to ankle in HV orange clothing. Eventually another vehicle rolled up behind and he immediately terminated his phone call, got out of his cab and marched towards it. There were more wild gesticulations and hands thrown into the air as a conversation ensued, but I assume the other motorist was a local who was able to enlighten him about the *modus operandi* at Scropton. He seemed a little deflated as he trudged back to his cab, even more so as the train whizzed past at that exact moment. The look on his face was priceless as I went down to open the gates. He trundled over the crossing with his head down unable even to make eye contact with me because of what I suppose was sheer embarrassment.

I don't blame people for being confused because, as previously stated, there were twelve different types of level crossing on the network at the time and, during the normal course of motoring, you may only ever encounter perhaps one or two types. (In fact, Scropton and Mill Lane were two different types of crossing within 200 metres of each other.) Also, there would soon be a generation of motorists totally unfamiliar as to the workings of a manned level crossing, simply because few such places remained. Even now, some motorists were shunting their vehicles backwards and forwards in the hope the gates would open automatically. However, if you do ever come across this type of crossing, just remember that revving your engine and/or beeping your horn doesn't make the train come any faster or the signaller move any quicker; quite the opposite in the latter case.

Over time, it became obvious to me that, not only were Scropton's gates interlocked with the signals, they were also interlocked with vehicles belonging to certain locals and both (Up and Down) Mill Lane Crossing telephones. I eventually concluded that there must be a pressure pad at the bottom of the box steps, which initiated a klaxon in the nearby houses whenever I was about to close the gates, and there almost certainly had to be a flashing sign on the main road, diverting everyone down the farm track – there was simply no other explanation for the frustratingly inevitable vehicular appearances.

I suppose this was my comeuppance for all the wicked things I'd done to Dungworthy when I was working as a groundsman at a large comprehensive school. Because the site was so big, I had access to one of the walkie-talkies that the site staff used, including Dungworthy, who was one of the assistant caretakers. My main work involved marking out the numerous playing fields – another solitary occupation – which invariably kept me at least 200 metres away from anyone else, but I could always spot the other site staff wandering around on their various duties from my unencumbered 360-degree view of the grounds. One of Dungworthy's duties was to deliver parcels to different departments around the school and I often saw him staggering around with his hands full. The radio procedure was even simpler than the military method and to call someone's attention we would just broadcast an extended 'hello', inserting the name of whomever we wished to contact at the end of it.

Whenever I saw Dungworthy on the horizon, overburdened with parcels, I could never resist calling him up. Over time, I'd perfected the art of prolonging the fun by leaving a deliberate pause between the 'hello' and the name. This I did now: "Helloooo..." I could see him visibly stiffen as his radio crackled into life and I knew he was thinking 'please don't let it be me', at which point I would insert "Dungworthy!" He would cringe, and I knew he was just dying to answer the call, but he would always ignore this first attempt and stagger on. He would however quicken his pace, hoping to reach a convenient spot to stow his parcels so he could respond to my call. He never, ever made it because I would only allow him a certain amount of headway before trying again – and he *always* cracked on my second attempt.

"Helloooo...Dungworthy!"
This time the parcels would be dropped in despair and he would angrily fumble for his radio.

"What do you want? I'm a bit busy now."
"Nothing, it's all right, it'll keep."
The radio would be shoved back into his pocket and the parcels would be picked up and balanced precariously in both arms again. I sometimes went for the treble and called him up again but was usually beaten to it by one of his colleagues. They all knew what I was up to, and within seconds, another voice would crackle over the airwaves.

"Helloooo....Dungworthy!"
This time the parcels would be flung down in fury.

Incidentally, it was around this time when I was introduced to two further SBO courses, namely Lifting and Handling and Conflict Resolution. They were standalone courses but, in Dungworthy's case, both would have been entirely appropriate if combined. Unfortunately, they weren't, and two full mornings had to be devoted to each of these weighty topics. The former involved numerous pictures of how to bend your knees to pick things up (so that's where I'd been going wrong all those years), before we took it in turns to lift an empty cardboard box several times (heady stuff). The trendy sounding Conflict Resolution seemed primarily concerned with how to be calm and passive to diffuse violent situations and not to simply hit first and as hard as possible as I'd previously thought. Neither course had much effect on us because neither course considered the real and unpredictable world that we inhabited. Dungworthy still carried his parcels as before, and as Conflict Resolution unfortunately gave no advice on what to do if the situation had already turned violent, I decided to retain my previous thought on the matter.

As was the case with Dungworthy, anger is often the result whenever you impede someone trying to go about their daily business, and nowhere more so than at level crossings. I've lost count of the arguments I've had, or the times motorists have aimed their vehicles at me, but I suppose their thought process is 'How dare he hold me up. My needs take priority.' But a train always takes priority, if not by law, then certainly by force. Only an idiot would argue priority with a train, but that's exactly what used to happen at Denby North Crossing.

Denby North and Street Lane were the last two trainman operated crossings on the Denby Branch, and to successfully marshal coal wagons in the sidings there, a train would have to shunt back and forth over both crossings several times. This operation could take between five and ten minutes and the road traffic would be stopped whilst it was carried out. Denby North was a quiet backwater and the road crossing only served a couple of houses at best, but whenever a train appeared, there was invariably trouble. One resident would become extremely agitated to find a coal train across his path and angrily remonstrate with the train crew.

In due course, a rapid loader was built which rendered Street Lane Crossing and its associated shunting obsolete. Unfortunately, this didn't improve matters at Denby North because the train would now proceed at slow speed (half a mile an hour) through the rapid loader towards the crossing, eventually occupying it for ten or fifteen minutes before propelling back. It would not be long before the embittered resident reappeared, more enraged than ever, so much so that he now actually threatened violence towards the train crew. I never understood why he got so upset but perhaps it was the contradiction of us going through a *rapid* loader at *slow* speed that irked him so?

Often, on these occasions I would be ensconced in the brakevan at the rear of the train and Big Bill would call me on the radio for assistance, causing me to hop, skip and jump along the ballast for 36 wagon lengths, brake stick in hand, for a futile attempt at mediation. The angry resident would usually have disappeared by the time I got there, so I would trudge back to the brakevan again. Sometimes, if Big Bill didn't have a very talkative secondman, he would call me up, claiming the resident had returned, just so he could have a bit of company – which is probably where I got the idea for Dungworthy's crank radio calls. I knew it was a ruse because Big Bill was not noted for his diplomacy and it was doubtful he would require my assistance in such matters: witness yes, assistance no. In fact, Big Bill would have made an ideal instructor for Conflict Resolution, *if* the course had been how I'd originally imagined it.

Compared with the Denby Branch, the crossings of the North and South Staffs were more regulated and there were generally fewer upsets. Hilton could be a little fraught at times and there used to be a family of weasels at Roddige who became agitated whenever I went near the crossing. Well, it may have been a family, but it was probably just one weasel. Every twenty seconds a furry head would pop up from a different place in the wooden decking and hiss at me, like a real live game of Whack-a-Mole, or in this case, weasel. There was also a domineering but short-lived peacock at Scropton, which would seemingly materialize on the crossing and delight in intimidating one of the relief signalmen. He claimed the bird was bullying him and would become extremely tense whenever he heard its unholy screech at sundown (it probably wanted to mate with him). It was not difficult to understand his concern however. The bird was bigger than Rod Hull's Emu, and just as unpredictable.

Tutbury was probably the source of most of my crossing friction though, usually just loud-mouthed youths in cars, but there was one incident where the threat of violence reared its ugly head again.

I'd dropped the barriers for an empty stock train on the Up, and just as it appeared under Sunnyside Bridge, a rat-like youth in a tracksuit climbed over the Up barrier and crossed in front of it. (Why do the unhealthiest looking people always wear fitness clothing?) Ordinarily this wouldn't have been too bad as most trains approached slowly to stop at the platform just beyond the crossing. Unfortunately, this train was non-stop and currently going at the permissible line speed of 70mph. Both these facts only became apparent to the youth when he found himself directly in its path. He just managed to dive clear and vault over the Down barrier, where I suspect he needed an immediate change of underwear. I raised the barriers and shouted the usual things you shout at someone whose actions have the potential to cause your telephone to become hot and your in-tray to stack up.

No doubt still grappling with the realization that he'd survived the encounter and wasn't currently a smear of strawberry jam on the crossing, he didn't seem to take my rudimentary but nonetheless accurate appraisal of his mental prowess and character in good part and strode back menacingly across the tracks towards the box. Ordinarily I am very receptive to visitors, but decided to make an exception in this case, partly because one of the residents had just mopped the floor and this person wasn't wearing the requisite plastic bags over his footwear necessary to enter. I grabbed the Bardic hand lamp from the block shelf, arriving at the top of the box steps, just as Tutbury & Hatton's incumbent (or so I assumed) village idiot arrived at the bottom. He wasn't so stupid that he didn't notice the solid lump of metal in my hand, or that I commanded the high ground, and wisely came no further. I mentioned something about him trespassing on the railway, which was obviously an issue that caused him many sleepless nights.

"Huh!" he snorted dismissively. "What's the maximum penalty for that?"

"Death," I replied simply, not feeling the need to elaborate further, especially as he had just avoided it by inches. I meant this comment to apply to his first act, but he must have construed that it may also apply to this current one too, and as common discourse seemed to weary him, and he evidently felt he'd been out in the sun too long, he eventually wandered off, no doubt to crawl under the stone whence he came.

The incident reminded me of how some of the old passenger guards used to deal with fare dodgers or troublesome travellers. These people were often 'encouraged' to leave the train by means of a 'persuader'. The persuader of choice for a freight guard was usually a brake stick (as previously mentioned) but a passenger guard always had their trusty Bardic, which, poaching terminology aside, I believe is where the term 'to lamp someone' or 'to get lamped' comes from. I do not advocate the use of weapons, or even violence come to that, but on a few of my previous jobs I was sometimes only one word away from violence and would have no hesitation in using such methods for self-defence.

I was first introduced to this way of thinking whilst on the Forces Junior Leaders course. A PTI corporal clone would turn up each week to instruct us in basic unarmed combat, only this clone happened to be a maroon-bereted Falklands veteran. He seemed to take great delight in re-enacting parts of the campaign, with him the sole member of the UK land forces and us a dozen fearful Argies. These encounters usually progressed from the relatively gentle application of restraint holds to a no-holds-barred melee, which seemed to be a cross between Judo and something akin to a Saturday night brawl in an Aldershot drinking establishment. I knew less about self-defence than almost anyone, and as a result was never very confident in using these methods, but where an opponent was physically superior or unpredictable, I liked the idea that all options were on the table and gentlemanly conduct didn't come into it. We were encouraged to achieve our self-defence/preservation objective by any means, including using everyday items that were immediately to hand as weapons. And this was from someone who had done it for real on the unforgiving slopes of Mount Longdon.

I tried to continue learning a bit of Judo when I was a trainman, but the class I joined practised the throws one week and the holds the following week. Working alternating shifts meant I could only attend the class every other week, so I only ever learnt to throw aggressors and could never hold them when, much angrier, they picked themselves up to have another go. As a result, I decided to just expand the unorthodox military method to include the brake stick and Bardic lamp whilst on the railway, and the use of other persuaders when working elsewhere. Not that I needed many during my second evolution on the railway, particularly since a sizeable German shepherd dog accompanied me on almost every shift.

In between agency HGV driving assignments, I once supplemented my meagre income with an eight-month stint as a part-time plain-clothes security operative for a national supermarket chain. A character like me stood out like a donkey's plonker in such an environment and it eventually became obvious that I was tailing shoplifters (and sometimes warehouse staff, as more stuff invariably went out the back than the front), but at some of the less salubrious areas I was sent to, I didn't even try to blend in. I never really got the hang of undercover detective work anyway because, at the time, I was driving around in a bright red Mark 2 Vauxhall Cavalier (faux Antibes) hatchback with a prominent black stripe around it.

Whenever I parked up at a stakeout, it wasn't long before the local ne'er-do-wells recognized my car and either (a) steered clear or (b) came to pick a fight. Starsky and Hutch never had this problem in their bright red Ford Gran Torino, and theirs had a prominent white stripe around it!

At one such location, the same character always turned up and tried to steal whatever he could lay his hands on. He was big and certainly unpredictable, but in addition to this physically imposing shape and manner he was known to sometimes carry a knife and had previously pulled it on a colleague of mine. There was no point trying to reason with such people and I didn't even try. I never tried to disguise my observation (or dislike) of him either and just hounded him all the time he remained on the premises. I became overt instead of covert. Whenever he turned around I was always there at the end of the aisle. I think I secretly wanted to goad him into action because he was a bully and enjoyed threatening people and being the 'big man'.

As soon as I became aware of his presence in the supermarket, I would purposely select the most expensive bottle of champagne from the Wines and Spirits section and keep it by my side. My plan being that the split second he made any aggressive move towards me, I would deliver it to the side of his head; an unforgivable waste of champagne, but a bottle of brown ale just didn't have the same clout, literally. I would act first, without hesitation because, unlike Starsky or Hutch, I had no partner and little prospect of assistance; I was on my own – the quintessential lone worker in the making. I would answer any assault charges later – the main point being that I would still be in a healthy condition to answer them. My plan was thought out with the recklessness and immortality of youth, and fortunately, I never had to follow through with the champagne. It was merely another persuader, one ideally suited for the retail environment.

In fact, apart from the odd playground fight as a kid and the occasional drunken scuffle and more challenging than normal citizen arrests I made in my twenties, at the time of writing, I've probably only had to physically defend myself properly just once. Quite an achievement considering I've travelled all around the world and have actually held jobs where physical confrontation was not just accepted but expected. That particular occasion however, was far more pedestrian (in both senses) and over in a matter of seconds. It was during trainman days and I was at Birmingham New Street, awaiting my back working to Derby (the midnight mail train, no less!) I needed some cash from the 'hole in wall' before departure but was aware that leaving the relative safety of the station to venture out onto the late-night city streets wasn't the wisest course of action, particularly to obtain cash. As the dispenser was just outside the door, I reasoned that I wouldn't be out there long enough to attract any undue attention. However, just after I'd pocketed my money and was heading back, a large shadow fell across my path and further progress was blocked by a huge man. As my eyes were trying to adjust to this sudden eclipse, I heard him say, "Your time is up Mr Railwayman," for I was wearing my BR badged orange coat at the time. In the nanosecond I had to interpret the possible meaning of those words, I sensed, rather than saw, in my periphery, a wild right hook swinging directly towards my left temple. As you can imagine, this was most unexpected but what surprised me more was my reaction to it. Almost automatically, and without even thinking, I bobbed down slightly and delivered a most excellent pile driver punch to my assailant's solar plexus, which caused his immediate deflation and incoming fist to drop like a stone. I had no idea where my punch came from, so I didn't expect him to. No doubt my maroon-bereted instructor would have urged me to destroy the threat, rather than to just neutralize it (and quite rightly, had it been the South Atlantic or any other theatre of conflict), but I was more than happy to leave this person doubled up on the pavement and extricate myself forthwith. Luckily for me, the mail train was always punctual.

The only other occasion, which was not a matter of self-defence but rather the rendering of assistance to others, occurred whilst I was working plain-clothes in Derby city centre. I suppose I had unwittingly fashioned myself along the lines of Detective Mick Belker from *Hill Street Blues*. I forwent the droopy 'tache and woollen hat but ate the same dodgy food and had the same scruffy clothes, rough stubble and cigar, (as well as arresting the same offender and suffering the same excruciating telephone calls from my mother every week – the parallels were really quite alarming). I even growled like him once when I assisted two of the company's uniformed security guards to restrain an exceptionally violent and (I assumed) drug-crazed lunatic. Even though the guards were big burly chaps, they were having a rough time of it, so, once again, with the recklessness and immortality of youth, I literally dived into the melee. I didn't bite this wildly flailing individual as Mick Belker would have done, but the only hold I could get on him was his left thumb, which I subsequently bent back as far as it would go. It was the only way I was able to subdue him. Hopefully readers can now understand the validity of my previous musings in respect of the Conflict Resolution course.

To sum up, not all my encounters have been railway orientated, but the same types of people very often had a starring role in them. Fortunately, unlike the Tutbury & Hatton village idiot most had the sense not to cross the line in my presence – physically or metaphorically.

17. A YEAR IN THE LIFE

I can't believe I'm writing 1 January in the Train Register Book again...another New Year! The passenger service runs as normal, but the shift itself is generally quiet as the local populace recovers from the night before. There is still that cosy Christmas holiday feeling and spirit of goodwill in the air, but a return to the real world is imminent.

Another classic photo by Bryn Davies, taken from Mill Lane and looking towards Scropton Crossing, February 2012. Note the distinctive pyramid roof of St. Paul's bell tower.

In an average year (if there is such a thing), 10,784 trains will pass Scropton, which equates to 32,352 signal lever pulls. With the distant signal lever pulls alone weighing in around 70kgs for the metre they are pulled in the box, that's roughly 755 tonnes over 11kms. To paraphrase Archimedes, 'Give me a lever big enough and I will move the World'. It's no surprise that signallers who regularly work here have reasonable upper body development. It's just the rest of the body that leaves a lot to be desired.

During box hours there will be around 4,642 authorised crossings at Mill Lane too – and a few that aren't authorised. There's not much to be done about the latter, as some motorists seem to enjoy the Russian roulette aspect of crossing without contacting the signaller, or they simply don't care, but one day their luck will run out. I often wondered if my shift would end prematurely with a loud bang, a plume of smoke rising from that direction and me having to urinate in a beaker. Not for any perverse pleasure you understand (and certainly not by choice), merely company policy after such an event. These selfish motorists are particularly noticeable on dark winter mornings when I go down for the gates. Looking up the tracks towards Mill Lane, I occasionally see the silhouette of a vehicle cross the lines and it is most unnerving.

Scropton will also arrange about 115 line blockages and be a controlling box eight times and intermediate box twenty times during engineering possessions. Someone will score a direct hit on Scropton Crossing with an on-train toilet about seven times (should this be classed as obstruction of the line or merely laying a new sleeper?), and at least five pigeons will disappear in a puff of feathers – due to being struck by trains and not because of the toilet effluent I hasten to add: human excrement regularly dumped outside your place of work – hardly world-class.

No one has ever bothered to count, but since a vehicle always seems to appear at the box crossing just as the gates have been closed to road traffic, it is reasonable to conclude that there will be a minimum of 10,784 vehicle crossings here. Trebling this figure however, provides a more realistic number. Quite a busy road crossing for an unremarkable and largely backwoods farm track, particularly as the population of Scropton was only 354 in the 2011 census. I would further add that perhaps only 25 of those 354 live on the 'wrong' side of the tracks, so the frequency of crossings is quite remarkable – or profoundly irritating if you happen to be the resident signalman!

Considering my shift pattern and time off, I probably signal about 4,688 trains a year, but before any ROC signaller gives a derisive snort, this equates to 14,064 signal lever pulls and a potential 9,376 times up and down the steps for the gates. Based on a 40-metre round trip each time, this is equivalent to going up and down Mount Everest 42 times every year, with a pull of 328 tonnes for the first half of the first ascent. Unfortunately, even with all this physical activity, the signalman's waistline does not seem to diminish, but inexplicably increases – but let no disgruntled driver dismiss me to the 'chaise' so casually now. Speaking of which, 4,688 trains also means 4,688 friendly waves to passing drivers, but I doubt I get the same amount in return. Some would rather chop their hands off than wave to a signalman. Nevertheless, I was always told to wave to drivers, just to make sure they were still alive, although I console myself that I am waving at the *train* rather than the driver anyway.

Spring is new life and unspoken promise but is also tinged with sorrow; an indefinable yearning for times past – for every beginning there must first be an ending. At the box, just before each sunrise there is a hush, an expectation, a single pulse of excitement, then the horizon is ablaze, and all sins are forgiven – a new day begins. Lambs prance in the fields and birds are busy nest building. One bird tugs furiously at a woollen strand hanging from a sheep, as the sheep itself looks on disinterestedly. A cloud of juvenile starlings periodically descends upon the bird feeder, but instead of sharing the bounty like the well-mannered sparrows, they constantly squabble amongst themselves for pole position. Even so, a full feeder will somehow disappear within the hour. A woodpecker occasionally intervenes and, like a belligerent yob, will head-butt any briefly victorious youngster off the feeder to gain sole occupancy. The woodpecker has a crazed look in its eye, but I suppose I would if I spent all my time head-butting things. A smartly attired rook will sometimes alight on the track twenty metres away and stride importantly along the rail head to investigate the commotion. If there were an avian cast for *Dad's Army*, the rook would be Captain Mainwaring. In quieter moments, a single robin picks up the pieces. It doesn't seem long however, before the short spring afternoons are merging into long summer evenings.

Summer is freedom and light. Its welcome warmth makes the shifts easier and the days seem carefree. It is freedom to arrive for work in the daylight and to return home at 22:00 still in the daylight. It is freedom to be in short-sleeves and have all the windows and door open. But summer is also dust, flies and stifling heat. Short-sleeves mean the subsequent development of a farmers' tan (face, neck and forearms only), which is never a good look, particularly when everywhere else remains bone white. Opening windows and the door, in a vain attempt to create a through draught, just means noise, dust and flies. The ordinary houseflies are frustrating enough, but Scropton seems to suffer a plague of tiny black ones about half a millimetre wide and a millimetre long, which are maddeningly itchy. They too enjoy short-sleeves and crawling all over exposed skin. It is a stark choice of whether to close the windows and slowly bake in the oppressive, but still, atmosphere of the box, or suffer the deafening roar of shuttling tractors, maddening black flies and sneeze-inducing dust.

With the sun blazing it quickly becomes uncomfortable in the east corner of the box on the early shift, then intolerable in the west corner on the late shift. The rise in temperature also causes the distant signal cables to expand and stretch to such an extent that upon pulling the lever there is little resistance and the repeater inevitably shows 'WRONG'. Several turns of the adjuster will correct this, but now it becomes more important than ever to ensure the repeaters are showing 'ON' when the lever is put back. This is the time of year when they seem to misbehave the most, sometimes flicking to 'WRONG' several minutes after the train has passed and the signaller has returned to a reclined position.

The trackside vegetation also threatens to take over and it becomes difficult to see the Up and Down section signals because of it. It is noticeable that the vegetation has become particularly bad when the Down Home starts to disappear too, especially since this signal is only about 80 metres from the box. The weed killing train may appear around this time, making its slow progress over the line and taking nearly twenty minutes to pass through the sections, so woe is the signaller who operates their gates or barriers too early. Sometimes the person operating the on-train spraying system forgets to moderate the jet, or simply doesn't bother, and the gates, box, crossing and steps are liberally doused with a noxious chemical, which is then inhaled, makes contact with the skin and is ultimately tracked back up into the box by the signaller. It might as well be spraying fertilizer anyway, for all the good it seems to do. I'm not sure which is worse, this or a direct hit from an on-train toilet.

I should be more familiar with the fickle ways of weed killing trains because it is by no means my first encounter with them. Crossover confusion notwithstanding, I was once secondmanning a ballast train and we were held in a loop. Our guard, who was riding up front with us, decided that this was an opportune moment to relieve himself and dived off into some bushes just ahead. Presently we observed his head poking above the greenery, and with his back to the track and a cigarette dangling between his lips, he had not a care in the world. Unfortunately, it didn't last because approaching in the opposite direction was a train of unusual configuration. The powerful jet of liquid shooting from it initially mesmerized my driver and me, particularly as it was easily reaching across to the cess side of the adjacent track. It took a few moments to register, but we eventually realized it was the weed killing train in spraying mode – and our guard was in the firing line! We whistled a warning, but the guard, thinking we were making a joke, just casually flicked two-fingers in our direction. That was his last discernible action before being blatted by the jet and promptly disappearing. He emerged from the undergrowth a few moments later looking rather dazed and bedraggled with a bent cigarette between his lips. I don't know what the liquid consisted of, but he ended up with a two-tone uniform; the front was standard BR blue, whilst the back was bleached white. He looked like Pepé Le Pew the cartoon skunk. Unfortunately, he smelt like it too and was banished to the back cab for the remainder of our journey.

The longest day comes and goes and then the schools break for the summer holiday. A couple of weeks after that, a subtle but perceptible change can be felt. It's still the height of the summer holidays, but there is a brief autumnal feel to the mornings and evenings now; a distinct crispness as the sun becomes increasingly sluggish at awakening, whilst the moon gently rises in a black sky once more. The vegetation is not as verdant as it was; yellows and browns are beginning to creep in now, dulling the once lush greenery. The wind has picked up too, from the still, stifling oppression of summer, to a fresh but constant harrying breeze.

With what must be a collective sigh of relief from all parents, the children return to school. From this point onwards, you are forever walking into spider webs invisibly suspended across doorways and pathways and constantly brushing yourself down – then the thing that strikes terror into the heart of the modern railway...the first leaves begin to fall. For some reason autumn has been re-branded 'leaf fall season', just in case people have forgotten what happens in autumn. There are now ten weeks of wearisome 05:30 starts as the RHTT blasts a path for other trains to follow. Obviously, for a resident on alternating shifts, there are only five weeks of this, but it doesn't excuse the sheer insanity of rolling out of a nice warm bed at 04:15, somehow making it downstairs then heading out into the cold, dark and wet. You don't remember anything about the journey to work, or even how you arrived at the box. You have some vague recollection of the RHTT going past, but no memory of signalling it. Someone must have done it though, as there is an entry in the TRB.

Autumn is golden melancholy, but each sunset is a daily work of art – a fiery masterpiece. Autumn is also spider season and the box becomes inundated with them, especially on the late shift – the perils of living in a wooden shed. Fortunately, most stay outside above the crossing spotlight and there are usually about 60 of them residing in this tiny triangle area of opportunity between window top and roof eave where the spotlight is fixed. They constantly jostle and fight for space on a silken carpet of web that covers the entire window. I do not know how they establish which web is which and it looks intolerably crowded, but food is plentiful as a multitude of gnats and moths swarm around and make continuous suicidal runs towards the spotlight. The webs are laden and sagging with bounty and the spiders cannot keep up against the onslaught. (The spiders don't get it all their own way of course. In summer they are sitting targets, with many plucked straight off their webs by some deft sparrow aerobatics.)

The relief signallers always want to brush them down and get rid of them, but it is best to leave them alone. If their outdoor community is disturbed, they tend to relocate indoors and much of a late shift can be spent evicting them. They are fascinating creatures but any with a leg span bigger than a fifty pence piece are unnerving. Most are larger than this, with one gaining the box record of three inches one year. I think it's the way they sneak up on you and the way they lurk. One minute the TRB is clear, you turn to tap out some bells then turn back after a second, and there is a big black thing sat there. Where it appears from in such a short time I do not know. Sometimes you hear them tip-tapping across the laminated notices on the wall, but they are never where you expect them to be. They are sneaky and resourceful, and I always feel like I'm being watched. If I spot one indoors, I can't really relax until it is evicted.

I've found a feather duster to be the best tool for this purpose, but a mug and a teaspoon work just as well. When I do spot one I steer it into the mug or position it adequately on the feather duster, ready for departure, then, with a triumphant flourish at the door or window, it's gone. I sit down again feeling quite pleased with myself until, in my periphery; I sense a black epaulette on my shoulder. I turn to look, and there it is again, horribly magnified at this range. This time there is no calm, methodical approach. I leap up, frantically brushing my upper torso, whilst trying to remove my HV vest. The vest drops to the floor and the eight-legged terror scuttles under the fridge. It will no doubt reappear at a similar time tomorrow, but I remain uneasy until a successful eviction is accomplished. Some nights they come in quicker than they can be thrown out. My oppo just used to squash them, but I always thought he'd be better off squashing certain signallers – at least spiders are useful. But as the 'enlightened one' himself (probably) said 'When a man has pity on all living creatures then only is he noble.' Besides, as already stated in Chapter 15, when alone in a signal box, you have to make companionship with what is around you.

It is Hallowe'en and small black clouds scud across the night sky, their outline briefly silvered by a high crescent moon. The weak watery moonlight bathes the top of the rails, making them glint ominously. St. Paul's bell tower is stark against this backdrop and a lonely owl hoots in the cemetery. As you go down for the gates, a bat flutters and swoops making several random passes then, once back in the box, all is quiet again. But what's that noise? Footsteps on the ballast! The scrunching becomes louder as something approaches the box. Could this be the headless trainman coming to wreak his revenge? No, it's just one of the local cats. They are usually quite clever and tiptoe along the top of the rail, but this one scatters ballast as it clumsily picks its way along the cess, glaring angrily at me.

I always remember one Hallowe'en in the Forces. I was on gate duty yet again, but a few of the lads had gone to a fancy-dress party in the clubhouse on the other camp, although the primary objective was really to get close to the local women who often attended. Apparently there had been a bit of trouble and the redoubtable and indefatigable Corporal Cole had been dispatched to sort it out. As I stood on the gate that crisp, dark evening, I could hear him in the distance, although it seemed he was heading my way at a vast rate of knots. I knew it was him; the phraseology was very distinct in the chill night air. "You people better get moving," and "I've got my eye on you people," and so forth. I turned to my partner who was covering from the sanger. He shrugged his shoulders; this was going to be interesting. Presently I could discern several shadows running towards me, but what struck me about these shadows was that they were not jogging casually, but rather appeared to be running for their lives.

First to emerge from the gloom was someone in a skintight skeleton costume and there was no stopping him as he zipped past me like an Olympic sprinter. "Who was that?" shouted my mate. I was about to reply that I had no idea when I was startled by the sudden appearance of Dracula, his cape fluttering wildly behind him. I got the impression that this Prince of Darkness hadn't got as many young virgins under his spell as he'd hoped tonight. He swept past breathless, but rather elegantly I thought, trying to keep his fangs in place. Frankenstein came clumping past next, complete with square forehead, green face and the inevitable bolt through his neck. It was Taff Evans from 3 Squad. Taff hadn't dressed up; he looked like that normally. To complete his outfit, he had donned some cumbersome thick-soled boots, which were unfortunately slowing him down. Every so often he'd cast a terrified glance behind him, which wasn't surprising really considering the most frightening character of all was right on his platform heels; one who needed no costume. Bent forward, heels digging into the ground, arms pumping like pistons appeared Corporal Cole. He fixed me with his trademark glare as he powered past. Well he may have done, it was difficult to tell with his dodgy squint, but I know he was just daring me to say something. No fear, it was just a normal, average night as far as I was concerned. I think skeleton man got clean away by the skin of his bodysuit and Dracula managed to slip back into his coffin unnoticed, but poor old Frankenstein was right-wheeled towards the guardhouse for re-education – which knowing Corporal Cole probably involved a swift kick to the *Groovy Ghoulies*. Taff's 'Monster Mash' was no match for Corporal Cole's Brecon Shuffle. The corporal didn't give up easily however and there was closer than usual scrutiny during the inspection next morning, specifically for traces of monster makeup behind the ears of his prime suspects.

I was once caught out myself on the school site. Sometimes it was my responsibility to lock up at night and I would trudge around the large complex with a torch, locking all the doors and checking for any open windows. As I made my rounds I shone my torch along the windows of the first-floor science labs. Window after window was clear, until my torch beam hit upon the last one, illuminating a terrifying figure staring menacingly down at me. Those meddling kids had positioned the resident anatomical skeleton at just the right angle, and had I been wired up to a heart monitor at the time, my readings would have been off the scale.

Back at Scropton it is Bonfire Night – the ideal night since all the leaves are off and the heaters and topcoats are back on. It is dark at 16:30 and a freezing fog hangs over the box like a wet blanket. It always feels two degrees colder here away from the warmer embrace of the city and it's back to chipping ice off the van windscreen and manhandling frozen crossing gates again.

Winter is contemplative and measured, full of bittersweet reflection and curious contentment. The bare trees are the only company now, but it is possible to see Sudbury's Down Distant and home/section signals from the west window and follow the tail lamps of a train as it describes a route around the large 'S' bend and disappears into Staffordshire. Immediately after its passage, Sudbury's bright green signals blink back to an intense red, and shortly after, bell code 2-1 is received and acknowledged – another train safely out of section.

The shortest day comes and goes, but an eight-hour shift is still eight hours, then Christmas comes to the box again – just one of many it has known. What was Christmas 1884 like here? I try to look back along the line of signalmen that have gone before. I am currently the last of that line, but who was the first? Did he sit here trying to look into the future, just as I sit here now trying to look into the past? Did he interpret his surroundings any differently from me? Have things changed so much? Only the ratio of trains to cars has altered, very little else. The method of moving trains from A to B has remained largely the same. We could exchange places, and both operate the box successfully, irrespective of the century. We also have Christmas in common too – he saw Scropton's first and, at the time of writing, I could very well see its last. The ghosts of Christmas past recede as New Year's Eve approaches.

Locking the box at 22:00 one New Year's Eve, I bumped into a chap out walking his dog. He bid me a happy new year and asked if that was it.

"Yes, until tomorrow." I replied.

He seemed a little surprised that anything would be happening tomorrow, so I enlightened him further.

"I'm not some chief executive on a three-day week and an indefensible half a million-pound salary!"

After personally overseeing the safe passage of over 4000 trains, innumerable safe road crossings and line blockages, it was a job well done and there was a deep fulfilment and satisfaction of the kind you just don't get from an enormous pot of money.

"I'll be back on New Year's Day to move some more trains around." I assured the dog-walker – which of course was exactly where we started.

Scropton Crossing, December 2014. *Bryn Davies.*

18. A BEAUTIFUL SKYE

(For absent friends who held the line – the front line and the railway line)

Whenever I was on late shift at Alrewas I would watch the sun dip behind the Armed Forces Memorial at the National Arboretum just up the road. War was still raging in Afghanistan and the sun setting over the memorial would be the same sun setting in that benighted country five hours hence. However, my thoughts didn't dwell exclusively on that. I was thinking more of an old school friend who had joined up at a similar time to me. We had also gone through the rigours of the Junior Leaders course together, and even competed for the same girl once, a long time ago. He got himself into a spot of bother during his first deployment to Northern Ireland and, unfortunately, could only see one way out. Taking a rifle from the armoury, he put the muzzle under his chin and pulled the trigger. It was another meaningless waste of a young life full of promise. That was twenty years ago, but not one has passed when I haven't wished I could have been there for him. I was going to find his name on the memorial, but I gathered it wouldn't be there, as he had not died in the line of duty in the true sense. Nevertheless, he had stood up to be counted when it mattered just the same.

One day in November I called in at the National Arboretum on my way home from the box. It was just before Remembrance Day, but I classed every day as a day of remembrance and, more importantly, I would always remember him, whereas this stone memorial would not. During my exceptionally brief but intense time on some perceived but now meaningless 'front line', I watched in awe, envy (and perhaps a little relief) as young men, many still teenagers like me, burst through the camp gates in an effort to discourage sniper fire, then, constantly covering each other and looking out for each other, disappeared down the grey street and into their place in history. How they did it day after day was amazing. In a few short hours I would be returned to the mainland and the safety of the barracks, trying to while away a Friday evening. I was unable to accompany them on that occasion, but they took a little piece of me with them nonetheless. Goodbye soul brothers.

There are many fine locations around the world to enjoy a sunset: the Egyptian Pyramids, the Grand Canyon, Ayers Rock (Uluru) or an island in the South Pacific. I've had the good fortune to see one in all these places, but I've found the sunset itself to be the main attraction, not necessarily the location. Few people would put a signal box on that list, but there is something special about sundown at the box. It feels like a theatre performance about to begin. First there is a hush as the light fades. The signalman basks in the afterglow, and then the signal lights come up softly like stage lights, just before the real stars of the show peep through the deep blue curtain backdrop. Parson Hawker summed it up best: 'Day melts into the west, another flake of sweet blue time into the eternal past.'

Sundown at Scropton Crossing, May 2014. *Author.*

'The stars are what bind the sky together otherwise we mortals would be crushed by the weight of its great silence.' So said someone with a lot more poetry in his words than me, but I could see why some of the old-time signalmen became amateur astronomers. Living in Derby city centre I rarely got to admire a starry sky, but in the semi-rural environment of Scropton, which suffered far less light pollution, I could watch the constellations recount their classical tales of adventure and romance on the celestial stage – a different star story for each season.

In spring, just above the horizon, Hydra, the water serpent, slithers across the southwest sky, with Corvus, the crow, and Crater, the goblet, on her back. The goblet remains forever out of Corvus's reach, as a reminder of why he is being punished. He pecks the back of Hydra with his long beak in a futile attempt the escape his fate. To the north, Ursa Major and Ursa Minor, the big bear and little bear, plod endlessly around the Pole Star, never being allowed to rest and set below the horizon, whilst the question-marked head of Leo, the lion, looks on.

Hercules dominates the summer skies. With his club raised, he kneels over the head of Draco, the dragon. Bootes, the herdsman, crosses the western sky, driving a strange menagerie of animals before him. Accompanied by Canes Vernatici, his two hunting dogs, he drives them all forever northwards. Virgo, the maiden, signifies the coming and going of the growing season, and to the west, Cygnus, the swan, swoops down the centre of the Milky Way.

The Andromeda saga fills the autumn skies, with Cepheus, the king, and Cassiopeia, the queen, in the north, to Perseus, the returning hero, and Pegasus, the winged horse, in the east, racing to save the princess from Cetus, the sea monster, who lurks low on the southern horizon.

In winter, the unmistakable shape of Orion, the hunter, stalks the southern sky, pursuing the sisterly groups of Hyades and Pleiades, who all flee his advances. Canis Major, the big dog, follows dutifully behind, with the bright jewel of Sirius on its collar. Lepus, the hare, hides at Orion's feet, and much like its earthbound namesake, is often difficult to spot. Taurus, the bull, blocks Orion's path with his large horns, forever staring him down with a menacing red eye, whilst Auriga, the charioteer, stands above. To the west, the Gemini twins fall hand in hand through space – the eternal embodiment of brotherly love.

Underneath all this high drama, trains pass up and down, cars go back and forth, and people carry on with different lives under the same patch of sky, but I would often take a moment to observe these swirling celestial performances – and generally marvel at eternity.

I lost Skye at the beginning of February 2014. She had been with me during my last few months as a relief signalman and nearly four years as a resident at Scropton – she never missed a day and died on duty. In the black months after losing her I did a lot of walking, up to twenty miles some days. They really were black months too, no colour at all. Mainly I think I was trying to walk off the depression, but strange as this may sound, I think I was looking for her too. Suddenly I was in an empty signal box, an empty van and an empty house and I spent many evenings wandering around at home, looking in every room hoping to catch some small sign of her. It didn't matter how many miles I walked though, it still hurt, but I think I went walking to try to find her out there – places we had previously been together – and perhaps I did in a way: perhaps she was all around me.

I used to drape my HV trousers over a chair in my bedroom and, one day, the sun shone through the leaded window, striking the reflective tape on them at just the right angle, scattering rainbow light across the floor. Was this what I was looking for? It reminded me of what someone once said about coming back from the colourless world of despair and having to teach yourself joy all over again, simply by looking long and hard at a single glorious thing. I was never able to recreate the effect but teaching oneself joy again was probably what little pieces of the previous chapter were about – the poetry of nature, the poetry of life.

Most people would think me foolish and over-sentimental, but I know some would understand. Skye was special, and we shared work and home so completely and were inseparable for four years. I couldn't make sense of her loss, but something good came out of it, for me anyway, because I started writing again. She was my inspiration. I laid much of the groundwork for this book shortly after her death and writing it kept her spirit alive. As time goes by parts of her character naturally fade from my memory, but this work kept (and will keep) her close to me. Along with my walks, it became a cathartic exercise. I know there is little to be achieved by living in the past or trying to live your life backwards, but sometimes you must retreat into the past to find some solace, mostly because there are times when the present can be too painful. That's the thing I've found about dogs though; they live totally in the present. They don't care about the past or the future, there is only now. Yesterday does not exist, tomorrow never comes, there is only today. Look to this day, for it is life. Maybe that's a lesson for us all.

Almost a year later, locals, box visitors and maintenance teams were all still asking after Skye, and whenever her name was mentioned it still had the power to take my breath away. It was another six months after that before my paralysing sense of loss began to abate. But that's how much of an impression she made on people – not bad for a previously unwanted dog. When my time comes, I doubt I will have as many people asking after me. Of all the things I've lost in life (including hair, sanity, good looks, taste in clothing – I'm lying about the last two because I never had them to begin with), this hit me the hardest. It wasn't until the end of the year, in fact the exact amount of time it took to reach and write this chapter, that I finally achieved some acceptance and was able to turn the page...as dear reader, you may now do.

Lux Perpetua – Skye snoozes in the signal box sunbeams. *Author.*

19. PULL OFF OR PULL OUT?

Much of the fun and magic disappeared from the job after losing Skye, but it felt as though my morale had been steadily eroding long before that black and terrible day. Since receiving the original notice of the box closures in 2011, my colleagues and I had suffered numerous people gloating, rubbing their hands and positively revelling that we'd all be out of a job soon – and some of those were actual visitors to the box, and even fellow NR employees!

Because morale was so low, and the re-signalling (as far as anyone knew) was still scheduled for 2016, I went through a stage of applying for suitable jobs on the internal vacancy list, primarily the recently created post of Level Crossing Manager. Who better for the role than a MOM trained signalman and former train crew member? I was interviewed on two separate occasions and twice I was informed that I was the ideal candidate for the job, which is why, of course, I still found myself working in a signal box. Apparently, it wasn't enough just to be skilled and experienced for the job, or to have an exemplary record, some interviewers wanted you to be 'passionate' or to embark on a 'journey' as well. I lost count of the times I was asked if I was passionate – only about the opposite sex and possibly small cigars – or to be told that a certain job was akin to going on a journey. Life is a journey, writing this book (and probably reading it!) has been a journey; I never found an actual job to be so. But signalling aside, I'd never been in one job long enough to find out. At times, I did wonder where else I might fit in after nearly a decade in a manual signal box. I had already accepted that when my time was up at Scropton, so too would be my signalling career. Even if there were vacancies at the Death Star I didn't want to go in there.

Another factor that tended to dull the enthusiasm somewhat was that any signaller now applying for another box had to re-sit the signaller psychometrics, even if the box they were applying for was the same grade as the one they already worked. One of the North Staffs relief applied for a vacant resident Alrewas position and was duly subjected to a day of testing in Birmingham, no doubt at great expense, even though he currently worked the box as part of his duties *and* had formerly been a resident there. Whoever implemented this costly and unnecessarily convoluted recruitment policy should really have had some cognition testing themselves. Unsurprisingly, it was revoked about six months later. The decision for most of us on the North Staffs was whether to risk staying to 'pull off' signals or to pull out altogether.

In similar extravagant style to the above, I was once selected for a 'random' drugs & alcohol (D&A) test and had to make the 300-mile round trip to York again, primarily to urinate in a beaker. I was not altogether sure how the random part came into it, being as I was given 48 hours' notice. Nevertheless, someone had to be drafted in to cover my shift whilst I travelled four points north (Chesterfield, Sheffield, Wakefield and Leeds) to participate in what would amount to a twenty-minute appointment. The negative breathalyser result was immediate, but my drug test result would be indeterminate for a further three days. I would therefore be signing on duty the following day, potentially in contravention of the zero-tolerance policy. I think whoever deemed it necessary for me to go all the way to York perhaps should have been breathalysed too. I was 'selected' for another D&A test two years later, which on that, and subsequent occasions, was conducted in the far more mundane surroundings of the box. I don't know if this worked out any cheaper for NR, but my instinct says not.

After my short but tense bladder emptying session under exam conditions in York I decided to make the most of being let out of my box and visit the National Railway Museum. I knew I would find little to thrill me there, being as most of the contents of Scropton box were equivalent in age to much of the stuff on display, but at least I could discreetly prepare an inventory of spare parts for the S&T fault team. Whilst ambling around, I was asked by one of the guides if I fancied having a go on their lever frame exhibit. He was somewhat taken aback by my rather abrupt reply of "You must be joking!" I was probably already on their list of dubious characters after my last visit. On that occasion, I'd stood for far too long gazing uncomprehendingly at a loco on display in the main hall (the old steam shed, formerly full of smoke where, ironically, smoking is now prohibited). It was a Class 56 loco I'd spent much time on in BR days, one hitherto roaring with life and power, but now just a silent and forlorn looking exhibit. If it was already a museum exhibit, where did that leave me? I left the museum feeling rather old and deflated that day.

A little-known fact, which I considered quite an achievement, is that I was probably the only person to get blacklisted for train driving at Derby twice. I don't know if the term 'blacklisted' can be used nowadays, but whatever colour list it is that renders someone *persona non grata*, I was firmly on it. The first occasion was during privatisation of BR in 1994 when all the redundant trainmen had gone their separate ways. Those not already accommodated elsewhere had been given the option of returning after two years, all except me and one other chap. I can't even blame a HR function (or non-function) in that instance because one simply didn't exist then. I wasn't bothered about returning to the railway at that point, I just liked to resurface every now and then to unsettle certain people. The second occasion was at the beginning of 2014, just after the most recent knock back from my final Level Crossing Manager interview. On the urging of several train driving colleagues, who thought that it was time I returned to the fold, albeit after twenty years, I applied for a depot driving position with East Midlands Trains (EMT), the current train operating company at Derby. I felt I was on a hiding to nothing, but as I really had nothing to lose, I allowed myself to be subjected to all the psychometrics, medical and formal interviews again. (Oddly enough, I passed the EMT psychometrics exactly 24 years to the day after the BR ones.) After this exhaustive process, I was verbally offered the position, which I accepted. But what happened next was totally bizarre and in all my previous engagements, was something that had never happened to me before. HR verbally informed me of a start date but neglected to furnish me with any written confirmation. Had I actually got the job? Was I just supposed to *sense* when to hand my notice in? I certainly wasn't about to terminate my current employment on some tenuous verbal agreement. (It's hard to believe now, but I had composed my letter of resignation and had started clearing my locker out.) Having heard nothing further, I phoned EMT to enquire about this rather unorthodox recruitment process, but for some reason, the female HR administrator I spoke to became distinctly huffy when I broached the subject and I was accused of not showing proper respect. Call me old-fashioned, but I still harboured a quaint notion that respect had to be earned and that it only *really* worked best when it was mutual, even if only grudgingly. It was around this point we found ourselves at an impasse and she promptly terminated the conversation – and I still had absolutely no idea where I stood.

As I never considered the telephone to be a good means of communication, I sent an email. Upon receiving no response, I then sent a letter requesting clarification, but again, received nothing in return (remind me which of us lacked respect again?) In the end, it took two weeks and a letter to the Managing Director before I finally managed to winkle out a reply from someone entitled 'Talent Manager'. I understand these people have some function in show business, but as to their value in railway operations I am rather vague. Unfortunately, this person got my house number wrong and dispatched the letter to my neighbour instead. Apparently, the job offer had been retracted shortly after my phone call, but no one had bothered to inform me until the unexpected arrival of my neighbour brandishing said letter. Sacked before I'd even started – a new personal best!

I was somewhat perturbed for a time, not because I didn't get the job, but because of their total incompetence. If I worked a signal box the way they worked their office, people would be maimed or dead. It was perhaps also the one and only time when I'd ever displayed any 'passion' regarding a job and I got severely pilloried for it. I did, however, manage to satisfy one of my curiosities; I still had what it took for train driving and was happy with that. What I found strange about the whole affair was that after submitting to a battery of tests, meeting the industry standard and being passed medically fit, it was possible to have the rug pulled from under you by someone you had never even met, simply because they happened to dislike your telephone manner. EMT constantly pedalled their company values of Teamwork, Honesty, Professionalism, Communication and Respect, but failed to meet every single one of them in my dealings with them. They may as well have just listed the Seven Deadly Sins as their company values. Those would have been much more accurate and achievable, at least as far as EMT's HR department was concerned. (Network Rail actually had Pride listed as one of their company values – so only six more to add then!) I much preferred BR's 1980s slogan of 'We're getting there'. No one was exactly sure where *there* was, but it was a simple honest statement and I couldn't understand why modern companies expended so much effort trying to promote values that should be inherent. I have worked for some dubious outfits in my time; once doing a day's driving for a company that went bankrupt later that same day. The truck was repossessed upon my return and consequently I received no wages, but after the debacle with EMT, I now tend to view that day's driving as one of my better engagements.

There were several footnotes to this tragicomic affair with EMT, in which, quite obviously, my name had not been passed through their HR computers beforehand. Several weeks later I was asked by an ex-colleague to (anonymously) re-edit and simplify their HST driver training manual, which I was more than happy to do. There was something curiously gratifying about the idea of the new recruits with whom I'd sat the psychometrics, studying my notes. Subsequently, I concluded that there would have been very little fulfilment for me in starting from scratch as a depot driver, so things worked out for the best after all. A couple of months later I was asked to contribute an article about Etches Park for their forthcoming Derby175 celebration/open day, which I largely sidestepped, although I would have loved to have seen the MD's face had my name appeared in their official programme. Finally, about six months after their incorrectly addressed 'dismissed before you start' letter, I received a personal letter (as did all NR employees on the East Midlands Route) from the managing director of EMT, thanking me for my commitment to customers and my sterling work during the year, albeit with Network Rail – that same drive and commitment so casually dismissed by his company not less than six months before! That letter actually arrived without any intervention from my neighbour. As it turned out, I also (eventually) had the satisfaction of outlasting many of the players in this tragicomedy, including the EMT franchise itself.

After that underwhelming recruitment venture, I decided to stay put at Scropton and be the last man out, unless some dazzling job opportunity presented itself, such as being a personal masseur for one of the top female starlets/models/singers of the day. Incidentally, the job of Lubrication Operative often appeared on the internal vacancy list, but as far as I could determine, this involved the oiling of points only and alas, not female body parts. I also considered taking early semi-retirement and living off the royalties from writing a good book – although on reflection, my first idea seemed much more realistic!

My overtime rate dipped slightly during 2014, partly because of my desire to keep personal tax obligations below a certain level, and partly because of a small influx of displaced crossing keepers and signallers after the Nottingham Re-signalling Project. These waifs and strays were easily absorbed, and with natural wastage continuing to outstrip any influx, it wasn't long before my overtime rate was back to 'normal' again. Because of the staff turnover though, about half the people on the roster were now unknown to me, and not being on the relief circuit anymore, they remained unknown. The management struggled to counter natural wastage because, understandably, few people wanted to transfer to a line that had apparently little future. New recruits were already only being employed on yearly contracts. That was quite prescient really, considering everyone on the North Staffs had received information about the voluntary severance scheme by the end of the year.

Receipt of the above correspondence notwithstanding, morale remained low for several reasons, although working under the threat of re-signalling was certainly the main one. My supposedly temporary oppo was still in situ (and remained so for almost three years before disappearing into the Death Star) getting paid over £5,000 a year more than me for doing the same job. It wasn't his fault and good luck to him, but that situation left me feeling rather devalued.

Another factor concerned communication, or rather the lack of it, again. Signallers were constantly monitored, and subsequently graded, on their safety critical communications, and having already offered my opinion of these methods I never really aspired to high grades. In all the safety critical conversations I've ever had (including countless level crossing calls), I knew a clear understanding had been achieved on every single one of them simply because no train dropped in the dirt, no motorist ever reported a near miss with a train (although several trains reported near misses with motorists who had not contacted the signal box before crossing), and more importantly, everyone I dealt with reached their intended destination alive and with all their appendages still attached. Surely an A grade every time? I likened getting an A grade on railway communications to getting an A rating on one of those property energy performance certificates. Both were nigh impossible to achieve for a 'normal' person in the real world, and both were just as meaningless. Therefore, I didn't tick boxes; I just worked them. But perhaps I should have adopted a more relaxed attitude to Network Rail's idea of good communication. They were the only company I knew of who promoted their zero tolerance to alcohol campaign on a set of beer mats and emailed fatigue management advice between 01:26 and 04:47.

Scropton's block shelf and associated signalling instrumentation was rewired in 2014 too. I never understood the sudden urge to do this because those electronics had not been touched since Alessandro Volta and Thomas Edison had originally installed them and any spare parts would almost certainly have to be looted from the National Railway Museum in York. But then I remembered the railway dictum stating costly renewals should always precede closure of a place, and in due course, a 'ponse unit' appeared in the compound. Once all the dust (topsoil) had been vacuumed (ploughed) from the back of the block shelf, I gathered by the look of horror on the signalling technician's face that the wiring was indeed somewhat below standard, but happily the work would only take four days. Unhappily, those four days somehow turned into ten stretching over six weeks, the bulk of which inevitably occurred on my early shifts.

The emergency lighting was replaced shortly afterwards, including an exterior light on the Up side of the box. I was enjoying a rare day off at the time, and returned on a late shift, unaware of this renewal. It only became apparent at sundown when the Up end of the box was completely bathed in a green glow. Modern lights now all seemed to incorporate a tiny but intense green LED, which remains lit regardless of whether the main light is on or not. That little green light may be a life-saver in a dark or smoke-filled environment, but at a manual crossing box it was potentially fatal, particularly if that box was controlling entry into an engineering possession or the signaller happened to be cautioning a train during the hours of darkness. I walked along the track to obtain a driver's eye view and it was horrendous! The green glow from the outdoor light dwarfed the red light of the Up Home signal. All a driver would see upon rounding the curve from Sudbury would be a green light, irrespective of the actual signal aspect. The green LED was swiftly masked with electrical tape. Honestly, I couldn't even leave the box for one day!

As a small aside, someone broke into the locking room the following year, damaging its door in the process. (Obviously some opportunist in this case, but with HMP Sudbury not far away, it wasn't completely unknown to encounter the odd absconder.) The door was replaced, but for some inexplicable reason it was painted bright red, which blended in beautifully with the existing LMS colour scheme. Is it so difficult to obtain a tin of gloss from the darker end of the ruby palette? But perhaps it was painted thus to counteract the green LED of the outdoor light that hung above it – one extreme to the other.

In the event, all the expenditure proved worthwhile, and the railway dictum was proved temporarily wrong, because in March 2015 we were informed that the re-signalling date had been extended yet again, until at least the middle of 2017. Whoever said life on the railway was dull? From potential redundancy to a two-year extension – what a rollercoaster! The whole thing was a bit like seeking the divine truth; the closer you thought you were to it, the further away it became.

Not long after, I had a close encounter with an old acquaintance of mine, namely the Sinfin Tanks train. This visit, however, was entirely unintended, as the Class 56 pulling it failed at my Up Home signal. (There seems to be a pattern emerging with this signal, as it has had numerous mentions throughout the book.) Before the train's arrival, but *after* I'd cleared my signals, I was advised by Sudbury that the loco was low on water and travelling very slowly. The latter part of this information was superfluous as there was, by now, the inevitable queue of motorists at my gates waiting for the errant train. It eventually came into sight and crawled to a stand at the signal. I went out and spoke to the driver whom, despite current difficulties, seemed an amiable chap. He understandably wanted to keep going but I suggested he end it here rather than foul a major road crossing, or indeed North Stafford Junction further ahead. He decided to give it one last try and I returned to view proceedings from the safety of the box. After much groaning, shuddering and black exhaust from the loco, I took the driver's subsequent finger across the throat and inverted thumb gestures to indicate that he was declaring it a failure. I walked back and informed him that I would return my signals to danger and allow the waiting traffic to cross, whereupon he shut the loco down and eventually joined me in the box. I noticed he had a camera with him and asked if he would take a few photos for me, possibly for inclusion in a book one day, (see Page 162.) As my telephone was becoming rather warm by this stage, I handed him an old copy of *Derby Trainman* and asked him to just send the photos to the email address inside the front cover.

"Oh, that's you is it! I've just been reading about you in here," he exclaimed, pulling out a railway magazine from his bag. (*Rail Express* was running a 20-part DTM series at the time.) As it turned out, this driver regularly sent photos to the magazine, and now two of its contributors were meeting in topical circumstances. It was another classic example of our small railway world.

Control was set whirring into motion and whilst they blew the dust off their 1884 Scropton map scrolls and arranged an assisting loco, I did what all proper railwaymen did in this situation and boiled the kettle. Unfortunately, I'd forgotten to bring milk, which could be construed as a gross dereliction of duty in railway circles, further exacerbated by the box being next to a dairy farm.

As this train failure necessitated assistance from the front, and it would be a while before the assisting loco arrived, the driver had made a call to his travelling shunter, who duly arrived in his van. They both then promptly disappeared to the supermarket in Hatton to obtain milk, leaving me with the life expired loco and its train blocking my main line: a most palpable *Mary Celeste* experience.

Assistance from the front also meant me having to operate the very reluctant crossover and the train crew returned just in time to see the duty MOM bouncing from one end of it to the other, liberally spraying oil on all the point slides. However, much of his bounce disappeared when I reminded him that, as the crossover had been officially booked out of use for over five years, I would require written confirmation if I was going to operate it. Of course, no one in Control would take responsibility for issuing such confirmation and I had to be satisfied with verbal authority over a recorded line. As I had a box full of people, who all agreed to back me up should this recording suddenly 'disappear' in the event of loco wheels touching ballast, I grudgingly accepted. I doubted whether the crossover could even be pulled after all those years anyway and suspected a PWay crew would be required to disconnect the rodding and force the point ends across. My suspicions were proved correct and I was informed that the assisting loco would pick up a PWay crew at Egginton Junction en-route to me.

It was roughly 90 minutes between the driver's declaration of failure and me acknowledging the impending arrival of the assisting loco into the section. I signalled it up to the box and stopped it just clear of the crossing. Climbing up into the cab to brief its driver I suddenly got a feeling of déjà vu. The loco was 37688 and the last time I'd been this close to it was 22 years ago when secondmanning it on a now largely forgotten freight job. I was expecting the cab to be full of burly orange clad bodies and was surprised to find only the driver and his secondman in residence. I was already laughing as I inquired if they had been supposed to pick up a PWay crew from Egginton.

"Ah, that's why all those blokes were waving when we sailed past the box," replied the driver, more to his mate than to me. "No one told us about that," he concluded, finally looking over his shoulder at me. I of course then looked over *my* shoulder in the direction of the Death Star, mentally chalking up another F grade for Control in communication.

"Welcome to Scropton!" I said.

Whilst we waited for the Keystone Kops to catch up, I outlined the plan of action to the ever-increasing assemblage of railway personnel, which now included a travelling fitter from EMT, whose primary responsibility would be to direct recovery operations should the loco fail to negotiate the recalcitrant crossover. The PWay crew finally arrived and set to work with gusto, and once the crossover had been reversed and secured accordingly, I verbally authorized the driver of the assisting loco to pass over it. I couldn't signal him in this instance because the cables for both ground signals had snapped three years before and had never been repaired. There was much wincing from the orange audience as the loco creaked over the points, but it crossed to the Up line without incident, whereupon the crossover was normalized, and the assisting loco finally coupled to the failed train.

As the relevant people made the necessary preparations for departure, I took the opportunity to consult my Rule Book on the sly, but the Class 56 driver caught me in the act.

"Having a review, are you?" he smirked, noting my guilty expression.

"It's all right for you; you just go when I tell you to. I have to make sure that you are protected from all directions. Besides, you don't begrudge me a rules review, do you? This situation only happens in my section about once every three years (which would account for the snapped ground signal cables) or one in every 32,000 trains. You just happened to be the *one*." At which point it was my turn to smirk and he to look guilty.

After blocking the Up line for nearly three hours, the Sinfin Tanks finally got underway. The orange bodies melted away and peace returned to Scropton, just as if all the feverish activity had never been. Unfortunately, this peace was short-lived, because I was plagued with requests for delayed line blockages immediately afterwards, but it had been a satisfying shift. I had really enjoyed all the humour of the situation and it reminded me very much of old BR days. Incidentally, the delayed line blockages were for cyclic S&T maintenance of the crossover ground signals. No repairs or renewals, just unnecessary inspection and lubrication of the already disconnected signalling equipment. As there was never any intention to repair the crossover, why continue with its cyclic S&T maintenance? The mind boggled.

A forlorn looking 56113 (6M65) declared a failure at Scropton's Up Home, with 37688 (*Kingmoor TMD*) eventually coming to its rescue, March 2015. Incidentally, the Sinfin Tanks were the last remaining regular freight working on the North Staffs, but even they were re-routed shortly after this incident. *Jim Scott.*

To add a further twist to this story, and to provide another classic example of the small railway world that we all inhabited, an old colleague from 4 Shed days visited the box a couple of years later. A former trainman, but now a driver for one of the freight operating companies based at Carlisle Kingmoor (the nameplate on the loco that came to assist coincidentally enough), we had lost touch in 1994, but had re-established contact after the release of *Derby Trainman* in 2006. He mentioned that, a week after the Sinfin Tanks failure, a train he was driving had failed near Warrington. When the assisting loco turned up, he had apologized to its driver (a stranger) for ruining his shift.

"Don't worry about it mate," came the reply "I failed with some fuel tankers the other week."

"Where was that?"

"Oh, you won't know it...Scropton...middle of bloody nowhere!"

"Was Tim, the Derby Trainman on duty in the signal box?"

"Yes...how the *hell* do you know him?"

I blotted my clean record of no signal cable breaks, when I had two in one month. First to go was the Down Distant, with its cable snapping mid-pull. There was a split second when I felt it twang and the lever suddenly go slack and I wondered how painful it was going to be. Instead of careering backwards as I was expecting, the large counter weight below yanked me forwards into the frame. It was painful, but I'd still not experienced the traditional 'flying backwards' cable break. I only partially experienced this with the Down Home, because, unbeknown to me, its cable had already snapped whilst the lever was still in the frame. Therefore, when I pulled it, expecting the usual resistance, any 'flying backwards' was self-inflicted.

The Down Distant failure had no major effect on train running, as the signal merely remained at caution. The Down Home however, was stuck firmly at stop and drivers had to be talked past it. Eventually, a S&T 'ponse unit' arrived, but inexplicably, they had no replacement cable with them. I confess to knowing very little about semaphore signal repair, but I would have thought that, other than a blown bulb, a snapped cable must surely be the primary reason for failure; therefore, replacement cable would have been foremost in my armoury. It was a lacklustre response and vindicated my continued removal of the first three letters from that word.

The company still stuck to their official closure date of August 2017 for the North Staffs and surveying pegs were even hammered in at the back of the box in July 2015, which, judging by their alignment, were for the supposed new automatic barrier crossing. During the following week however, locking fitters and other maintenance staff kept turning up to ascertain how much more life might be squeezed out of the existing equipment (perhaps they should have checked the signallers too!) Therefore, considering these visits, I strongly suspected that the company timescale for closure would not be met again. Rumours of 2020 were now circulating, but I don't think even the high command knew what was supposed to be happening, or more importantly, when.

By the end of summer, for me, came a general feeling of acceptance. The wider world of signalling didn't really impact on my little fiefdom and ridiculous new company initiatives aside, I returned to being fairly content with my lot. Whatever was to happen would happen. Extended box life or redundancy; either was fine by me. I decided to stay and 'pull off' signals, but some of my colleagues did in fact pull out altogether. Towards the end of September, came the official announcement we'd all been expecting. Because of financial constraints (something possibly to do with the company being £50 billion in debt), the North Staffs re-signalling would not be completed until April 2019, at the earliest. Although there was no handshake, repeat back, initiative or indeed official announcement of any kind, the project ended up being shelved about two years later, with no set date for completion. It was now likely that the box would see me out, instead of the other way around, which, when I started writing this book, was certainly an ending I never envisaged.

My new (permanent) oppo arrived in August 2016 and he became the fifteenth signaller that I had trained at Scropton. That made an average of 1.5 signallers a year – the half signaller being quite apt in some cases, although not in his I was happy to find. Part of the crossover was also removed shortly after his arrival, but it continued to be rigorously inspected and maintained. Why? We couldn't operate it *before* a length of rail was removed, what chance now? I suppose there was a reasonable case for PWay still Inspecting the trailing point ends, but why S&T was directed to continue maintaining the ground signals (officially disconnected in 2014) remained a mystery? I suppose I shouldn't have been so mystified. A level crossing manager once told me that he was still inspecting all the crossings on the Denby Branch five years after the track had been lifted and responsibility for the track bed had passed to the local council. It would seem there is a right way, a wrong way and the railway after all.

Scropton's complete but officially out of use crossover in August 2014. *Author*.

20. FOR WHOM THE BELL TOLLS

(...never send to know for whom the bell tolls; it tolls for thee)

The above is an extract from John Donne's Meditation XVII, which explores the interconnectedness of humanity. In his case, the bell was funeral tolling, which caused me to briefly ponder how much of life, well, *my* life at least, is governed by a bell. After several years' absence, the hour and half hourly strike was reinstated at St. Paul's, so along with block bells, I had church ones to contend with again. At home, I lived within the sound of bells from three churches. The nearest church, also called St. Paul's, was closest to the railway (St. Mary's North Junction), with both having a distinctive and regular beat; bells and the rattle of trains through the junction respectively, much like St. Paul's at Scropton and the rattle of trains through the crossover there. There was no escape. At home and at work, bells filled my days and permeated my nights. They marked the passage of trains and the passage of time: interconnectedness at its best, even if it sometimes felt like self-imposed tinnitus.

The passage of time was marked in other ways too and it was November 2016 that I found myself notching up a decade of service. This was celebrated in the traditional style of being sent for a medical, providing yet another thrilling opportunity to urinate in a beaker. Considering the number of times I've had to do this, it's just as well I have plenty to spare! At least the medical was conducted in Derby this time and I didn't have to travel to some far-flung location. I suppose it was fortunate that the company rail warrants didn't extend to use on the Trans-Siberian Express because if there was an occupational health clinic in Vladivostok, I was certain they would try and dispatch me there. It wouldn't be long before DVLA were demanding I take a medical too, but as I would doubtless be charged some extortionate fee for the same results I was about to receive gratis, I decided I would decline their generous invitation when it came. As a result, I would be stripped of my HGV licence. When I first obtained it at the age of twenty-one, reaching my mid-forties seemed so distant it was almost inconceivable, but now that I had firmly crossed that threshold, it merely came as a surprise. At least my true age coincided with my physical appearance now, with or without the cigars.

Just before my medical, a fifteen-year-old schoolboy had visited the box on work experience and had asked how long I'd been there. To him, ten years was a LONG time. It was two thirds of his life, but only a fifth (or thereabouts) of mine. The decade had slipped past, almost frighteningly imperceptibly for me, but then time didn't seem to have much meaning at the box. It was only really the changing seasons that marked its passage. Perhaps that should be the standard measurement of time for a manual signaller?

This passing of time finally hit home when a new relief signalman came to learn the box after having recently passed for Egginton. I told him that

I'd worked the last train off the Test Track, and consequently one of the very last trains over the junction.

"What year was that?"

"1990."

"That was the year I was born."

It took a brief moment for me to compute this, because he'd said it so casually that it might well have been last month. I didn't feel any older and, up until that point, we'd been conversing on an equal footing. He disrupted my mental computations still further when he mentioned later that a friend of his was doing up a classic car.

"What car?" I asked, for some reason expecting it to be a Mark 1 Jaguar, or even an unassuming Morris Minor.

"It's a Mark 2 Vauxhall Cavalier."

Bloody cheek! That was my first motor. It was no good; I had to face up to it. I was now officially an old man.

As if to confirm my new doddery status, I had a close but unplanned inspection of the box steps one afternoon. I was just in the process of ascending them to take duty when the fifth step gave way, causing me to partially disappear through the gap; much like a condemned man on the gallows just as the hangman had pulled the lever for the trapdoor. This sudden and unexpected descent expertly stripped all the skin from my left shin (I still have the scar) and twisted the attached knee a little more than its original design specification. I was particularly aggrieved as I'd spent most of that week painting the box interior, and that was how it repaid me! (I'd only embarked on this painting spree because S&T had started on the frame then never returned. As I couldn't rest with an unfinished job, particularly one I'd originally planned to do, albeit a mere six years previously, I decided to complete it myself, inevitably expanding to the walls.) The only consolation was that I had not expended any time or effort painting the steps.

During the 2009 refurbishment, the wooden steps, in my opinion, should have been replaced with metal ones, but a new set of wooden ones had been put back (largely because metal ones had been deemed unsafe!) Unfortunately, these were cosmetic rather than practical and had been constructed from thin softwood, with the treads not jointed correctly. After seven years of weather and steel toe-capped boots thumping up and down a minimum of eight times an hour, they were thoroughly rotten and a veritable death trap. These facts only became fully apparent when I found myself in the unique but uncomfortable position of being eye-level with the eighth step; hence the above detailed report as to their woeful condition. Ironically, the LOM had just pinned a poster up in the box promoting the latest safety initiative. It was entitled '5 Steps to Safety' – a statement I found to be wholly untrue at Scropton. I did, however, become a minor celebrity in the safety briefings for a time: I had unwittingly provided a genuine, real-life safety concern for them, instead of the measly offerings that had previously been served up. Around that point, management had become so desperate that they were coming out asking if *we* could think of anything to talk about for a safety conversation. They had run out of ideas, even SBO ones!

Someone suggested using a ladder as a temporary solution for box access, but aside from me, no one else held a ladder-climbing certificate, so new steps had to be hastily constructed by the maintenance department and secured into position. Unfortunately, as it was such a rushed job, their design failed to meet the building regulations, something that was somehow left to me to point out. The builder couldn't really see what all the fuss was about (not enough tread, amongst other things), but then he didn't have to go up and down them a minimum of sixty-four times during an eight-hour shift. I was more concerned that I might be sent on a stair-climbing course – there is a limit to my SBO course tolerance.

Five weeks later, a new set of steps was constructed and attached to the box – painted red of course. Given enough time, the box might be one uniform colour in the end, if enough rotten woodwork drops off before closure.

Speaking of aged things, Scropton's rather tired and worn level crossing was 'replaced' in February 2017. I think its renewal had been put off whilst they decided whether the re-signalling would take place or not, but now that date was indeterminate, my oppo and I looked forward to having a new crossing deck installed. Unfortunately, we didn't get the shiny new crossing we were hoping for because the contractors made a right mess of it. Over the years there had been countless photos and surveys of the crossing but perhaps unsurprisingly, no one had bothered to consult this superabundance of information before starting work. Point and gate rodding was suddenly in the way (surprising at a mechanical signal box!) There were electrical cables that hadn't been accounted for, which obviously were for the gate releases and road warning lights. Also, there were a mixture of wooden and concrete sleepers under the old deck and the new rubber deck slabs could only be seated on concrete sleepers. This mixture had actually been discovered seven years previously, but again, unsurprisingly, had not been made known to the relevant parties. Five nights of road closure were scheduled for the work, whereupon the contractors replaced the old for the new on the first night, pulled up the (uneven) new and put some of the (now damaged) old back on the second night before largely abandoning the job on the third night, resulting in the remarkable achievement of the crossing now being in a worse state than it was before. Not only were there still mix and match sleepers underneath, there were now mix and match slabs on top, so much so that the deck resembled a piano keyboard and 'level' crossing became a distinct contradiction in terms. Two slabs on our walking route had not been replaced at all, so there was now a danger of falling between the rails. Not content with negotiating that obstacle, there were also three large potholes to avoid too. The crossing surface resembled the runway at Port Stanley after the Vulcan bomber had paid a visit in 1982 and it was now actually safer to walk across the tracks than the crossing. The contractors also neglected to replace the wooden gate stops. This perhaps wouldn't have been too bad, except that it happened to coincide with the arrival of Storm Doris. Anyone unfortunate enough to be operating the box that particular night had to chase the gates up the track after every train. After complaining to control, the duty MOM came out to have a look.

"Did they do the job in the dark?" he exclaimed incredulously.

"Well, yes," I replied "but one presumes they had the benefit of spotlights." Judging by the state of it though, I began to doubt that statement. It was six months before another team came out and tried again. They made a slightly better job of it, but to be honest, they couldn't have made it much worse. I didn't have high hopes to begin with because one of the contractors arrived wearing a combination of HV vest and Hawaiian shorts. I didn't know which bit of this bold ensemble was more eye-catching, but there was no danger of him not being spotted on the track.

Mentioning dodgy characters, it was around this time that someone pointed out that a photo of me on the box steps was being used as the heading for Scropton's Neighbourhood Watch web page – ironic really, one of Scropton's most suspicious characters fronting the campaign.

What remained a mystery to me was that I worked in a wooden shed, essentially in the middle of nowhere, and yet it seemed to be the centre of the universe; a Mecca for the unending stream of vans that continued roll up. With a mixture of weary resignation and grim fascination, I once kept a record of them during a week of early shifts: eighteen out of a total of thirty-five early shift hours interrupted and eighteen hours' intrusion of the dreaded outside world. (Not to mention a grand total of fifteen vans.) For a lone worker who valued his solitude, early shifts were a good working definition of Hell. The box probably had more visitors in a day than Sudbury Hall just up the road, which is National Trust attraction, and signposted!

The buildings maintenance during that week was an unexpected 'bonus', with more bits of rotten woodwork replaced and painted the wrong colour. These paint jobs always seemed to be conducted in the same manner: two vans, five blokes, but only ever one paintbrush amongst them. A complete repaint was initiated, but never completed. (What is about people who start a paint job then never finish it?) This underwhelming endeavour left the front rotten and untouched, the rear in undercoat, the west side in primer and the east side finished in a colour scheme resembling that of a seaside ice cream parlour. I was seriously considering sliding back the window and selling cones to passers-by. There was also an asbestos survey, which was a definite oddity, being as the last – and one assumes decisive – had been conducted in 2009. No asbestos had been identified on that occasion and it would have been somewhat unorthodox for the company to add any afterwards, (although I wouldn't have put it entirely beyond the bounds of possibility). I informed the inspector of this, but he merely pointed to a panel above my head.

"That looks suspect."

"Well if it is asbestos, don't you think it's a little late to worry about now, being as I've spent nearly a decade underneath it?"

"It's only dangerous if it's damaged or disturbed."

"You mean like when someone cuts into it to take a sample?"

He gave a dismissive wave, bid me stand in the porch whilst he donned a respirator, then climbed his ladder and gouged into the panel with a knife.

"Well, is it asbestos?" I enquired, from the through draught of the porch.

"I don't know. I'll have to send it to the lab. It could take a while."

With box closure indeterminate, I now faced the possibility of many more years underneath a previously untouched but now disturbed suspected asbestos panel. If ignorance is bliss, this was Eden.

A year later, I found out that it was indeed asbestos, which then required it to be inspected annually. Unfortunately, a different company seemed to win the contract each year, and with the previous survey reports not passed on, each new inspector would start from scratch, literally! Therefore, the asbestos and I were disturbed every twelve months. Still, I suppose I was considered a bit too long in the tooth for it to make much difference. For my part, I simply added it to the already lengthy list of other volatile organic compounds in the box, not least of which being all the Bakelite fixtures.

One day, an orange clad NR chap, who looked very familiar, visited the box. I couldn't place his face, but there was something about his manner and appearance that, in the past, and at another box, had caused me some concern. I just couldn't remember what or how. He informed me that he was doing an asset inspection, but after further interrogation, the light bulb moment still eluded me, and I had to get the gates for the next Up train. He followed me out to continue his inspection. After closing the gates, I returned to the box and was just about to clear the Up Home, when, much to my alarm, I saw him standing at the top of the signal post ladder peering over the arm. Then it suddenly struck me: it was the former lamp man who used to top up the paraffin reservoirs. I was surprised recognition had taken so long, but, to be fair, this was the only position I'd ever really seen him in; wobbling precariously twenty feet up a signal ladder, his head directly in the path of an arm that was about to chin-chop him. I still shouted a warning, and he still looked. The spirit did live on after all.

About two years after my partial disappearance through the box steps, I got the impression that someone was trying to give me a subtle hint. A sign stating 'Your Safety Starts Here' was attached to the box at the foot of the steps, no doubt to be observed before ascent. However, I still deemed it wholly untrue in my case.

I don't know if Foley Signal Box had the same sign, but it was certainly untrue there, when a local ne'er-do-well, under the influence of drugs, assaulted the duty signalman, gained entry to the box and started interfering with the signalling equipment. He even managed to make an emergency broadcast on the GSM-R – something that most of us had never done (or could even remember how to do). Who says you can't work under the influence?

It wasn't long before other signs started appearing. The outdoor toilet was re-branded as an 'Approved Welfare Facility' shortly afterwards, as opposed to going behind a bush, which one assumes, was no longer approved. A key safe was also attached to it, which no one seemed to know the combination for. This wasn't a problem until one of the relief signalmen decided to lock the one and only toilet key in there upon completion of his late shift. I arrived to take duty the following morning in, shall we say, some discomfort, and was unable to gain access. I phoned Control to ask if they knew the combination (I should have known better really):

"I need access to the Approved Welfare Facility."

"The what?"

"The outdoor bog. I need the combination for the key safe at your earliest convenience, or rather mine."

"No idea."

"Never mind, I'll find a key."

I grabbed a screwdriver from the van and broke in; it took all of five seconds. It's amazing what you can do when you're desperate...and I was! Incidentally, Network Rail had a process for reporting safety concerns called Close Call, but even though I classed this as one, I doubted they would.

Of course, sitting alone in a signal box year after year made it increasingly difficult to relate to people anyway, but then I thought it might be the ideal training for politics, local government, HR, the retail industry or *any* public facing role for that matter. Sometimes, without being fully conscious of it, I found myself pacing up and down the box like a caged animal. Perhaps some graduate psychologist can do a study on the 'last of the lone workers'; there should be a doctorate in there somewhere. I accept you must be a little 'odd' to survive in this job – although I prefer the term 'eccentric' – otherwise you would run off screaming, as a few in fact have.

It wasn't all doom, gloom and despondency however; visitors (some official, some not, some invited, some not) still popped up occasionally. The unofficial and generally uninvited ones were the best and it was always interesting to note the expressions of these people. Young people tended to shrink away from a mechanical signal box, no doubt concerned that if they stayed too long they might get press-ganged and find themselves stuck there indefinitely. I'm sure most of them wondered how anyone could survive in such an austere and out-of-date environment – no personal electronic devices allowed officially remember, apart from perhaps a radio, and even then, only under certain circumstances. That we were *still* using pen and paper to record the passage of trains in the TRB, instead of electronically inputting and uploading all this dazzling information, must have been a shock in itself – how very twentieth century. I expect a SBO course in the use of pen and paper at any moment but knowing the railway it will probably be quill and parchment. It wasn't just the younger generation that perhaps felt this way. The same could be said about some of the visiting MOMs and LOMs; those that always hovered closest to the door for a quick getaway. It was no surprise. For most, it was an environment they had escaped and had no desire to return to. Older visitors or those with little railway knowledge were always shocked to find that trains were still signalled in such a manner. I'm sure some of them thought it was all an elaborate wind up or that a stage set had been built and that I was operating it solely for their benefit. One female visitor asked if I was a volunteer and, for once, I didn't have an answer. Well, not until I had stopped laughing anyway. The only person I didn't see, certainly during my 'temporary' oppo's residence, was the Railway Chaplain. He must have considered him heathen and me beyond redemption. Maybe he was right on both counts.

I had ceased doing any early shift overtime by the beginning of 2017, just making myself available for late shift overtime – on the assumption that it was when I could mostly get a bit of peace. But after the East Notts re-signalling in 2015 – from which I'd gained my new oppo – the North Staffs found itself in the hitherto unknown position of having almost a full complement of staff. However, it wasn't long before natural wastage outstripped this influx again: more 'mental health' casualties, people on medication and individuals totally unsuited to signal box life. There were so many signalmen and crossing keepers being accompanied at one point that I thought we were running a crèche instead of a railway, but with the imminent threat of box closure lifted, I no longer felt the need or desire to chase excessive overtime anymore, fully staffed or not. Even so, I regularly notched up a 60-hour week over seven days of late shifts, and still the occasional thirteen in a row, if I'd happened to swap shifts with my oppo. On those occasions, box visitations and interruptions were happily kept to a minimum for me, but my oppo was still plagued on the early shifts. He even managed to add another obscure one to the ever-growing list; apparently a contractor had turned up to take photos of lineside weeds, (not feeble railway personages, but unwanted flora). Not to remove them or to even spray them, but to take photos. It must have cost a fortune for a contractor to do this shoot, and for no tangible result whatsoever, unless you count the fascinating slideshow of lineside vegetation that he must have accumulated. It sounded like a job Dungworthy should have been entrusted with, and it was he who often sprang to mind whenever those sorts of characters popped up.

At the school site, as well as working on the grounds and occasionally covering night security, I had also stepped in to help with buildings maintenance when necessary. This was because demand for Dungworthy's expertise in such matters had come to an abrupt end after he was once directed to fit a new closer to a fire door. Unfortunately, he attached the entire mechanism (piston and arm) to the door itself, the result being the fire door having a similar range of movement to a Wild West saloon door. After a lengthy investigation he eventually concluded that one end of the closer had to be attached to the frame and the other end to the door, but then somehow managed to fit the whole thing upside down, the result being that it now took a minimum of six people to force the door shut. I can only assume that Dungworthy eventually went on to become a well-respected and much consulted figure in Network Rail's inspection, maintenance and renewals department, although I can offer no hard evidence for this assumption.

The beginning of 2017 was also the first time I'd started to feel the cumulative effects of operating a mechanical signal box (not counting all those times up and down Mount Everest too!) I'd had pain in my right elbow for a while, then in October, the soft tissue around my left knee became inflamed – the two main stress points for me when tugging levers. It wasn't just bells taking their toll, repetitive strain was too and old injuries were coming back to haunt me. For the first time in eleven years, I had to book myself unfit for duty, remaining largely hobbled at home and left to ponder my future working a mechanical signal box. Odd really, because I always thought my back would be the first to go. I was now, however, one of the longest serving Scropton residents in recent times (most had only lasted six years, on average), but it wasn't really a record to celebrate if joint damage was the result. My elbow pain felt like permanent tennis elbow, but was (eventually) diagnosed as golfer's elbow because of repeatedly gripping and swinging the gates and levers. With an average 50kg pull for each lever, it was one hell of a golf swing! My knee was the main stumbling point (literally) and it was three months before the pain subsided and the joint reverted to its normal size. There were periods where I didn't want to return to the box and periods where I wondered if I'd even be *allowed* to return. Psychologically, I had moved on. Perhaps it happened when I lost Skye, in my heart at least anyway. I visited on several occasions, primarily to deliver my doctor's certificate and it was interesting to note the subtle changes – life at the box, of course, had moved on too. Ironic really, after all those years under the threat of closure, the re-signalling finally got shelved and I might be invalided out. After Christmas, I had a change of heart. I didn't want to finish under those circumstances. If I was going to move on, I wanted it to be on my terms. I had to adopt a smarter way of working, even though I had already sensed that this was the beginning of the end.

I returned to the box at the end of January 2018 and, along with a few other minor adjustments, alternated between my usual southpaw lever pulling stance and an orthodox one, thus reducing some of the stress. (Well, it worked for the Italian Stallion in *Rocky II*, so why not me?) Although it made me look clumsy, and I still had pain, I managed to avoid any further bouts of inflammation. Having not seen my LOM for nearly four months, he miraculously appeared that first shift. Not to check on my welfare as such, but to ensure I didn't delay the Royal Train, which just happened to be the third one I signalled. It's always nice to know how you stand, but apparently not too well in my case, either physically or socially.

The bell wasn't tolling exclusively for me. After a valiant ten-year resistance against cancer, it finally tolled for my father four months later. In Meditation XVII, Donne also talked about being diminished, and I was.

Almost without me realizing, another two years rolled by, but there were several noteworthy events within that time. The bell tolled for Derby PSB too, when it was incorporated into the EMCC during the Derby Re-signalling Project in September 2018. According to NR's 'Future Vision' the North Staffs Line was supposed to have gone in first, which I always thought was odd. Derby is far more important than us, but what did I know? What I *do* know is that the decision reversal really ruined the ending of this book! But just as I'd thought my other box pastime of article writing had dried up, I managed to produce one documenting the Derby re-signalling work, a piece which inspired me to go on and pen the Lost Lines series.

The next GSD (Sybilla) arrived in May 2019. Even though she was my mother's dog, and excellent companionship for her, we decided to dog share. But even now, I am still unsure as to which half is mine – the teeth end or the tail end. I only brought Syb to the box a couple of times, but she took to it straight away.

A young Sybilla supervises Scropton Crossing, June 2019. *Author.*

As briefly alluded to in Chapter 19, EMT lost the franchise in August and the remaining Class 15x fleet had their bodysides hastily rubbed down and East Midlands Railway (EMR) stickers applied. The following month I released a second edition of DTM, along with the Derby Days series of articles – my last major burst of literary creativity in the box.

Yet another trainee appeared in March 2020, and whilst I was explaining the process and pulling the levers for the next Up train, I got the third (and final) cable snap of my career. However, I didn't know it had snapped until the driver phoned to tell me that he had just passed the Up Section at danger. This revelation confused me initially, as I knew I had cleared the signal and had definitely not put it back in front of him, my trainee being witness to such. I did, however, detect a distinct slackness when I replaced the lever, and further investigation revealed that the cable had snapped at the exact moment I had locked it out of the frame.

By mid March, the Coronavirus restrictions were in place and about three months of stores were delivered to the box in one go. The train service was reduced to six a shift, no visitors were allowed, except for essential repairs and maintenance, and even the MOMs and LOM stayed away. It turned out there was an upside to this virus after all! Our shifts were temporarily altered to six hours (07:15-13:15 and 13:15-19:15) at the beginning of April, allowing just one signaller to work both shifts if necessary. I ended up running the box single-handedly that first week, which was a novel, if not entirely unexpected experience for me. (The line returned to normal hours, although not a normal train service, about six weeks later.) Of course, I was on early shift when the lockdown was eased and endured a succession of visitors that first Monday. I think they had all been queuing around the corner waiting to pounce: it had only taken a national pandemic to stem the flow, but somehow the box had managed to function perfectly well without them. In fact, I would venture to say better, in most cases. The first visitor informed me that he was there to survey Archers Crossing, with a view to removing it at a later date.

"I didn't even know it had been closed." I said, genuinely trying to sound surprised.

"Yep, a year ago."

"Thanks for letting me know. I only supervise it."

It was nice to see the noble art of communication was still alive and well and, with an increasingly heavy heart, I awaited the arrival of the asbestos surveyor.

The Coronavirus did provide one last humorous health and safety snippet. A safety alert was issued in July regarding the alcohol based hand sanitizer that had been supplied to us, which apparently could explode at high temperature. As the mercury had already nudged 38C inside the box a couple of times during June, we had inadvertently been sitting with a ticking time bomb in our midst. This story was almost as good as the one I'd heard about when the company once presented one of its outgoing chief executives with the 'Sword of Safety'. I hope it had a cork on its pointy end. What's next, the Grenade of Gratitude? But perhaps they were trying to give him a hint that he should fall on it. If so, they should have presented it sooner, being as £65 million had been wasted on the ill-conceived Safe Work Leader project during his tenure – a project that was promptly abandoned after a twelve-month trial on the East Midlands Route. That made the manager who once tried to arrange a dark hours assessment during the summer solstice look good.

Since around 2018 though, I had been getting itchy feet – the kind which foot powder does not alleviate; I needed a new challenge. I occasionally glanced at job vacancy lists during this time and tried to imagine myself elsewhere. It got me through those temporary blips, but again, without really realizing that these blips were becoming more frequent and prolonged. I also unwittingly fell foul of several rules and policies – a misunderstanding largely on my part – and suffered the terrible wrath of the great management machine. My only 'crime' was that the world had changed and I had not changed with it. But when I was brought to account, I was glad it was for an off duty indiscretion rather than on duty incompetence. It's strange how someone can set two trains on a head-on collision and effectively get promoted or squander £65 million and is feted, but fall foul of the safety rules whilst off duty and it is regarded as the crime of the century. Nevertheless, it all happened at the right time and unwittingly provided my way out. The old knee was continually firing warning shots and, more importantly, I had the care of an elderly mother and a (now) large, boisterous GSD to consider: circumstances incompatible with a full-time safety critical job. Besides, I had already been offered other work and was keen to accept. The end was going to come sooner or later and now seemed a good time as any. After all, 'now' is all we have.

21. TRAIN OF THOUGHT

(In search of Skye)

It was August 2020 when I finally took my leave of Scropton Crossing Signal Box, a place that had been a home, a haven, a prison, a workshop, a visitor centre, a way of life, and yes, perhaps even a 'journey'. My salvation and ruination rolled into one. My last late shift was exactly like my first all those years ago, pleasant, peaceful and measured. And that is what I will take away with me. It is also what I have tried to recreate in this book: my view from the signal box. There aren't many jobs like this now, having the freedom of working alone and the time to observe nature's dance. I remember absorbing all those sunrises at the box; breathing them in, and, for a few brief seconds, feeling that same golden uplift in my soul and thinking that perhaps the world wasn't such a bad place after all.

During my tenure, I had trained twenty signallers and MOMs, signalled 63,000 trains, and filled in 56 TRBs, using 14 Bic pens and 16.8 miles of ink, all within a temperature range of minus 12C and 40C. I've also outlived three sets of steps at Scropton (well, most of the box really, as it ended up like Trigger's broom after all the replacements), three white vans and several rail franchises. I watched the local children grow up, people come and go and relationships change as frequently as the seasons. I'd also lost my father and two canine companions during that time, and perhaps even myself once or twice. I may have lost them but I believe they still exist out there somewhere. They are only invisible because they happen to occupy a different time frame: that is all. That's why I continue walking...and searching. Taking in a view or a sunset, or feeling a constant reassuring breeze on my back, I know they are out there somewhere, and one day, when I pass beyond the last protecting signal (as might be said in this business), I'll be out there too and we'll be together again. That will be a great day. George Bernard Shaw said 'There are two great sorrows in life; one is losing your heart's desire, the other is finding it', and he was right.

Even after all the disappointments, foolishness, hypocrisy and apathy that often came with the job, there still remained a deep personal satisfaction too, but a non-specific satisfaction, something in the background that sustained me year after year. I only really felt it when alone and, funnily enough, only at sunset after the day's physical work had been done. I used to feel it at Washwood Heath after the train had been unloaded, usually around dusk. I'd climb into the back cab of the loco for the journey home, food would be consumed, it was warm and comfortable (well, the cabs were decidedly spartan, but a damn sight more comfortable than the discharge point I had just spent several hours standing in). I had the night skyline of Birmingham as the backdrop for my little back cab apartment and, with a good imagination, it could almost be Manhattan, except for Washwood Heath's landmark of two gasholders. But that was the point, the body might be a prisoner but the mind was free. I was living inside my mind. It was similar to being in the signal box at sundown or on an evening departure in the brakevan from Willington Power Station after the travails of the Denby Branch or completing the last drop when truck driving then heading home – just me and the open road, mission accomplished – satisfaction. But still, like Washwood Heath, even though I was close to life, I was always on its periphery; part of it but separate somehow. Perhaps that's how it's been all my life?

Whilst researching and writing the article 'Echoes of the Denby Branch' (see *Derby Trainman 2nd Edition & Lost Lines*) in 2015, I walked the remnants of the line, recalling that it traversed the nearby Bottle Brook nine times; they were entwined – which must have caused a few headaches for surveyor George Stephenson and the Midland Railway engineers that followed. My fate seemed similarly entwined with the branch, certainly during my school days and early career. It was almost as if it were a nexus. During those walks, I often found myself in the green space between the former Denby North and Street Lane crossings, facing my old comprehensive school. On one of my last days there, I had looked at some of my fellow students and wondered what might become of them and how far in the world they might go. Now I laughed out loud. Nearly three decades later I hadn't got very far at all, just the other side of the road! Sometimes it felt as though I'd never left, and even though I'd been around the world and played many roles, those days never seemed very far away. I was also still walking...and searching. For what, I didn't truly know, absolution perhaps, or maybe I was just searching for my youth; the boy I left behind.

In 2005, I started *Derby Trainman* with an extract from T. S. Eliot's 'Little Gidding': 'We shall not cease from exploration/and the end of all our exploring/will be to arrive where we started/and know the place for the first time', without *really* knowing why, and it wasn't until that walk, a decade later, that those lines became clearer to me.

I have undoubtedly run out of time, and inclination, for a third evolution on the railway, so, in closing, I paraphrase the last few lines of *The Worm Forgives the Plough*, by John Stewart Collis, a work I've always admired:

The rails will remain, long after the last manual signalman has gone. In the summer they will glitter and shine for him, and in the winter, mourn.

An azure sky, February 2020. *Author.*

APPENDIX

Absolute Block

What follows (plain English aside) is the standard method of AB signalling. Although the operation of the block instrument would rarely differ from place to place, each box could, and often did, have a different signal or track layout, as well as individually tailored special instructions for the movement of trains. Incidentally, Scropton was the best match on the North Staffs for the standard AB method.

Imagine three signal boxes (A, B and C) alongside two railway tracks. One track is for trains travelling in the Up direction (towards London); the other is for trains in the Down direction (away from London). Communication amongst the boxes is achieved by use of the block instrument, and box B contains two, one for each direction. On a standard BR 'domino' block instrument, a block bell and tapper are housed at the bottom. Directly above is a switch (commutator) that has three positions: Normal, Line Clear and Train On Line. Next is the block indicator, which mirrors the current position of the commutator. Finally, the block indicator above that shows the position of the commutator in the advance box. If the direction of travel is A to C on the Up, box B will have box C in advance on the Up and box A in advance on the Down...I know, you're weakening already!

	REAR	ADVANCE	DOWN >
< UP	ADVANCE	REAR	
C	B	A	

To move a train between A and B on the Up, the relevant block indicator at B will showing Normal and the instrument will be operated as follows:

A sends 'call attention' (1) to B.
B acknowledges by repetition.
A sends bell code description of train (aka 'Is Line Clear?')
B acknowledges by repetition and turns the commutator from Normal to Line Clear. B has now confirmed the line is clear and has accepted the train. This will remain the case unless an obstruction or some other emergency occurs. The above action also unlocks the signals at A, allowing them to be cleared for the approaching train.

A sends 'train entering section' (2).

B acknowledges by repetition and turns the commutator to Train On Line. (Offers train to C).

Train passes B.

B calls attention of A and sends 'train out of section' (2-1) then turns commutator back to Normal. B is now able to accept another train from A.

For each direction, the signaller at B will clear a minimum of two semaphore signals: a home/section (stop) signal and a distant (caution) signal. These will be 'unlocked' by the relevant box in advance after they have acknowledged 'Is Line Clear?' from B and turned their commutator to Line Clear.

II

Additional DTM/TOL published material – my thanks to Jane Goddard (Derby Telegraph) and Paul Bickerdyke (Rail Express):

Traction:
'On the Denby.' (DTM Chap. 10.) December 2005.

Derby Telegraph:
'Crossing the shed's threshold...' 11 January 2013.
'Bringing up the rear on freight trains.' 20 February 2013.
'Ups and downs at St. Mary's Goods Yard.' 24 December 2018.
'Remembering the tracks of our years.' 28 January 2019.
'Keeping the test track open proved to be a bridge too far.' 01 April 2019.
'Travelling at 60mph in a garden shed...' 08 April 2019.
'Walk *fuelled* memories of long-lost branch line.' 29 April 2019.
'Pictures that signal changes at Goods Yard over 30 years.' 16 March 2020.

Rail Express:
'Playing by the rules...' March 2015.
'Going hands on.' April 2015.
'Things get messy...' May 2015
'Know your onions!' June 2015.
'Language Timothy!' July 2015.
'Tough brake!' August 2015.
'Fright night!' September 2015.
'What a banker!' October 2015.
'So the brakes work then?' November 2015.
'Odds and sods.' December 2015.
'Signs of trouble.' January 2016.
'It's your turn son.' February 2016.
'Put your back into it!' March 2016.
'From gogglebox to signalbox.' April 2016.
'Nightshifts on shed.' May 2016.

'A white-knuckle ride.' June 2016.
'WAR: what is it good for?' July 2016.
'Milking it!' August 2016.
'Like a limestone cowboy.' September 2016.
'A fistful of dust.' October 2016.
'A year at Scropton.' (TOL Chap. 17 abridged.) August 2017.
'Calling at Derby.' January 2019.
'On a roll to Royce's.' August 2019.
'45 not out.' November 2019.
'Industrial relations.' December 2019.
'20s aplenty.' January 2020.
'47s R Us.' February 2020.
'Goyles vs Tractors.' March 2020.
'The great 08s.' April 2020.
'HSTease.' May 2020.
'In the frame.' November 2020.

(See Rail Express back issues 226-245, 255, 272, 279, 282-288, 294.)

DVD
On the Denby. (Cab ride November 1991.) Released 2007.

GLOSSARY

AB	Absolute Block
AHB	Automatic Half Barrier
Bardic	Railway hand lamp
BR	British Rail
COSS	Controller Of Site Safety
EMCC	East Midlands Control Centre (Death Star)
EMT	East Midlands Trains
GPR	General Purpose Relief
GSM-R	Global Systems Mobile-Radio
HMRI	Her Majesty's Railway Inspectorate
HST	High Speed Train
LMS	London, Midland and Scottish
LOM	Local Operations Manager
MOD	Ministry Of Defence
MOM	Mobile Operations Manager
NR	Network Rail
PSB	Power Signal Box
PTI	Physical Training Instructor
PTS	Personal Track Safety
PWay	Permanent Way
RHTT	Rail Head Treatment Train
ROC	Rail Operating Centre
RTC	Railway Technical Centre
S&T	Signal & Telecom
SBO	Stating (the) Bleedin' Obvious
SBSI	Signal Box Special Instructions
SLR	Self-Loading Rifle
SPAD	Signal Passed At Danger
TCB	Track Circuit Block
TD	Train Describer
TPWS	Train Protection Warning System
TRB	Train Register Book
TRUST	Train Running System
UWC	User Worked Crossing

Printed in Poland
by Amazon Fulfillment
Poland Sp. z o.o., Wrocław

63994933R00107